The A-Z of INTERMARRIAGE

The A-Z of INTER-MARRIAGE

RABBI DENISE HANDLARSKI

NEW JEWISH PRESS
an imprint of University of Toronto Press
Toronto Buffalo London

© Rabbi Denise Handlarski 2020
Published by New Jewish Press
an imprint of University of Toronto Press
Toronto Buffalo London
utorontopress.com
Printed in Canada

ISBN 978-1-4875-0678-0 (paper)   ISBN 978-1-4875-3483-7 (EPUB)
                                   ISBN 978-1-4875-3482-0 (PDF)

Library and Archives Canada Cataloguing in Publication

Title: The A–Z of intermarriage / Rabbi Denise Handlarski.
Names: Handlarski, Denise, 1979–, author.
Description: Includes bibliographical references and index.
Identifiers: Canadiana (print) 20190209585 | Canadiana (ebook) 20190209615
   | ISBN 9781487506780 (paper) | ISBN 9781487534820 (PDF)
   | ISBN 9781487534837 (EPUB)
Subjects: LCSH: Interfaith marriage. | LCSH: Marriage – Religious aspects
   – Judaism.
Classification: LCC HQ1031 .H36 2020 | DDC 306.84/3 – dc23

University of Toronto Press acknowledges the financial assistance to its
publishing program of the Canada Council for the Arts and the Ontario Arts
Council, an agency of the Government of Ontario.

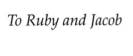

To Ruby and Jacob

CONTENTS

ACKNOWLEDGMENTS

This book could not have been written without the many couples and community members invite me into their stories and their lives. Thanks to everyone whom I have been honored to serve. Thanks to all of my colleagues, congregants, and many communities of which I am lucky to be part. Thanks also to Natalie Fingerhut at University of Toronto Press, without whom this book would not have made its way to the world. Your humor and insight are a marvel. Thanks to my dear family and friends. Thanks most of all, and much love, to my partner, Charlie, and our children, who fill the pages of this book as they fill the days of my life.

INTRODUCTION

When I was a teen, I attended a talk called "The Disaster of Intermarriage." At that time, I remember seriously wrestling with the idea that if I married someone who wasn't Jewish, I'd be giving up my identity. I also, however, had a tinge of a feeling that this was racism or xenophobia, in some way. Couldn't you be both proudly Jewish and open to creating a family with someone who was different? There are many thousands of intermarried Jews in North America,[1] most of whom are raising children Jewishly, practicing Judaism in some way, and participating in Jewish community. Yet the narrative of intermarriage as "disaster" remains firmly in place.

Why a reference guide to intermarriage? There is no how-to guide for marriage or for life, but perhaps we can come close to creating one. *The A–Z of Intermarriage* is a compendium of story and strategy; a coming together of religious source material, cultural context, personal narrative, and the learning I've done along the way.

The reason I am so passionate about this book is that I am intermarried and serve many intermarried couples in my role as wedding officiant and rabbi in the Humanistic Jewish movement. In this movement, we serve cultural and secular Jews, offering community, celebrations, and ceremonies without the language of prayer. Because we let go of what Jewish law tells us we have to do and, instead, use Jewish ethics to guide a sense of what we believe to be ethical and just in the contemporary moment, we were officiating and celebrating intermarried weddings long before any other Jewish group. This wasn't a marketing ploy or done as a way to ensure our own continuity, although our communities have no doubt grown and thrived as a result of our openness. The goal was simply to serve the people in our communities well. And to do that, we had to recognize that intermarriage is a positive result of the openness of North American society (and other societies too). We are accepted! We are even loved! This is great news for a people who have been expelled and excoriated in most corners of the globe. It is my goal to use my experience and expertise as an intermarried rabbi, one of only a handful in the world, to try to help others create meaningful, engaged, wonderful lives.

I am a believer in the power of intermarriage. I think it is healthy for individuals and families to experience and express pride in who they are, in the diversity and divergence that makes them (us) who they (we) are.

I believe intermarriage can be a positive and healthy-making force for Jews, Jewish families, and Jewish communities. Judaism has traditionally denounced intermarriage, even excising and rejecting folks who want to join in Jewish activities and groups – all while worrying about Jewish population numbers and the decline of communities. I have often found there are two parallel threads, completely in contradiction with one another, in Jewish life: (1) "*Oy vey*, there aren't enough Jews" and (2) "You aren't Jewish enough, so-and-so isn't Jewish enough, let's keep really tight boundaries to keep 'others' out."

Look, I get it. We are a minority and minorities have felt and continue to feel under threat. Many people talk about assimilation as the greatest threat Judaism has ever known. And they're not wrong! Assimilation is a threat, but the anti-intermarriage narrative only intensifies that threat. When the Jewish community is insular, closed-minded, and exclusionary, many of its members will choose to leave. No one is itching to join a club that does not respect their families, and their values. Many Jews today welcome universality and equality and celebrate justice and openness. Even for those who do not choose to intermarry, openness to intermarried families is attractive to many contemporary Jews who want their own groups to be diverse and welcoming.

But this is not a book about all that. That's backdrop. This book is meant to be both practical and entertaining; it is meant to be a book and an experience rooted in text and philosophy and rich with real-world experience. This book is written for people who

- Are intermarried, open to intermarriage, or considering intermarriage
- Have family members who are intermarried
- Are interested in points of view about intermarriage they've never considered
- Would never get married but are in/considering an intercultural relationship, so close enough
- Love how-to books
- Want to know about Jewish approaches to life, learning, and love
- Think of the alphabet as their jam

Here's what you'll find in this book:

- An "A–Z how-to manual" for intermarriage; what issues arise and how to deal with them; useful concepts to consider
- An introduction that begins each of the A–Z listings to explain key concepts being discussed under that particular letter
- Select concepts under each of the letters that have been chosen to best exemplify ideas and practices that are meaningful to intermarried couples and families
- Jewish and other religious source material
- Personal experiences and anecdotes of real people who have experienced these real issues
- Ideas, inspirations, and illustrations for how to live a happy and balanced intermarried life
- Cross references throughout the text that can easily locate topics of interest; for example, see "H" for "Holidays" and see "C" for "Children"

With literally thousands of Jews, and millions of people across religions/cultures, choosing to marry someone outside their own culture, there is a growing population searching for ways to make their marriages and families culturally engaged so that they feel authentic and inclusive. This guide is also something that will interest the parents and families of people who are intermarrying, so that they can learn more about their child and how to support them. If you are intermarried or you love someone who is intermarried, this book is for you!

Why Is This Book on Intermarriage Different from All Other Books on Intermarriage?

Intermarriages are on the rise. Our most recent American statistics come from the Pew Research Center's study on American Jewish life. The study showed that prior to the year 1970, 17 per cent of Jews married non-Jews. In the years 2005–2013, it was 58 per cent. The *2018 Survey of Jews in Canada* showed a slightly slower, but still growing, intermarriage rate. (Note: The survey called it "outmarriage," signaling the authors' own bias as researchers and interpreters of the data.) What the data shows in both the Canadian and American studies is that the population interested in intermarriage is growing. The research also shows that the population is young, connected, and likely to be in search of something affirming and engaging. And yet when I meet with wedding clients and they ask me for a resource, I am a little stuck. There is no adequate book currently on the market for these people.

Of the few books about intermarriage, none of them are authored by a rabbi/officiant who is intermarried, sharing her experience and those of her intermarrying clients. Also, most books about intermarriage approach the topic with seriousness and almost solemnity. This tone lends credence to the negative thinking intermarrying couples have already heard. That this is going to be hard. That it is going to be a lot of work. Of course, any marriage is work! But this book is for couples who are celebratory of intermarriage and who want to do relationship work in a way that is fun; they want to explore the possibilities that intermarriage creates, not just the problems.

How to Use This Book

This book is organized alphabetically A–Z but can be approached as you choose your own adventure. Read it in order or jump around. If you are currently struggling with an issue, you can skip to a particular section about that (for example, see "C" for "Conversion" or "H" for "Holidays"). Use the table of contents to find what you're looking for. Of course, the book can also be read from beginning to end so that the stories, Jewish texts, examples, and anecdotes cohere into a picture that conveys the full and rich life of intermarriage.

The A-Z of INTERMARRIAGE

It is fortuitous that "A" begins the alphabet because some traditional and typical concerns like "assimilation" can be dealt with quickly and we can move on to issues that actually tend to concern intermarried people. I mean, assimilation as an overall concept does concern intermarried folks, but no one wakes up in the morning with the sudden awareness that they are intermarried and likely to assimilate. The couples I work with are deliberate in choosing their partners and the expressions of their cultural identity. Some might choose to let Jewish practice go, but the majority are engaged Jewishly, decidedly unassimilated. The fear of assimilation is something that is often imposed on intermarried people, but not something that they are often or overly concerned with themselves. Also discussed is the biblical story of Adam and Eve and how the textual first couple might give us clues as to how to forge a successful intermarriage. They were different, yet they found each other and found that they complemented one another.

I write here about how attitudes to intermarriage have shifted, both within couples who see intermarriage as a wonderful dynamic in their relationships, and beyond each couple to the communities that are embracing them. Relationship dynamics such as accepting one another (including your partner's family!) and how to take action to make the relationship strong and fulfilling are also discussed.

Acceptance

The reality is that intermarriage is an unstoppable phenomenon (not that I wish to stop it) precisely because Jews are so accepted in contemporary society. Yes, there is still antisemitism and when we encounter its expression, it can be terrifying, but we are, largely and widely, accepted.

What Jews sometimes are not so good at is accepting ourselves. It is difficult for people to accept change. Yet change has always been part of Jewish life. We began as a culture of religious rites that revolved around a central temple. If we had been unwilling to change, we would not have survived. We have adapted and adopted aspects of cultures from every place we've lived across our long histories of exile and diaspora. We are proud to be speakers of Yiddish and Ladino, as well as all the languages of the world. We delight in "Jewish food" that is a mix of foods we have inherited and encountered in the many places we have lived (the latke is the product of Eastern Europe, hummus is common to all Middle Eastern cultures, Chinese food is not inherently Jewish but Jews seem to really like it for the most part).

We need to accept that Judaism is changing, and will continue to change, as a result of our intermixing with others. We also need to understand that such change is nothing if not traditional from a Jewish perspective. We have always adapted, adopted, and accepted aspects of the cultures around us. We are shapeshifters, and we continue to shift.

Paul Golin, the current executive director of the Society for Humanistic Judaism, the Jewish movement with which I affiliate, has devoted his career to studying and educating about intermarriage. Once, at a talk in Toronto that he gave while working for the organization Big Tent Judaism, he asked the audience to raise their hands if they practiced Judaism differently from their grandparents. Almost all hands went up. We can imagine why. Some of these people secularized, some perhaps adopted a more traditional practice than their parents. Some were not born Jewish at all but "married in." Some were Jews by choice. Some simply created new traditions to serve their contemporary needs. Almost all of us do it differently than our grandparents. Golin said, "Then why should we be surprised or anxious about the Judaism of our grandchildren looking different from our own?" This is the key question. Every generation has made changes to keep Judaism relevant, and this is good. Judaism staying relevant, continuing to be meaningful to us and influencing our lives, is the point.

We need to work on being accepting of that which we cannot control. We need to work on being accepting of difference. And, above all, we need to work on being accepting of one another. There is such destruction amongst Jews when we criticize and insult each other because we have different ways of expressing or practicing Judaism. This is serving no one. I firmly believe that it hurts every Jewish *neshama* (soul) and self when we hurl insults and judgments; it actually hurts the one doing the hurling more, for their own humanity, their opportunity for complexity, is compromised when they cannot see the humanity and complexity of their brethren.

We must find a way to be accepting of ourselves, our partners, our changing families, and our people.

Action

The key to a successful intermarriage is in the doing. If you are currently in or considering an intermarriage, here are five things you can do right now to set yourself up for success. To help, think of the handy acronym LATKE:

LISTEN: Ask your partner and ask yourself these questions, and attentively listen to the answers: What is essential to my identity and cultural practice, what can I let go of, what can I adopt?

ACT: What is one thing you can do this week to help each partner feel affirmed? Is it celebrating Shabbat (sabbath)? Is it sharing a text from each culture? Is it buying or recycling the Christmas lights?

TALK: Say out loud the one thing that scares you most to tell your partner about what you are wanting but not getting, or are hoping to introduce into your lives about your own cultural practice.

KINDNESS: Whatever your partner has just said, respond with kindness. Perhaps you'll need negotiation, perhaps you'll need mediation, but right now, do one kind thing in response. Tell them you hear them. Give them a back rub. Clear out a drawer for the holiday paraphernalia they are asking for. Whatever it is, respond with kindness.

ENERGY: We are all busy and sometimes it is difficult to find the energy to have the tough conversations and put our goals into practice. So, find one energizing thing you can do right now to free up space for this work. Meditate together for five minutes. Go for a walk. Relax with a bottle of wine as you have these conversations. Make the work of creating a successful intermarriage part of what energizes, not de-energizes, your life as a couple and a family.

Adam and Eve

According to Judeo-Christian biblical tradition, Adam and Eve were the first couple. There was no intermarriage at the time the story takes place, but there is strong evidence to suggest that there was intermarriage at the time the story was written.[2] Some of the cultural anxiety around intermarriage stems from trying to create, and then maintain, a discrete people. In order to assert that there is a group such as Israel/Jews, the logic of the group maintained a strict standard for the insider/outsider. Yet, throughout the textual tradition, we see examples of those who chose to leave or join Judaism via marriage. There has never been "purity" of any people, and this is a good thing! But we are getting ahead of ourselves. Adam and Eve are the first couple. There isn't anything called intermarriage yet, but there are power dynamics in their relationship that, later on, do inform intermarriage dynamics.

The text posits two competing stories for the creation of woman. In chapter 1 of the Bible, the text says: "And God created man in His image, in the image of God He created him; male and female He created them" (1:27).[3] In chapter 2, the creation of Adam and Eve, we find that Adam, lacking a "fitting helper" (2:20), was made to sleep so that God could "fashion" Eve into a woman from Adam's rib. In the first chapter, man and woman are created at the same time and as equals. They are both created in God's image and they exist side by side. The Adam and Eve creation story is more narratively interesting. It is written as a story, as opposed to a factual record. Through the narrative, we glean attitudes about women at the time. Eve is created just after Adam has named all of the animals, thus establishing his dominion over the living things. Eve is created to be Adam's helper in administering to these things but, given that she is named along with the animals Adam tends, and given that she comes out of his body, the text implies that she is to be subservient to him.

Every partnership includes power dynamics that, ideally, shift and settle into, if not equality all the time, equilibrium over time. In an intermarriage, the power dynamic may influence how the cultural life of the family takes shape. If one partner is domineering, we may find that their partner assumes more of their cultural traditions. If one partner lacks power, their own culture may become eclipsed.

Ultimately, Eve eats of the tree of knowledge and she and Adam are cast out of the Garden of Eden. All of us have our own journey from innocence to experience. To me, Eve is rather heroic: I'll take knowledge any day! But they have thrown their lot in together and must experience life – paradisiacal or earthly – together. Just as we all must with our own partners of choice.

Aggravation

All of this is not to say that intermarriage is always easy. When both partners assert their beliefs, their goals, their values, there may very well be conflict. All partnerships must encounter conflict and compromise and, for intermarrying couples, discussing religious and cultural aspects of life may present in this way. Of course, two Jews marrying may experience similar aggravation if one intends to follow Jewish law more stringently than the other. For example, if one partner wishes to follow the kosher dietary laws, the other may feel put out. If one partner wishes to send children to Jewish day school, or attend synagogue at least weekly, the other may feel their own approach to Judaism and to life is eclipsed. There are many ways of being and doing Jewish, and all couples will find themselves experiencing aggravation. In my experience of working with intermarrying couples, I find they are ahead of the curve in dealing with this aggravation because they have already encountered some of these conversations. Usually, a couple dating across cultures will have thought about what their culture means to them, where they are willing to sacrifice or change, and where the sticking points are. By the time they are marrying, they have covered this territory.

If you were to show me a couple who never feels aggravation in negotiating the terms of their relationship, I would show you a couple who were either lacking in equality between the partners or lacking in depth and integrity in terms of how they were living their lives. The work of defining who one is as an individual, and who people are as a couple and a family, is real, deep, difficult, challenging work. Anyone who is not asking themselves and their partner difficult questions is missing out on the fullness and complexity of how we find a life we feel is worthwhile, fulfilling, and reflective of who we wish to be as we move through the world.

Aggravation is part of the territory when it comes to relationships. Finding ways to deal with it together as a team, to turn aggravation into acceptance, is the work of creating a deeper, fuller, and more meaningful relationship.

Antisemitism

Another concern that Jews have often had is antisemitism; that our extended families, if we intermarry, will harbor antisemitic thoughts and feelings that will only end up hurting the Jews who have married into that family.

It is my belief that we all have internalized bias, even when we are open and loving in our conscious minds. We may have picked up some beliefs or stereotypes about our partner's culture along the way, and we need to be doing our best to unlearn stereotypes and to challenge our internal biases (see "U" for "Unlearning"). However, what greater sign is there that antisemitism is waning than the fact that so many people want to marry Jews? Part of antisemitism is that many people do not know any Jews, and so never have their stereotypes challenged. Now that there are Jews in so many families where previously there were none, Jews are challenging and changing the way we are seen societally.

My teacher, colleague, and friend Rabbi Adam Chalom tells a story that came from a cruise ship. A man said something antisemitic and his wife slaps him and says, "You idiot! Your son-in-law is Jewish!" And so it goes. That man had antisemitic ideas his whole life and now his daughter has chosen a Jewish person to live with. Statistically speaking, any grandchildren that man has will be raised with some degree of Jewish identity and culture. It is difficult to continue to hate people who, actually, you love. Intermarriage is a win for those worried about antisemitism.

Assertiveness

Feeling able to assert one's cultural values and cultural practices is not only a sign of being secure in one's culture, it is a sign of being secure in one's relationship. For most people, we need to learn the skills of asserting our needs concerning our religion or culture. No one has taught us those skills. Throughout the sections of this book, we'll see examples of couples figuring through how they can come to understand and assert their needs. Our biblical first couple, Adam and Eve (see above), are an interesting first test case.

My advice to my clients when they are entering into an intermarriage is to have a discussion about how the cultural or religious aspects of their identities might look in the context of their partnership and, if applicable, their family. There may be disagreements (see "Aggravation"), but it is crucial that everyone feels heard.

A$$holes

Part of the aggravation that a couple may experience is what happens when we need to deal with a$$holes. Here's a story from my own life: I was studying in Israel as part of my rabbinic training and had just married my non-Jewish partner the summer prior. I mentioned to some acquaintances I met in Israel, Canadian Jews who had just made *Aliyah* (moved to Israel), that I had married someone who was similar to me in that we were both atheists, but different from me in that he wasn't Jewish. They looked at me like I had just told them I was a serial killer and exclaimed boldly (and rudely): "I hope you don't have children, then. The children of intermarriage are f*cked up." So, this is what I mean by a$$holes. First, plenty of people who are not children of intermarriage are f*cked up (including, some would argue, the people who insist on judging others and telling them how to live). Second, children of intermarriage are often extremely happy and well-adjusted in all areas but, in particular, in terms of their religious and cultural identities. I doubt this couple had ever actually spoken to a child of intermarriage about their experience, but I have in my work. At my congregation's Sunday school we have many children from intermarried families and they can speak eloquently and intelligently about what we adults might call hybridity, syncretism, multiple identities, and complexity.

Being a product of intermarriage does not make you messed up. What is really messed up is that much of mainstream Judaism has empowered people to speak to one another like that. Again, this is a serious turnoff for people who are intermarried. I am so grateful my husband wasn't there for that conversation; he doesn't need to be exposed to that kind of hatefulness. And that kind of hatefulness repels me and many other Jews from mainstream Judaism.

When I was a teenager and felt constantly bombarded with anti-intermarriage messaging, it really undermined my sense of belonging in Judaism. I felt this politic of exclusion and xenophobia really reflected poorly on my own people. It had the opposite of its desired effect: it made me want to look outside of my own people to see what perhaps we were lacking or, put another way, to find out what these Jewish authorities were so afraid of.

Here's a story of a couple whom I married: they had been told that intermarriage was wrong and evil from both sides – he was Jewish and she was Hindu. Both had felt their respective communities were too insular. When they began dating, they discovered that there were so many cultural similarities. At their wedding, we compared the Jewish *chuppah* or canopy with the Hindu *mandap*, both used in the marriage ceremony. Both wedding traditions involve circling. Although both sets of parents were nervous about this union at first, they all danced together at the wedding in Jewish and Hindu style (think the *horah* meets Bollywood). Through this couple, the worlds of both families expanded.

I have many stories like this. Most of the time, family members come around. However, in this intermarriage A–Z guide I feel it needs to be said: some people are going to be a$$holes. We can't change that. All we can affect is how we respond. We can ignore them; we can try to educate them; we can badmouth them in a book we eventually write about intermarriage. These are the choices we have. It is always my advice to focus on the beauty and good in one's life and, if others can't see it, to understand that their smallness does not have to become ours. We can transcend it.

Assimilation

Certainly one of the Jewish communal concerns about intermarriage has been assimilation. Jews of my generation grew up hearing that if we were to marry outside of Judaism we'd be completing Hitler's work (see "A" for "Attitude"). Of course, assimilation is a notable concern for those who deeply care about Judaism and want to see its continuity. I always find there are two competing strands in mainstream Judaism on the issue of continuity. On the one hand, there is anxiety about Jews and Judaism "dying out." On the other, there is a strict adherence to in-group and out-group politics. I have mentioned already that there is no "purity" amongst Jews; we are a diverse group racially, linguistically, and culturally. And yet so many Jews insist on drawing strict lines about who is "really" a Jew. It has always seemed to me that if we are serious about Jewish continuity, we should welcome those who wish to be part of us. Keeping people "out" when one is worried about their group dying out is contradictory at best and exclusionary at worst.

The reality is that Jews in North America and Europe are often quite assimilated, and this is good; this is of our own choosing. We feel as equally Canadian, American, British, Brazilian, South African, and so on as we do Jewish. This is the consequence of the lack of antisemitism, at least state-sponsored antisemitism, that we have enjoyed for the past several decades. And so, yes, there is assimilation. What keeps us Jewish, then? We *want* to be Jewish, we choose it. We feel affinity for Jewish history, religion, text, culture, family. We see being Jewish as part of the many aspects of identity that make us whole and complex.

It has not worked, in fact it has backfired, to try to scare Jews into being, marrying, and staying Jewish. The fear tactics suggest that there is nothing inherently beneficial or, dare I say, fun about being Jewish. Rather, we owe our identities to our forebears. This is ridiculous. If Judaism is to continue, it will be because Jews find it meaningful. Our work is not to draw strict lines of who is in and who is out. Our work is to make it meaningful so that more people will want in.

Table 1. Jewish child-rearing

	Among those who are parents/guardians of minor children in their household, % raising their children …					
	Jewish by religion (%)	Partly Jewish by religion (%)	Jewish not by religion or mixed (%)^	NOT Jewish (%)	Other (%)	N
NET Jewish	59	14	8	18	1	907
Jews by religion	71	15	7	7	*	764
Jews of no religion	8	11	11	67	2	143
Married	61	12	8	18	1	808
Spouse Jewish	96	2	1	1	0	551
Spouse not Jewish	20	25	16	37	1	257
Not married	45	24	9	21	1	98
Orthodox	97	1	–	2	0	278
Conservative	88	4	1	7	1	125
Reform	60	20	9	10	1	276
No denomination	19	17	16	47	1	177

Source: Pew Research Centre, *A Portrait of Jewish Americans: Findings from a Pew Research Center Survey of US Jews* (Washington, DC: Pew Research Center, 2013), p. 67. https://www.pewresearch.org/wp-content /uploads/sites/7/2013/10/jewish-american-full-report-for-web.pdf.
Note: Figures may not sum to 100% due to rounding.
^Includes those who are raising their children Jewish but not by religion as well as those who are raising multiple children Jewish but in different ways (Jewish by religion, partly Jewish by religion, and/or Jewish but not by religion).

Recently, this has been happening. The 2013 Pew Research Center report on Jewish Americans is the most recent and the most in-depth population survey ever done on Jewish life in America. The way the report interprets the numbers on intermarriage makes it seem, according to the typical Jewish narrative, that high intermarriage rates are leading to high rates of assimilation. The researchers focus on the people who are *not* raising their children to be *primarily* Jewish by religion. However, if you read the data, it is clear that the *majority* of people identifying as Jewish either by religion or by culture or ancestry are raising children of intermarriage with at least some Jewish identity (see table 1). The majority! True, these children might be "Jewish and …" but they are Jewish, and often proud of and practicing their Judaism.

This is such a win for those worried about assimilation! We can also see that things have shifted by generation. The dynamic is cyclical: when intermarriage was seen as so taboo that your parents might disown you, there was no possibility of or attraction to retaining Jewish identity and practice. So, naturally, Jews who intermarried left Judaism. But recently we have been seeing a new cycle: as Jewish communities have become more open and accepting of intermarried couples and their children, more Jews are finding ways to bring Jewish life into their families and

Table 2. Spouse's religion (% by age)

	CANADIAN TOTAL	AGE						AMERICAN JEWS
		18–29	30–44	45–54	55–64	65–74	75+	
Religion of spouse								
Jewish	77	84	74	75	79	80	82	50
Christian	11	10	11	11	12	7	11	31
Other religion	1	2	1	1	2	1	–	2
None	9	6	15	11	7	11	5	17
TOTAL %*	100	100	100	100	100	100	100	100

Source: Brym, Robert, Keith Neuman, and Rhonda Lenton. *2018 Survey of Jews in Canada: Final Report* (Toronto: Environics Institute for Survey Research), fig. 5-1. https://www.environicsinstitute.org/docs/default-source/project-documents/2018-survey-of-jews-in-canada/2018-survey-of-jews-in-canada---final-report.pdf?sfvrsn=2994ef6_2.
* Totals may not equal 100% due to rounding.

Table 3. Raising children Jewish (% of those with children, by Jewish identity)

	CANADIAN TOTAL	JEWISH IDENTITY				
		By religion	By ancestry /descent	By culture	All three	Other combination
All children raised in Jewish religion	86	93	65	83	95	85
Some children raised in Jewish religion	7	4	14	9	3	6
All/some children raised Jewish, but not by religion	2	4	3	2	1	4
No children raised as Jewish	5	–	18	5	1	5
TOTAL %*	100	100	100	100	100	100

Source: Brym, Robert, Keith Neuman, and Rhonda Lenton. *2018 Survey of Jews in Canada: Final Report* (Toronto: Environics Institute for Survey Research), fig. 5-3. https://www.environicsinstitute.org/docs/default-source/project-documents/2018-survey-of-jews-in-canada/2018-survey-of-jews-in-canada---final-report.pdf?sfvrsn=2994ef6_2.
* Totals may not equal 100% due to rounding.

their families into Jewish institutions and programs. This reenergizes Judaism in turn, thus making it more appealing to more people.

It may seem paradoxical, but if one is worried about assimilation, celebrating intermarried families is our best bet for Jewish continuity.

A recent Canadian survey took this on directly and argued that intermarried folks don't raise their kids Jewish as often. However, the researchers' own data seems to contradict that takeaway (see tables 2 and 3).

The Canadian data show that Canadians are less likely to intermarry than their America counterparts (although, the younger one is, the more likely one is to intermarry, which is common to both American and Canadian findings). However, the vast majority of folks are raising their kids with a Jewish identity and with Jewish practices, regardless of intermarriage.

The Canadian survey, unfortunately, describes intermarriage as "outmarriage," even though its data make clear that the majority of these folks are Jewishly engaged. Assimilation is a problem, but the attitudes around intermarriage contribute to that problem.

Attentiveness

The flip side of assertiveness is attentiveness. As our partner explains their anxieties, their feelings, their wishes, and their values, we need to honor and listen to these concerns. This is how it went with my husband and me. I told him early on that it was important to me to raise Jewish children. Not all intermarried families make this choice but this was important to me. He explained that he was open to that, but his own family traditions at Christmas, for him a secular affair, were important and he would like to keep them.

We disagreed over certain points: whether to put up Christmas lights (yes, if they are blue and white) and a Christmas tree (I'd rather not have one in the house but let's help decorate the tree at my in-laws' place). We still sometimes disagree. The point is that, I hope, we both attentively listen to what the other says. Sometimes we need to listen for the statement behind the statement. When I say I'd rather not have a Christmas tree in the house, what I mean is that I see that as a symbol of a culture with which I do not identify, and it feels like too great a compromise of my identity and culture to have one occupy the center of the place I call home. What my husband means (I believe, but I suppose we'd have to ask him to be sure) when he says he wants the tree is that he has a strong association with this cultural symbol, and his attachments to that symbol are tied up with positive memories he has of his childhood and his family, and that it is important to him to create such memories and bonds with our own family in our home.

None of this gives rise to the solution. The reality is, one of us is going to have to compromise. But at least we know what we are talking about; attentively listening to the statement behind the statement our partner makes brings us on to similar terrain and helps us find our footing. It is an act of empathy and love. And, done well, it helps strengthen the relationship even as these negotiations and aggravations take place.

Attitude

Attitude makes all the difference in creating a successful intercultural or inter-religious relationship and family. If you believe you are doomed to fail, you will. It's natural that the negativity around intermarriage as a phenomenon can negatively impact the success of the intermarriage as it is practiced. That is, if pressure from family, or from yourself, means that the relationship is constantly under scrutiny and critique, there is less chance of a healthy intermarriage dynamic. The relationship may thrive, but it might be too hard to swim against the stream of criticism and, in my experience, in these circumstances one partner almost certainly gives up their culture or religion entirely. It is too hard to constantly combat negativity. The good news is your attitude can work the other way too! Many of my clients are excited about the cultural connections they forge with their spouses. When your attitude is right, you can discover that the Jewish wedding canopy, the *chuppah*, is similar to the wedding *mandap* from the Hindu culture. When you are positive about your partner, you can find that you love experiencing a holiday you never got to have as a child. There is so much good in the sharing of cultures through family and marriage. Delight in it!

Attitude is everything. How do you approach your partner's religion/culture? Their feelings about it? Is there openness? Is there defensiveness? Does the love you have for your partner make you open to learning about their cultural history and beliefs? Does the power of that love make you scared you'll end up sacrificing your own? In intermarriage as in life, "A" is for "attitude," and it really is a foundational building block in intermarriage.

Here, we talk about how learning about your partner's background can enrich your own cultural or religious identity and experience. We talk about what the Bible actually says about intermarriage, including dispelling some common myths and stereotypes. And we talk about the beauty of intermarriage that can be created when couples work well together. "B" is about how cultures borrow and blend from one another and, when we learn about how that has worked in our own cultural contexts, intermarriage becomes all the richer for the blending of its own. Finally, "B" is about the idea of a *b'shert,* that someone is intended just for us.

Backgrounds

When people think of intermarriage, they often think of religion or culture as being the primary marker of identity in someone. Sometimes it is, and sometimes it isn't. Take me as an example: I'm deeply rooted in my Jewish identity; I practice Jewish ritual and celebrate Jewish holidays; I study Jewish history and text; I work for a Jewish congregation. I am very Jewish. And yet when I was selecting a spouse, Judaism was not the primary aspect of identity I wanted to connect over. I wanted someone who cared about social justice the same way I did. I was seeking someone who was funny and kind, who wanted children and whom I believed would make a good parent. I was looking for someone who felt rooted in the city in which I live because I wanted to stay close to friends and family. I wanted someone educated, employed, eager to make the most out of life.

Some people seek out a partner who is like them so that they may bond over their mutual interests. This is, of course, terrific if it works for you. But I was not like that. I wanted someone who would challenge me, who had his own interests, who would expose me to new ideas and experiences. For these reasons, finding someone who wasn't Jewish was actually attractive and exciting. I could share my culture and background. I was not explicitly seeking out someone who wasn't Jewish; I had dated Jewish people. But I was open to any partner whom I felt complemented me and the many aspects of my identity that were important to consider, not just my Jewish identity.

So when people ask a potential partner what their background is, I always wonder if they are talking about educational and employment background, experience with skiing or making music, background in previous relationships that inform any new relationship, exactly what kind of background they mean.

Everyone has a story. That story is made up of the very many aspects of life that shape our complex and multifaceted identities. Some Jewish stories come from the Hebrew Bible known as the Torah. In Jewish circles, we say that there are seventy faces of Torah (this comes from rabbinic commentary on the Bible – Midrash to be more precise and, for those who know Midrash, *Bamidbar Rabbah* 13:15–16). The "seventy faces of Torah" remind us that there are multiple ways of interpreting a story. Perspective matters. The background of your partner will certainly inform their perspective and, at times, may conflict with your own perspective. This is called marriage. We all hold on to our own narratives and the blessing of marriage is finding a way to join stories, to integrate someone else into the narrative of your life, to write a new story, to work on negotiation, perception, interpretation.

Beauty

There is so much beauty in a relationship in which both parties are committed to learning about and celebrating the heritage and culture of the other. My favorite part about being a rabbi is being able to meet couples before I officiate their wedding. I always include their story of how they met and fell in love as part of the ceremony, and so I get to ask them questions and hear them express how they came to be life partners. This is my favorite part of the rabbi gig! I love getting to know the stories of how people fall in love, what they come to adore in the other. So often intermarriage is painted in such a harsh light that we forget that all intermarriages are marriages and all marriages are based on love and, therefore, deserve celebration. Okay, not *all* marriages are based on love, but if you are reading this book then you care enough about your partner or the person in your family who intermarried that you want to foster a good relationship with them. Love is everywhere. It is beautiful, it is meaningful, and it is precious.

Belief, Behavior, Belonging (Bonus: B Mitzvah[4])

I realize it is cheating to put all of these words together, but they really go together! The three Bs of belief, behavior, belonging tell you a lot about who a person is. Research suggests that in a religious or cultural context, it is these three things that lead to affiliation and fulfillment. We are shaped by what we think, what we do, and where we go. And these become mutually constituting and reinforcing factors. If I attend a great lecture or service, it might change my thinking, which might influence my actions, which might affect the next choice I'll make in attending a lecture or service at that same place.

What is important is not whether your partner shares your culture or religion. What is important is that there is enough common ground in the three Bs to make the relationship sustainable.

Here's an example: My partner and I share a belief around the idea of God. We are not the types of atheists who try to prove to others that there is no God. But neither are we believers. We do not pray, and we do not believe God will solve our problems or the problems of the world. We believe in a humanistic philosophy that says if something needs doing, it is people who have to do it. This grounds our sense of personal responsibility, of morality, even of ambition. It is much easier for me to be married to someone who shares these beliefs with me than to be with a Jewish person who has a different idea about cosmology, the efficacy of prayer, or anything else to do with belief.

In terms of behavior, my husband and I both act similarly when it comes to things that count. In terms of culture, we believe in family celebrations and try to make the other's special and meaningful. We do not believe that giving gifts for any holiday should be its main thrust. We act in concert and consistency when it comes to instilling morality and responsibility in our children. You can see how shared belief gives rise to shared behavior.

In terms of belonging, the belief and behavior again correspond. We are both members of my Jewish congregation. (Note: It is *very* important for intermarried people to find a community that not only "tolerates" but celebrates intermarriage. See "C" for "Community" and "A" for "A$$holes.") You both deserve to feel welcome and at home in the community you choose. It is fine if this community serves the needs of one partner more than the other. Some people belong in two communities and some in one and some in neither. But community serves a really important role in our disconnected world. You deserve to find one that celebrates you and your family.

My group of friends are almost all intermarried. In fact, almost all of the couples closest to me are comprised of a Jewish woman and a non-Jewish man. This is a community! We celebrate Passover together and everyone is very welcome and participates. We understand one another's challenges and experiences. We feel a shared sense of belonging based on our shared beliefs and behaviors.

The three Bs of belief, behavior, belonging really tell you what you want to know about a potential partner. Please do not misunderstand me and think they always have to align perfectly! There are plenty of behaviors my partner has that drive me up the wall (and vice versa, to be sure). But in terms of the aspects of life that matter most to you, it's good to find some common ground over the three Bs. If they don't align yet, it's a worthwhile conversation to have to find out if they can. And how. And who needs to change what to make that happen.

What does all this have to do with B Mitzvah? Well, very often intermarried folks struggle with how to mark this important coming of age ritual, and I think the answer can be found in the three Bs. The traditional way one has a B Mitzvah is to read from the Torah as part of a prayer service, and then have some kind of celebration. The celebrations used to be a small luncheon at the family home, and now can be as extravagant as the most opulent celebrity weddings. With my clients, I tell them to focus on what matters: the three Bs.

The whole point of the B Mitzvah is to help this person, moving from childhood to adolescence, articulate who they are, what their identity values are, and how their identity and values will be enacted in the way they move through the world. My clients have the choice to read from the Hebrew Bible, but they all also have to do a research project, in English, on a topic of Jewish significance. Most adults I know who had a B Mitzvah can't remember their topic. In the Humanistic Jewish movement (see the introduction for a definition), we want people to be connected to their topic enough that they'll be able to tell their own children about it. We want it to be meaningful, and an articulation of their interests and values. We also require community service, learning, and an affirmation of identity and beliefs. Those who choose to do a reading from the Bible work to find one that touches on matters close to their heart (we don't stick them with the assigned reading for their particular date; we aren't doing the B Mitzvah in the context of a prayer service, so we are free to use the full text as we wish). Their interpretations are usually deep and meaningful, because they are writing on and interpreting something they care about.

The end goal is not that they have memorized and chanted some sounds in a language they don't speak, from a text they don't understand or care much about. This is, sadly, often the B Mitzvah experience, which ends up putting the focus on the party. I'm pleased that families plan the party that makes them happy, but the focus for me is on the ceremony itself. I want it to matter. Because I want the B Mitzvah person and event to be focused on the three Bs: belief, behavior, belonging. Who are they Jewishly and as a citizen of the world?

Bible

What does the Bible say about intermarriage, anyway? Some people who are against intermarriage will use the Bible as justification for their point of view. Are they correct? Well, yes and no. There are seventy faces of Torah (see "Backgrounds" for this discussion).

In the best-known biblical story of Exodus, Moses leads his people to freedom from Egyptian bondage. He does this with the support of his siblings, Miriam and Aaron, and his wife, Tziporah, the daughter of a Midianite priest and a loyal companion. Wait, what? Tziporah is a Midianite? Thus not an Israelite? The man called *Moshe Rabbeinu*, Moses the great rabbi and teacher, was intermarried?! You'd think that the many Jewish and other religious leaders and organizations who have spoken of intermarriage as "fulfilling Hitler's goal" would find this to be an uncomfortable contradiction. I don't know whether they do or don't, but I do know that if Moses can intermarry, not all of "Judaism" can be against it.

There are plenty of biblical narratives of people marrying into other tribes. The biblical Book of Ruth has a very famous example of what is, essentially, a conversion. Ruth, a Moabite, has married into an Israelite family. Sadly, her husband dies. Her mother-in-law, Naomi, entreats Ruth to return to her people, aware that, as a woman and a widow, Naomi can't take care of her. But Ruth is fiercely devoted to Naomi, in a beautiful biblical expression of true affinity and love between women. So Ruth the Moabite says to her mother-in-law Naomi, "Your people shall be my people and your God shall be my God" (Ruth 1:16). This story is often pointed to as a sign that conversion is kosher. Ruth is fully a member of the Israelite people (and, note, she didn't need a year of conversion classes to get there). I also see the story as a powerful reminder that love happens across lines of culture and community. For more on the Book of Ruth, see "S" for "Shavuot."

Of course, there are seventy faces of Torah and so one can easily find prohibitions against intermarriage. Moses (the same Moses) gets chastised later in the Exodus narrative for being with a Cushite woman. (There are really interesting implications in this story for Jews and race, as "Cushite" implies darker skin. When Moses' siblings object to this union, there may be a racist motivation and/or an anti-intermarriage one.) There is also the disgusting story of Phinehas (or Pinchas), who commits murder due to his outrage over an Israelite–Midianite tryst and is seen as a hero for it. Again, this very configuration was celebrated when it was Moses with Tziporah. There are contradictions in the text.

What all of this means to you is dependent on how you view the Bible. Most of the couples I see who are intermarrying believe that the Torah contains narratives that have served as the cornerstone for religious and cultural learning, debate, practice, and community. They can find meaning in some of the stories, or find them interesting as literary works. But they do not think that the Torah is a legal code that needs following nor, and this is the part that is controversial, do they necessarily think it was divinely written or inspired. Whatever your belief in the origins of the Bible, I challenge you to consider its weight in your life. If there are other prescriptions you ignore, why pay attention to the ones around intermarriage? Given the contradictory nature of some of these stories, making important life decisions such as whom you will date, marry, or co-parent with based on the Bible seems only logical if the Bible similarly affects other aspects of your life. If it does, I can appreciate how intermarriage may be difficult for you. You may be reading this because you have a child or someone else in your life who is intermarrying and you wish to understand it. In that case, let's remember that there are seventy faces of Torah, and what you take from it – as rich, beautiful, and inspiring as it may be – will not necessarily be what your loved ones take from it.

Blending

Some couples choose to blend cultures in their relationship, taking some aspects of each person's tradition and combining them to create family traditions, rituals, practices, and connections. I know plenty of couples who celebrate "Chrismukkah," a perfect example of blending, where they take traditions and combine them. One can buy Christmas tree toppers in the shape of the Star of David (see "S" for "Shopping – Stuff" for a story about what happened when these were featured in the airline magazine *Skymall*). I've been at dinners where both Christmas ham and Chanukah latkes are served. Some people find these things shocking and disturbing, and others find them to be exemplary of the many compromises one makes in creating a home with a significant other. What is your reaction to those examples?

My home is a mixed home in some ways, but blending isn't really my style. I like to celebrate traditions from my Jewish holidays Jewishly and traditions from my partner's family without any Jewish influence. But this is not about me and how I do it. This is about you and how you make traditions and practices meaningful for you. Do you like the idea of blending? Are you a Chrismukkah kind of family? If so, there are a lot of practical ways you can approach blending to make sure everyone feels heard and represented. Sit down with your partner and discuss how you'd like your calendar, with its many holidays and traditions, to reflect both or all of your family cultures and traditions. Use the acronym BLEND:

BEND: Which of your traditions can you be flexible about to make room for those of your partner? Where can you compromise?

LEARN: What do you need to know more about from your own or your partner's celebrations and culture to incorporate these meaningfully? You'll enjoy foreign holidays or practices much more if you learn their significance to the culture and to your partner.

ENTERTAIN: One of the best ways of actualizing some blended traditions is to host your families. One of the many benefits of intermarried families is that there is no competition for holidays; whatever it is you celebrate, your in-laws are probably free. So invite them over, share what you do, and make them a part of it. They may be resistant (see "A" for "A$$holes"), in which case be the host for friends, acquaintances, other intermarried families. Make your home the place to be to do blended traditions right.

NEGOTIATE: It's a word that comes up a lot in this book. Unlike "bend to blend," negotiation (see "N") is both about flexibility, and also articulating your hard lines. Where are you unwilling to bend? What is necessary for you to feel like you are getting what you need out of blended traditions?

DREAM: Just because you've never celebrated a mix of Diwali and Chanukah, or Passover/Easter/Bengali New Year, doesn't mean you can't! I'm not making up that example of Passover/Easter/Bengali New Year. I did a baby naming for a family that was an intermarriage between a Jewish Canadian and an Indian Christian. We brought in elements of all three traditions: Christian candlelighting led by a minister; a discussion of the Passover symbols of spring for rebirth and fertility led by me; and Bengali poetry read by the baby's father. This not only made for a really fascinating and fun baby naming, but it showed the parents how to raise a child with blended traditions that are beautiful and meaningful and, here's the key, that bolster and lend significance to the other traditions. When blending is done right, all of the traditions and rituals are made *more* significant, not less. Dream up your ideal scenario and then work with your partner to make it a reality.

Borrowing

Borrowing, like blending, is about mixing cultures together. Jews are really good at borrowing. Think latkes, languages, lifestyles. Latkes? They became popular in Eastern Europe but came originally from Italian pancakes. Languages? No one would deny that Yiddish or Ladino are "Jewish" languages, but they came about because of where Jews happened to be living, borrowing from the dominant language around them. Lifestyle? A Jew living in Ethiopia likely has a pretty different lifestyle from a Jew living on an Israeli *kibbutz*, which is pretty different from a Jew living in New York. And these are contemporary Jews. Think of the difference in lifestyle between a Jew today and a Jew 150 years ago, or 1,000 years ago. The reality is that, for most of us, our lifestyles are determined by the time, place, and surrounding culture in which we live. And Judaism also influences our lifestyles: we may eat *door wot* (a chicken dish) if we're in Ethiopia, falafel and hummus if we're in Israel, bagels with lox if we're in New York. Our experiences and lifestyles may be Jewishly inflected, but they also involve borrowing from the surrounding culture.

The cool thing about borrowing is that it works in multiple directions. I remember finding it so amusing when I heard a child, not Jewish, an immigrant to Canada from China, use the word *schlep*. This is amazing. We have not only borrowed from the cultures we've lived in and near, we've changed those very cultures. There is an area of Toronto called Kensington Market where many Jewish immigrants settled towards the beginning of the twentieth century. They established credit unions, shops, restaurants, aid societies, and more. Today, the area is largely Asian, often with the very same types of services and stores being run for immigrants from China as they were for immigrants from Eastern Europe a century earlier. We have had tremendous influence on Toronto and on immigrant populations that followed us, in ways we could never have imagined.

Borrowing, like blending, means we enrich one another through our interactions. So much more so when those interactions come from loving connections.

Bridges

One of the unspoken benefits of intermarriage is the bridge building that happens because couples and families engage in this kind of borrowing and blending. As a result, people know more about Jews and Judaism (what better antidote to antisemitism is there?) and we know more about the world. The negotiations that go on in families symbolize and catalyze negotiations that need to go on cross-culturally, for better intercultural and interfaith dialogue, towards a better world.

I teach at a fantastic university called Trent University in Ontario. It has a beautiful campus with a river running right through it, and a bridge connecting the two sides of the campus. (Note: The two sides are called "East Bank" and "West Bank" and once, seeing the university's address include "West Bank Drive," my father asked me if this was a political statement about Israel.) I do multifaith work on campus with leaders and students from many sects of Christianity, from Muslim and Baha'i cultures and religions, from Sikh communities, and more. Just as the campus couldn't function without the bridge that gets you to the academic buildings on either side, I believe it couldn't function without the dialogues and debates that forge bridges across the communities of people on campus – that is, people of all religions and people of no religion.

When we work out the dynamics of blending, borrowing, compromising, and negotiating, we build bridges within our relationship and between our families. This bridge building is a powerful tool for creating a more peaceful world. If we could learn to get along with people who are not like us, we would solve a lot of problems. I'm thinking specifically of problems like antisemitism and xenophobia, both of which Jews have suffered due to perceptions about us. While I'm on that subject, I want to offer a nudge to Jews today who are xenophobic. Sometimes we are so focused on antisemitism and being the "other" that we forget to examine our own biases, fears, and assumptions.

When Jews get married, we often do so under a *chuppah* (Jewish wedding canopy). When I officiate at an intermarriage, we often talk about both the construction and the meaning of the *chuppah*. In its construction, I encourage couples to find a way to incorporate both heritages. For example, I had a couple who used the groom's Scottish family tartan as part of the fabric. He was not Jewish, and she was. The *chuppah* was created to be a bridge between their respective cultures. Or using a *tallis* (prayer shawl) interwoven with another garment of significance to the other partner, such as a baptismal article of clothing they wore as an infant. I also discuss the meaning of the *chuppah*, a structure open on all sides like the tent of the biblical Sarah and Abraham. Their tent was open for reasons of hospitality, so travelers would see their home as a place of refuge. We speak about how the marital home will be open as a place of refuge to family and friends, with openness and acceptance as symbolized by the wall-less structure. Moreover, I discuss how marriage is like a home without walls – it is vulnerable to the winds of time and change, and also open to the warming of the sun. And the *chuppah* can serve as a reminder that a good marriage is a place where bridges, not walls, are formed.

My own *chuppah* when I got married was not symbolic of my intermarriage, but was still symbolic. A close friend of mine constructed her *chuppah* for her wedding out of bamboo poles and a beautiful piece of fabric from a store selling handmade goods, fairly traded by people, primarily women, in developing countries. I loved the fabric, it was a lovely pattern, incorporating burgundy and gold, some of my favorite colors, so I used it for my own wedding. After I used it, several others from our close circle of girlfriends used it. We called it the "sisterhood of the traveling *chuppah*." The home we build includes our partner and family, but it is also useful to incorporate symbols of all those who are special, welcome in the home, and part of the fabric of the relationships housed there.

B'shert (a Jewish Word Meaning "Soulmate")

After all, what it's all about is finding and fostering the relationship that sustains you the most. And any relationship that is worthwhile takes compromise and conversation. I am not a believer in the idea of a soulmate. I don't think there is one perfect person out there for any of us. It is too incongruous; with all the millions of people in the world, how would any of us find a partner if there were just one out of all of the options? I don't believe in predetermination or any kind of fatalistic "master plan." What I believe is that commitment is a choice. It's a choice we first make when we set out to build a life with someone, and it's a choice we keep making over and over again as we live out that life.

There is a Jewish concept of *"b'shert"* – a Yiddish word meaning a predestined soulmate. If you've ever been in love, you probably know the feeling that you sometimes get when you cannot believe your luck to have found this person and you cannot imagine your life without them. It's a nice feeling. It's the feeling of *b'shert*.

So I don't want to wreck that feeling for you, but I do think marriages only survive if we recognize that that feeling is not there all the time, and nor should it be. I am always suspicious of couples who feel completely happy all the time with their partners. It suggests to me a lack of individuality and a lack of growth. There should be times that you, with your own identity and deeply held views, will come up against your partner's identity and deeply held views. This will be hard. But when you find ways through those hard times, your relationship will become better and stronger and more fulfilling.

To me, the idea of *b'shert* is less of a lived reality and more of an intention. I don't believe my husband is the only one in the world I could have built a life with. But I chose him for good reasons and I am committed to him and our family. I want to live each day *as though* he were my intended, my one and only. I want to treat him that well. I want to work out each conflict with him as though it were a foregone conclusion that we'd always work out each conflict. And when we get that feeling like we could never be with another, it is because we have earned that feeling. It didn't happen to us; we made it happen.

"C" is a big section because of the question of children and how they are raised in terms of religion: Mixed? None? Part? These words are used by some and are offensive to others. This section covers both research and case studies about what couples have done to instill religion or culture in their children. I have included detailed questions to discuss when planning a family, and some helpful communication tools to get the job done. These conversations can be fraught, but they can be fun too! There is also focus on community and how to build or join communities that are supportive and that help the family thrive. I'll give some examples of how people are raising their children and creating communities that work for them.

Calm

Once when I was in the throes of new motherhood, and stressing about everything from sleep to poops to baby acne to who knows what, I read a great article. It was championing a new style of parenting! It was going to revolutionize mom circles the world over! It was the CTFD style of parenting. What is CTFD? Calm The F*ck Down. I needed to CTFD as a new mom.

I want to bring the CTFD model to Judaism and, especially, intermarriage. Sometimes when I'm at a talk or conference or something and someone is railing against intermarriage and how it's destroying the Jewish community, I answer with all my academic and rabbinic statistics and social analysis and experience. But what I really want to say is "CTFD."

If you are the parent of an adult child who is intermarried or intermarrying, and you picked up this book to figure stuff out, this part is for you: CTFD. I say that with gentleness and love (really, I mean that). But, truly, the calmer you are, the better it's going to go for you.

Recently I spoke at Limmud, a day of learning on Jewish topics, with a sociologist about trends in the Toronto Jewish community. Intermarriage featured strongly in both our talks. Afterwards a lovely woman approached me and said something like, "After my son married out, I find it really hard to get him to come to holidays or do anything Jewish at all." She was sad. It made me sad. I gently and respectfully told her that a good place to start might be to stop saying he "married out," especially to him. I invited her to consider whether she gave him a hard time about this marriage, whether she had projected some anxiety onto him, and whether all of that might be affecting his desire to engage with Jewish stuff, especially on her turf. I suggested she approach her son and apologize for any hurt she had caused him and his partner. Then tell him why she so valued him AND HIS NON-JEWISH SPOUSE at the holiday table. Mostly, I told her to try to lose the anxiety and make the holiday table somewhere they would all want to be. In short, CTFD.

If you yourself are intermarried and are freaking out about how to raise your kids or incorporate traditions or why your partner never mentioned that they expected you to go to church or whatever your particular thing is, please, take my advice: CTFD. It doesn't mean these things aren't a big deal. It's precisely because this is all such a big deal that I want you to approach it with a cool head. Everything will be okay.

Camp

I'm going to say something kind of controversial here: I'm skeptical of Jewish summer camp. Survey after survey shows that a key indicator of whether someone will identify as Jewish in adulthood is whether they attended Jewish summer camp. Not all Jewish adults attended summer camp, but it looks like the vast majority of kids who attend Jewish summer camp stay Jewish. A bunch of those folks also intermarry, so you'd think I'd be the biggest champion of Jewish summer camp around. But here's what's discomfiting about it to me: I worry that the "Judaism" of summer camp is, at best, lacking in substance and, at worst, pretty chauvinistic. It can also be very uncritically Zionist, which might work for some families but does not work for all.

I used to be a summer camp director and, while we were not an officially Jewish camp, lots of our kids were Jews. On the first day, one kid came off the bus chanting, "Jews are the best! Jews are the best!" He had come from a previous Jewish summer camp experience where that was a normal thing to do when getting off the bus. The camp staff pumped the kids up about their "chosenness" even before arriving at the camp. I had to explain to this kid that he needed to cool it in an environment where not everyone was Jewish. And we had a pretty interesting conversation about the difference between pride (feeling good about who you are) and chauvinism (feeling better than others). I worry that too much Jewish pride actually comes from a sense of superiority (it's why the whole "chosen people" thing doesn't work for me). I'm not saying all Jewish camps have their kids chant "Jews are the best" on the bus, and I fully understand how a Jewish camp was an oasis in an openly antisemitic world for the boomer generation, but it did make me wonder why Jewish camps are so successful at instilling identity.

As a child, I attended a Jewish summer camp for only one summer. The only Jewish thing about it was that we dressed up for Friday night dinner. Maybe there were Shabbat candles? There was no Jewish programming. There was certainly no discussion of Jewish text or values. It was basically a bunch of Jews hanging out with each other.

If Jewish summer camps are a predictor of Jewish identity, I have to wonder why. Some are better at the Jewish values stuff. I adore a local camp called Shomria, for example, both for the Jewish teaching they offer kids and for a very special program they run, called Heart to Heart, that brings Jewish and Palestinian Israeli kids to the camp for important coexistence work. That's a camp I can get behind (and support with my time and my dollars).

What's the point of all this? For intermarried folks, you might want to check out Jewish camp. It might be awesome for your kid. But if it's the kind of camp where people are chanting "Jews are the best" and not everyone in your family is a Jew, you might want to think twice.

Children (and a Bonus "C" – Circumcision)

Most of the traditional anxiety around intermarriage has to do with fears over "confusing the children." I was so aghast when people told me that my kids would be "f*cked up" if we raised them as "both" (see "A" for "A$$holes"). In my experience, kids are pretty adaptable. They're smarter than most adults give them credit for. They're fine.

In *Being Both: Embracing Two Religions in One Interfaith Family,* Susan Katz Miller speaks about meaningfully teaching her children Jewish and Christian practices, texts, and values, and instilling a firm identity as "both." If this works for you, awesome! I wanted my kids to identify as Jewish and early on my partner and I decided this is what we would do. He has no religious or cultural identity he wishes to instill, anyway. We are both atheists, so that part is easy and requires no compromise. So if you ask my kids if they're Jewish, they'll say yes. If you ask if they celebrate Christmas, they'll also say yes. Our kids go to public school, and that is where they learn Christmas songs and see images of Santa and a decorated tree. Plenty of kids managed to go to public school and emerge Jewish (including yours truly). At home we don't have Santa but we do have a little tree. But my kids feel Jewish and do so much Jewish stuff that there can really be no confusion. We do Shabbat each week (and my daughter's teacher says she talks about it all the time). We celebrate most holidays (not the weird minor fast ones but, you know, lots and lots of holidays). We read Jewish books. We talk about Jewish values like *chesed* (lovingkindness). We hang out in Jewish spaces. We go to Jewish Sunday school and community programs.

Here's the thing: if a little Christmas cheer can make your kids reject their Jewish identity, you aren't doing Jewish very well. You aren't showing your kids what's exciting, wonderful, and fun about Jewish practice and tradition. You aren't giving them an identity rooted in meaning.

It's not just me who wants you to relax about the kids. We have hard data now to show that the majority of intermarried folks are raising their kids with at least some Jewish identity and practice. And more and more kids are identifying as Jewish as they grow up. This is in spite of generations of us being told that if we "married out" our kids would choose to align with the dominant culture. Guess what? Kids know what's up. Not everyone chooses to raise their kids with Jewish identity and practice. And that's actually fine with me. Everyone gets to decide how they want to parent their children and, for some people, their Jewish identity is not something they desire to pass on. But the majority of people who are Jewish and intermarried *do* want to pass on some Jewish identity and practice. The problem is that they've been told that, because they are intermarried, their kids will choose the other partner's religion or culture, especially if it is the culture that is most common where they live (so, for us in North America, kids will choose to celebrate Christmas because it's reflected in and a part of the dominant culture). But it doesn't have to be this way! If you to do want to transmit Judaism to your kids, this is how: Make it clear that being Jewish is awesome. Show them. And, for Pete's sake, make it easy for them to connect. When communities are welcoming of intermarried folks, their kids, if not the whole *mishpachah* (family), are more likely to want to engage.

When welcoming a new child to the family, it is traditional to have a ceremony. Actually, the tradition only extends to babies assigned male at birth, and it includes a circumcision. Modern Jews do a ceremony called a *Brit Shalom*, which means covenant of peace. (Sometimes the ceremony is called something else. For girls, it is sometimes called a *Simchat Bat* – celebrating a girl.) Circumcision, or *Brit Milah* (covenant of circumcision), is a long-standing tradition. It is also sometimes a sticky subject, as some people don't like the practice. Intermarriage can be a factor; sometimes the family who isn't Jewish doesn't understand the practice. It is sometimes not an intermarriage thing, many Jews today also question whether they wish to circumcise (see "O" for "Oppression" for a story about a family who disagreed about circumcision).

I have a lot to say on this subject but, to boil it down, I think everyone needs to chill. Having a baby is hard enough without judgment on all sides of this issue. I know folks who are pressured to circumcise by parents on one side and pressured to avoid it from parents on the other side (for more on this, see "G" for "Grandchildren"). This is tough. Ultimately, it is the decision of the parents. If you're intermarried and making it choice, there are resources to help you. Speak to doctors, religious and spiritual leaders, and, most importantly, each other. This decision, like all others in an intermarriage, is about deciding how to live your values as a family.

Communication/Chrismukkah

People make choices about how to honor their ceremonial and holiday traditions. Some folks take a separate-but-equal approach. Others choose to blend symbols and rituals. Figuring out how to unite the symbols of the *mandap* and the *chuppah* at a wedding, the *tzedakah* and the *zakah* in the home (see "Culture" below), or any other blended tradition takes some work. The place where much of that conversation happens is around the "December Dilemma" – how people do Christmas and Chanukah. There are many approaches to this time of year, but before we go there I want you to shift the focus from "dilemma" to "delight." That is, this is all supposed to be meaningful and fun. Framing it as a dilemma is part of the problem. And it reflects a larger communication problem that couples have, and came by honestly because they grew up with a narrative of crisis around what it would mean for a Jew to have a Christmas tree. The communication problem here is thinking that all this is going to be So. Very. Hard. Look, sometimes it's going to be hard. But the harder you expect something to be, and the more you brace yourself and get defensive and be all in your head about it, the harder it is sure to be. Chill. This is an opportunity for "December Delights" – creating traditions that make you happy and reflect your values. Frame the communication in this positive way and I guarantee the communicating will be much more fun.

People intermarry for all kind of reasons, the most important being that they love each other. So remember that love and communicate from there. What is important to you? To your partner? Where can you bend? Where can they? What can you let go of? What is a dealbreaker? How can you do stuff to make it all fun?

All marriages require that the partners communicate on a number of issues. Whether it is money, differences in parenting approaches, family dynamics, or culture or religion, you're going to have to figure out how to talk to each other, how to hear each other, and how to make sure everyone is getting what they need. For help communicating, you may want to see a therapist or coach. Some rabbis or other religious or cultural leaders excel at these kinds of conversations. And if it's the "December Dilemma" versus the "December Delights" that you want help with, check out my "December Delights: Creating a Crushing Chrismukkah" guide in the appendix.

Community

The real tragedy in the fear-mongering over intermarriage is how destructive it has been to the Jewish community. So many people have been hurt, truly harmed, by rejection. I'm talking about the kids of intermarried parents who grew up hearing they're not a "real" Jew (usually by the kid who ate bacon for breakfast and wouldn't know a Shabbat candle if it smacked them in the face). I'm talking about the parent of the kid having a B Mitzvah who isn't allowed on the *bimah* (podium) because they aren't Jewish. I'm talking about people who can't get married by their family rabbi, people who get dirty looks in synagogue, people whose families won't welcome their spouse to the Passover table. *Oy vey*. We have caused some real damage. Why? Oh, you know, "Jewish continuity." It was so important to continue Jewish communities that we excluded a bunch of people who wanted to be a part of them. Now, not enough people want to join us, and we don't get why?

The reason more people are raising their kids with a Jewish identity and practice, are connecting to communities, and are breathing new life into Judaism is because (finally!) there are communities that will welcome them. I'm a proud member of the Humanistic Jewish movement, founded on the principles that secular or cultural Jews need celebrations and communities that do not use the language of prayer but instead focus on human and earth-centered concerns. Because the movement's founder Rabbi Sherwin Wine, along with the other leaders and community members who started this branch of Judaism, was less interested in what Jewish law had to say and more interested in what would serve human needs, Humanistic Judaism was completely groundbreaking on intermarriage. I joined this movement partly because I appreciate serving communities that maintain no barriers for intermarried folks, from participation to board leadership to who a rabbi can marry (in officiating or in their own spousal relations) and so on. We were visionaries (despite being "non-prophet societies"). Other movements and some independent congregations are catching up. It is now more possible to find your rabbi, find your people, and find your space, and so more people are more likely to engage.

And I do want you to find your community. I am such a believer in the power of community for so many reasons. We live lives that are overwhelmingly busy. We juggle so many demands. If we have to come up with all our own spiritual programming and learning, it's going to sink to the bottom of a long to-do list. I think we need teachers and leaders who inspire and challenge us. We need peers who offer support and friendship. We need people to eat *challah* with. We need people to sing with.

Notice, the tragedy of the anti-intermarriage garbage was not that it hurt the intermarried people. That is awful, of course. But, to me, the tragedy is what it did to our Jewish communal spaces, turning them into places built on a model of fear and scarcity, meanness and a lack of compassion. Frankly, it's all pretty un-Jewish. Judaism, the way I understand and practice it, is about being welcoming, kind, giving, and good. At Passover we say, "Let all who are hungry come and eat" not "let all who agree with and practice like us come and *kvetch* (complain) about how other people do it." We lost out on all those families and folks who could enliven us with different points of view and experience. We lost out on all those kids who, after being told they weren't a "real" Jew, went on to become many wonderful things but not in our Jewish spaces. The good news is that the spaces are changing. Find one that will see and welcome you for who you are and for who your family is. You need community, and your community needs you.

Compromise

All the communicating is going to lead to some kind of compromise. You're not always going to have things be exactly as you would want them. Welcome to marriage! People talk about intermarriage as though there are going to be so very many sacrifices and *oy vey* how will it all work out and there will be hand-wringing and more. Please. Working out the cultural practices in my home are the least of the compromises my partner and I make to have our home function. We agreed to have a primarily Jewish home with some Christmas cultural stuff thrown in to honor his childhood traditions. Yes, we had to compromise about things like lights and a tree. He has had to learn new Jewish traditions, holidays, and vocabulary. None of this has been that hard. You know what's hard? Figuring out who gets to sleep in on Saturday when the baby never lets anyone get any rest. Debating who is going to the friend's party when you can't find a babysitter and you both want to go. Understanding that you don't get to spend as long in the bathroom as you once did if everyone is to get out of the house on time. I can't tell you the compromises I've had to make in terms of scheduling, sleep, *schlepping*, and *schmoozing* – all the good "s" words. If you can't compromise, you can't be married (or happily married, anyway). And it shouldn't always be the same person compromising all the time, either! You both got to give to get. You both should *want* your partner to be happy. Marriage is like improv comedy. You have to say yes as often as possible to keep the show going.

Conversion

In Judaism, it has often been seen as a victory if the partner converts. And it may indeed be a victory for that person and their partner, but only if the conversion comes out of a genuine interest and feeling of affinity for Judaism. Conversions of convenience really serve no one. In fact, I believe they detract from the health of the cultural life of the family as they foreclose the possibilities for conversations about how to bend, blend, and borrow from various cultures to create the cultural life of a family that works for everyone.

It is precisely because so many couples are "intercultural" rather than "interfaith" that the whole question of conversion has become a little ridiculous. In cases where you have a religious Jew, and by that I mean one that believes in the God of the Bible and values praying to that God, and you have their partner who shares those beliefs, it makes sense for the partner to convert. But this does not describe the vast majority of conversions that happen for marriage. Conversions by spiritual seekers who come to Judaism and choose it for themselves are very different from the conversions of convenience that people have gone through to satisfy the requirements of a rabbi who has been asked to officiate.

This is not to knock Jews by choice and the meaning in their conversions. Quite the opposite! I think we make a mockery of that serious process and Jewish *neshama* (soul) when we ask people to do the same thing when they are not believers, when they don't really wish to become Jewish, and when the Jewish partners don't know or believe the majority of what the non-Jewish spouses are being asked to learn, practice, and believe.

Most people who were born Jewish (outside orthodoxy) are not that Jewishly literate. Most don't attend synagogue regularly, study text, or mark most of the holidays. So how can we ask their partners to do all that stuff? We are setting people up to have to make a difficult choice between pretending to believe something they don't or having their partner leave their community. It's an awful choice. I don't want to spend a ton of time on that here because it is so well documented in the work of Keren McGinity, Kerry Olitzky, and many others. Here's what I'm saying: Don't convert! (Unless you want to.) That is, no one gets to tell you who you are and how you live. It's absurd that Jewish leaders make people jump through so many hoops. Luckily, things are shifting. Find a rabbi who will welcome you as you are, not ask you to pretend, not ask either partner to say stuff and do stuff that isn't really what you believe or feel like doing, and will help you figure out how to create a Jewish home or a blended home that does fit your values. Can't find such a rabbi? Call me. It's what I live for.

Cost

A lot of people feel priced out of Jewish life. Day schools, supplementary schools, synagogue memberships, Jewish Community Centre

(JCC) memberships, hiring a rabbi to do a baby naming or a B Mitzvah (see "B").

All of this is expensive.

People spend money on what's important to them. In my family, it's important that my kids are educated Jewishly, that they have big holiday celebrations, that they get to do Jewish programs. I spend money on that. That's my value. But I send my kids to public school, not (just) because of the cost of Jewish day school but because I want my kids to be in a diverse environment and I care about public education. Those are also my values.

I'm in a position where I can determine how much to spend on certain extras. Some people aren't. And some people are but may choose not to invest in Jewish stuff if it comes at the expense of ski lessons or a vacation.

If you are in a position to spend some money on Jewish life, it can be a gift to you, your partner, and your kids (see "Community" above). If you are not, free options are available. The PJ Library (pjlibrary.org) sends free Jewish-themed children's books to families in the US and Canada each month. Many community events at synagogues and JCCs are free. Many congregations will be happy to offer you a subsidized spot. Don't let money be a barrier to living the life that corresponds with your values. And, if you can, support with time, commitment, and dollars those values and Jewish institutions that do welcome and make great space for intermarried folks.

Creativity

Sometimes a successful intercultural home requires some creative thinking. One of the things I adore about my intermarried home is how we get the kids involved in figuring out ways to celebrate our holidays. They create art, they sing songs, they make our home the cozy, celebratory place we need it to be. I love my partner for his ability to come up with creative solutions to problems. He approaches things from such a different perspective, really operating from a place of possibility and offering creative ideas and solutions that I could never think up. I love that we have learned how to communicate and compromise, partly because we are intermarried, and that has had a positive ripple effect across so many areas of our marriage. Life can be complex, often confusing, and full of conflict. The "C" of creativity is the antidote to all that. Keep calm (see above) and creatively figure out how to carry on.

C

Culture

Often when people talk about intermarriage they refer to it as "inter-faith marriage." I get that this was the traditional term because people were very rooted in faith-based communities if not in their faith itself. But now? Most of the people who intermarry are not really "faith" types. Of course there are exceptions to this. Susan Katz Miller's book, *Being Both*, is a wonderful resource for those looking to practice two different faiths in their home. The people I serve, people like me, are not really interfaith. We are intercultural. For some people, blending faiths is a challenge because the tenets are opposing. Is Jesus the messiah or isn't he? Do we believe that there are many Gods or just one? These are questions that might make it hard for a Christian-Jewish or Hindu-Jewish union. These are questions of faith. The cultural tenets, however, are not really opposing. Everyone has to figure out how they make it all work, but there is nothing inherently or explicitly conflicting in putting up a Christmas tree and lighting a *menorah*. The wedding symbols of the Hindu *mandap* and the Jewish *chuppah* dovetail nicely. I can already hear critics saying, "But this is watering down our tradition! It is much deeper than that!" I couldn't agree more! The Jewish value of *tzedakah* (charity and justice) corresponds nicely with the idea of the Muslim pillar of *zakah*. Christianity teaches to love your neighbor. So does Judaism. Cultural practices, including ritual elements such as lighting Shabbat candles, Passover Seders, planting a tree on Tu B'shevat, all of these can be layered with meanings from other cultures to enhance their value for an intercultural family. All cultures value light, freedom, appreciation of nature – so you can blend how each culture approaches these things. Shabbat, Passover, and Tu B'shevat are Jewish containers, but they can be filled with a mixture of meanings.

Borrowing from Brené Brown's work on "daring greatly," this section talks about how to use daring to communicate both with one another as a couple and with other family members who may have questions or objections to intermarriage. The concept of daring is perfect because it is rooted in a sense of love. When you love someone and you love yourself, the ability to be daring arises naturally. We will defend what we love. Let's talk about dancing. If you can think of your marriage as a dance, you can figure out how to move in time together. The reason to speak of death is that one of the issues for intermarried couples to work out is how to honor cultural traditions in difficult times. If someone dies, do you follow the religious or cultural rites of their family or those of the partner left grieving? Can you be buried together in the cemetery of your choice? Different places have different rules. This section provides coaching on how to navigate some of those difficult conversations. It also gives space for beautiful approaches to marriage/intermarriage such as how to dream together and pursue those dreams, and how to create a do-it-yourself (DIY) cultural landscape that helps you build and make meaning in your family life.

Daily Life

Sometimes it seems the Jewish community expects that for intermarried couples their intermarriage is the main feature of their lives. But it is rarely front of mind. No one wakes up and says, "*Oy vey!* I'm intermarried." Life is filled with mundane and meaningful tasks: breakfast, hygiene, carpool, school drop-offs, work, dinner, bed, rinse, repeat. For many of us, our daily lives are not actually that infused with cultural or religious practice. In these scenarios, being intermarried will only come up occasionally. And that's just fine.

For some, they wish to infuse Judaism and/or other cultures into their daily lives and the home. Some keep kosher. Some offer blessings. Some hang a *mezuzah* on the doorframe as a daily reminder of the Jewish elements of the home. Some do Shabbat, Havdallah, or other regular practices.

Part of why I started SecularSynagogue.com, my online community for cultural/secular/spiritual-but-not-religious people, was that I wanted Judaism to be a daily (or at least regular) feature in the lives of people wanting to connect. I think we benefit to think of the values of *mitzvah* (good deeds), *chesed* (lovingkindness), or *tzedakah* (charity and justice) regularly. I think learning about Jewish topics and discussing issues pertinent to Jewish life can add meaning to one's day. The majority of the people in SecularSynagogue.com are in intercultural relationships. They are interested in Jewish culture and practice, and they are also incorporating other aspects of their multiple identities. It's so vital to have communal space that can support and inspire the daily practices that add depth to your days.

If you are intermarried, some daily stuff might be a solo project. I do a lot of daily stuff on my own – the newspapers and periodicals I read, the conversations I have online and in person, the films, concerts, and public lectures I attend without my partner. Your partner cannot and should not be everything. It's fine to do some things separately. In fact, it's healthy. You might also bring your partner in for some of these things. For us, we do Shabbat as a family, my partner even keeps it up if I'm not home. Some daily and weekly stuff happens alone, some together. Everyone gets what they need and no one has to do what they're uncomfortable with.

Dancing

There is a Jewish proverb that says "You can't dance with one *tuchus* [bum] at two weddings." The idea is that you can't be in two places at once and also that one shouldn't overextend oneself. It's a nice metaphor for intermarriage because you can't be two people at once, and a couple can only really have one direction for their family life. What's the lesson? Decide on your dance. Set the music, learn the steps, and then rock it. Make your homelife dance your own.

Daring

For so much of my life, the Jewish community was concerned with preventing intermarriage. There were multiple programs, speakers, sermons, all aimed at reaching out to those "at risk" of intermarrying. But these resources were all trying to solve a problem that no one actually had. No one, myself included, wakes up in the morning and thinks, "*Oy vey*, I'm intermarried!" Or "Hmm ... if I'm not careful, I might accidentally intermarry." The people drawn to these programs were usually already against intermarriage and had no interest in it. The people whose values make it possible to intermarry are more secular, more culturally Jewish; they value diversity; they see Judaism as a family that one can join and, for them, can't ever fully leave. These people were not interested in those programs and, therefore, not interested in a huge chunk of what Jewish life had to offer for decades. If you were someone, like me, for whom prayer was not interesting or meaningful, you would not be drawn to a Shabbat or other holiday service at the best of times. If the rabbi spent all their time on a diatribe against intermarriage, instead of something inspiring, you might just never return. And that's what happened. People stopped going and stopped engaging.

The issue is that what was presented as "Judaism" was completely fear-based. The community was operating from a place of scarcity, worried that people "marrying out" or "diluting" the religion, or some other made-up concern, would end the religion and community as they knew it. However, people are generally not drawn to places and people that operate from this scarcity mindset. People are drawn to abundance. People are not drawn to fear; people are drawn to love.

Social researcher Brené Brown has written several books that get into these issues. I like her work because it is both deep and accessible. Her first groundbreaking publication was *Daring Greatly: How the Courage to Be Vulnerable Transforms the Way We Live, Love, Parent, and Lead*. Oh, how I wish the Jewish leaders of my youth had had this book. They were so unwilling to be vulnerable. They should have just admitted they were scared of what was happening to Jewish life. They should have said to those intermarrying, "We're nervous here, but let's figure this out together." They should have realized that the problem might not have been with the people intermarrying; the problem might have been how they were practicing Judaism and whether it was attractive.

We all need the courage to be vulnerable. Our communities are beginning to be daring. We are beginning to ask big questions, get uncomfortable, and show that we are nervous but willing to work to make what we have to offer, and who we are, great.

If I have one piece of advice for couples intermarrying, it's this: Don't be afraid to be vulnerable with your partner. Show them why your cultural values and traditions are important to you. Share them with openness. Be equally open when your partner shares theirs. This may feel strange or foreign to you, but if you can witness and learn and, eventually, practice the traditions of your partner (see "C" for "Compromise"), you can get through so much of what is required in and of a marriage.

Death

All great poetry is concerned with love and death. And so is this book! Why talk about death at all here? Well, it's something to consider if you're intermarried. Different cultures and traditions handle death differently. It's worth discussing your end-of-life wishes and plans with each other. Do you want to be buried or cremated? Do you wish to follow the customs of your culture of birth or the culture of your partner? Do you wish to be buried together? If so, can you find a place that will do that?

In Toronto, where I live, my congregation, Oraynu Congregation for Humanistic Judaism, was the very first to offer a Jewish section of a cemetery where people of different cultures and religions could be buried together (non-Jews can't be buried in a traditional Jewish cemetery). We also allow for people to be cremated (also a no-no in Jewish law) with the option of burying the remains. It has been so important for intermarried folks to have this option. Other groups are now following suit but not everywhere has options like this. It's worth doing some research.

Definition

The Jewish community writ large is overly and somewhat oddly concerned with the "definition of a Jew." Many spend a lot of time worrying about the three Bs (not my three Bs of belief, behavior, belonging; see "B") of budgets, buildings, butts (as in attendance; butts in seats).

This is made obvious when people show up at events and then, when they do, all those people hear about is the "definition of a Jew." What counts, who's in, who's out, boundaries and rules. Could there be a more boring preoccupation?

I hang out in secular Jewish circles. We get called, and call ourselves sometimes, everything from atheist/agnostic/heretical/secular/spiritual-but-not-religious/cultural Jews. Self-definition is important. Identity and identification are important. What is super unimportant is stressing out over whether the person in the next pew over from you is a "real" Jew.

It's so destructive when kids tell other kids at Sunday school or camp that they are "not a real Jew" (see "C" for "Camp"). As if Judaism is a zero-sum game and there isn't enough Jewish to go around. As if we have to hoard it or lord it over others. It's so yucky.

If *halachah*, Jewish law, is your thing, the definition of a Jew is someone who was born to a Jewish mother or who has converted. That's it. Not someone who believes in God or prays or pays synagogue dues or keeps kosher or even someone who gives to *tzedakah* (charity) or calls their mother often. These can be meaningful and wonderful expressions of Jewish values, but none of it is required of Jews. What is required is that you have been born Jewish or have chosen to become Jewish.

That means that Jews (whether by choice or by birth) who intermarry are still fully Jewish. End of story.

So let's stop using terms like "marrying out." There is no "out" in Judaism (well, you can convert but some will still say you have a Jewish *neshama,* or soul). You are a Jew once you are a Jew, and it doesn't matter what you do.

Why all this stressing over a definition? It's that scarcity, fear-based stuff. We all need to let it go. If Jewish practices and communities are inspiring, engaging, and create opportunities for growth and connection, Jews of all kinds (and their non-Jewish partners and families) will want in. If Judaism sucks, people will want out. Let's make it not suck.

Recently I was speaking to a university Jewish studies class. I talked about who I am, what I believe, and what I do. I mentioned that I was intermarried and work with intermarried folks and everyone's attention focused on that. I got question after question like: What if people you are marrying lie to you about how they plan to practice Judaism? (Answer: I don't have requirements; I help them figure out what will work for them. They have no reason to lie.) Will you do a B Mitzvah for a child if the dad is Jewish? (Answer: It is such an honor to help people become B Mitzvah; I would be so delighted.) Do you worry about people being Jewish in the future? (Answer: No. If Judaism is meaningful for people it will continue. If it isn't, no one will miss it.) I don't mind answering tough questions but it did strike me as sad that these questions were top of mind. There were no questions of Jewish wisdom, meaning, how cultural Judaism works to make people's lives or the world better. Just the fear-based stuff I grew up with too. We could all be and have so much more.

Destiny

See "B" for "*B'shert.*"

Divorce

Like death, divorce is obviously an unpleasant topic that people wish to avoid. But it's important for intermarrying folks to consider what they'd want in the event of a divorce. The Jewish tradition (usually in addition to civil divorce) is to go before a rabbinic assembly called a *beit din* and request a *get* (writ of divorce). The stipulations depend on the *beit din*. In the communities where Jewish law is applied more strictly, these courts favor men and often are truly harmful to women. I know many people who would sooner die before requesting a *get* from a rabbi. But if you might want one, it's worth thinking about whether your partner would go through this process with you if they aren't Jewish. Sometimes these things are best discussed before marriages fall apart. Of course, ideally the marriage stays intact. However, it might be an important commitment you make to each other that you will honor your agreements around culture and religion even in the event that things turn sour. (See "L" for "Legalities.")

DIY

Because we may not have had models in our past or in our communities on how to build a Jewish life, I encourage intermarried folks to do it yourself (DIY). Figure out how to have a raucous, hilarious, joyful Shabbat dinner. Or, if it's more your speed, gather resources all through March so that your Passover Seder can be filled with learning, discussion, and study. The Jewish internet is huge and growing. There are online text sources like Sefaria, community resources via "Jewbooks" (Jewish Facebook groups), ritual support via Ritualwell and My Jewish

Learning, and a wealth of resources via InterfaithFamily that are geared specifically for folks who are intermarried, including content to make holiday celebrations, how to find officiants, and much more. There are also many print resources, speakers, how-to events, cultural community and congregational programs – in short, all kinds of resources you can access to figure out how you want to do Jewish in your house. If you aren't finding a community you like (see "C" for "Community"), find one online, or build your own, or be a community unto yourselves. DIY traditions can be most meaningful because they are built to serve the needs of you and your family. You've invested the work into making them so you care about them. Bonus points if everyone in the home participates, regardless of Jewish identity or lack thereof. Judaism is a primarily home-based culture, so opportunities to DIY abound!

Dogma

As you can tell, I'm no fan of dogma. Jewishly, there's the dogma of those who think we should take the Bible literally. There's the dogma of those who think *halachah* (Jewish law) should be followed as closely as possible. There's the dogma of the "Are you a real Jew?" types that would have people prove "how Jewish they are" by producing their Jewish credentials and experiences. For some, the dogma works. Some people like the structure and the feeling of following rules. But some, like me, kind of bristle against rules. I want to be able to chart my own course.

I don't think Jewish dogma is the essence of the spirituality of Judaism. In Judaism there is a distinction between *keva* (letter of the law) and *kavannah* (intention) (see "K" for these definitions). I'm a real *kavannah* girl. It's almost never meaningful for me to follow rules for the sake of doing so. Judaism is full of wisdom and beauty, and to access it, especially for non-traditional and/or intermarried folks, one needs to transcend the idea of what "should" be and focus instead on the possibilities of what "could" be.

Dreams

Part of "daring greatly" (see "Daring" above), I think, is to dream big. I want your life to be rich. I think people deserve to be fully themselves, to luxuriate in the traditions and practices that nourish them. I think dreaming is an important part of marriage too. You are building a life together – what dreams do you share, both individually and together?

How will you support each other's dreams? Often those dreams have to do with raising children or home ownership or travel or career goals. But do you have spiritual dreams? Might you want to make a pilgrimage? Do you have a dream of hosting a huge Passover Seder for your entire extended family? Is part of your dream life a really solid Shabbat practice? Share your dreams with your partner. Be big and bold in your dreaming. Your marriage will be stronger if you help make one another's dreams come true.

"E" is for "energy" and "excitement." If you are excited about your cultural practice, it is more likely your partner will be interested in it too. If you bring energy to learning about your partner's beliefs, it'll deepen your connection. "E" is also for emotional load, related to the energy and excitement you bring to exploring your marriage/intermarriage. Part of the dynamics of figuring out how to live in an intermarriage is related to the dynamics of marriage in general. Who is in charge of the emotional caretaking? Is it equitable? Talking and thinking through emotional load can be part of how to navigate any issues intermarriage itself gives rise to. In this section we speak about elevation, both literal (have you ever been lifted up on a chair at a Jewish celebration?) and figurative. We speak about the importance of the everyday – how life is the sum of small moments. Finally, this sections considers "eats" and how a lot of what we experience in sharing culture has to do with food. More than a simple act of nourishment, food is a cultural transmitter of history, knowledge, community, geography, and more. Moreover, food brings families and communities together.

Eagerness

At a Jewish wedding, the couple and their family get lifted on chairs (see "Elevation" below). My favorite moments are when the non-Jewish parents of the intermarrying couple get up on that chair. This is such a leap of faith in so many ways. It's a tradition that's likely new to them. As mentioned, it's a little scary. But they put their bodies on the line and say, "I'm not missing out on this. I'm here for my kid. I'm willing to learn any new tradition that'll help this family come together. Sign me up for the joy."

I've seen some beautiful willingness and even eagerness on the part of non-Jews to get to know Jewish customs and community so that they feel connected to their new family by marriage. It's a beautiful thing.

Ease

I have an unsteady and erratic yoga practice, so I'm no expert when I say this, but I understand that yogis try to incorporate something called *sukha* into their practice. This is not to be confused with the *sukkah*, a little hut we build to help us celebrate the Jewish holiday of *Sukkot*. *Sukha* means something like "ease." It is the focus precisely when things are not easy. Note that subtle difference between easy and ease. If you are in an easy marriage, first, congratulations, and second, are you sure it's easy? For both of you? My experience is that marriage is only easy if someone is sacrificing too much. Marriage shouldn't feel like torture, but it should sometimes feel like work. After all, we all have foibles and flaws. In yoga, when you are trying to hold a posture that is offering some kind of intensity or discomfort (not pain, discomfort), the goal is to settle into that pose with ease. The teaching is that sometimes we all need to lean into discomfort. Resisting it or complaining through it only intensifies the discomfort. Finding ease in moments of tension helps soften things enough that we can actually move past the discomfort. What happens next? We get stronger.

Are you still with me or are you in downward dog all of a sudden? I don't love doing the "chair" pose (also known as "intense" pose), but I know that how I react to it in the moment matters. If I'm like, "Ugh, this is haaaaaard. I hate it," the pose will feel like it will take forever. If I decide to practice *sukha* or ease, I remember that my thoughts are mine to control and things are rarely as bad as they seem. And then my quad muscles get stronger! Marriage and intermarriage are the same. Sometimes there will be tension. Find ease. You and your relationship will get stronger.

Eats

There is a rich world of food that intermarriage can open up. I had a Jewish client who married a woman from India and he was so excited about learning how to cook *aloo gobi*. My own husband will tell you that his favorite part of marrying a Jew is experiencing regular bagel brunches and *babka*. While this may seem trivial, food is such an important part of culture. It matters! And it is delicious!

One of the best ways of smoothing things out with extended family is to invite them over for dinner. I'm not saying this is the moment to introduce oddities like *kishka* or *gefilte fish*. But share your culture through food. Have them taste some *matzah* ball soup, some homemade hummus, some *hamentaschen*. The side that's not Jewish should also share some of their family recipes. This is a great way for people to get to know each other, and each culture, in a non-threatening and safe way (and did I mention delicious?).

Education

Whether it's the in-laws trying to learn about Judaism, or either spouse learning about their partner's culture, education is important. The usual way people have gained this education is either in premarital counseling with an officiant or in conversion classes. Premarital counseling can be a wonderful thing! But if your officiant isn't on board with your intermarriage, you may experience pressure to follow their religion/culture. Conversion can also be a wonderful thing! However, most people today don't really wish to convert simply because of the person they are marrying. (If you want to convert, terrific! Welcome to the Jewish people! But it shouldn't be required of you if you're not interested.) We need better options for Judaism 101 for people joining Jewish families. Some of these programs exist. Organizations like InterfaithFamily (InterfaithFamily.com) offer a wealth of resources online and in-person programs in some large urban centers. Getting familiar with Jewish beliefs and customs will help make everyone feel comfortable.

Education is also, of course, an important consideration when people have children. What kind of cultural/religious education do you wish them to have? Some people go to Jewish and Greek school. Some people go to Jewish supplementary school three times a week. Some go to a learning program that offers pluralistic religious instruction. Some people don't have any formal Jewish or other religious/cultural education but parents take time to educate at home.

We know that education helps instill identity. If you want your child to identify as Jewish or Jewish and something else, it's a good idea to consider some kind of education. You can DIY it. There are tons of resources from the PJ Library (pjlibrary.org), which sends free Jewish-themed children's books each month to families with young kids in Canada and the US, or the BimBam (bimbam.com) website that offers animated videos for Jewish learning. I do recommend some kind of teacher-led education if possible as well.

Sometimes we fear what we don't understand. The more everyone in the family gets educated about Judaism, the less strange it may feel.

Elation

Do you remember some of those earliest moments of falling in love? Walking around sort of drunk on joy and with a goofy smile plastered to your face? That's elation; the high of love. You can recreate that feeling but, ironically, it takes some work. The first time you kiss your partner you are elated. The ten billionth time you kiss your partner, as you race out the door with a screaming toddler attached to your leg, it may not feel quite so, well, uplifting. There are different ways to get back to that feeling of elation. One is to make a list of things you value and feel gratitude for in your partner. Another is to plan a date that is silly and thrilling – ride a roller-coaster or see a scary movie. Sit down some evening and talk about all the things you love about each other, things that are pretty unique. Miss each other! I am a big believer in spending some time apart so that you genuinely miss your partner and are excited, even elated, to see them again. And, when all else fails, have a dance party in the kitchen. I feel that's the answer to many of life's problems.

Elevation

In Jewish weddings, there is a custom of the wedding couple being lifted up on chairs (see "Eagerness" above). If you've never been hoisted and bounced up on such a chair, let me tell you what it feels like: it's super fun and scary as hell. Many of us worry about being dropped. Many of us don't love heights. Let's be honest, it's a little weird that your Uncle Morty, your friend from high school, and your brother-in-law come together to hold the chair legs that are supporting the chair that's supporting your body – doing all of this as they dance around. The tradition is for the couple to reach for each other, often using a napkin they each grab onto. I'm going to tell you that this moment, found at many weddings of intermarrying folks, is the perfect metaphor for your marriage.

There are going to be ups and downs. You're going to be supported by your family and community. That support can be a little precarious and there is the risk of falling. You will reach for your partner but will also feel a little separated by the craziness going on around and between you. The root of it, though? Joy. Pure joy. Drink it in.

Emotion

What's the emotion that comes to mind when you hear the word "intermarriage"? For some of you, I bet it's anxiety, or tension, or even anger. I'm going to gently suggest to you that everything will be easier and better if the primary emotion we all start associating with the word "intermarriage" is love. I bet when you think of the word "marriage" you think of love (they go together like a horse and carriage, after all). Every intermarriage is a marriage; a union of two people who are willing to bet on each other in our turbulent world. We are talking about two people who are committed to one another, who care for one another, and who want to build a family together. This shouldn't provoke anger, anxiety, or tension. But it does, partly because of our own fears sometimes, and partly because of the fears imposed on us by the Jewish community. Guess where those fears come from? Also love. It's not the best expression of love, but if you are a parent who has a hard time with your child's intermarriage, it is your love that heightens the emotion of fear. The Jewish community is afraid of intermarriage because the people who comprise it love their Judaism and are nervous about what it will mean for them and future generations if it changes. It's all love. We're all better off when we remember that.

Many couples approach me to officiate their intermarriages, and expect me to say something like "I won't officiate" or "Here are my stipulations." But every single time the first thing they are going to hear from me is "*mazel tov* and congratulations!" This is a marriage, folks! Life is too short and love is too precious to start anywhere but celebration.

Emotional Load

E is also for emotional load. The work of Keren McGinity shows that there is an interesting gender divide amongst intermarried couples. Everyone should go out and read her books immediately; they are fascinating and brilliantly researched and written. But here's a taste of her findings: Her research looks at heterosexual couples (with full understanding that there are, of course, many intermarried queer folks). For Jewish men who marry non-Jewish women (who "marry in"), they are more likely to remain Jewish and practice in the home. The opposite is true for Jewish women who "marry out." Gender dynamics play a role here. Women often will take on the work of converting, or learning about Jewish practices to incorporate in the home. The opposite is also true: Sometimes when non-Jewish women "marry in" they still have to do the lion's share of the emotional load, including making a Jewish home. McGinity does a great reading of a scene from the television show *Sex and the City* when Charlotte, who has married a Jewish man, prepares a beautiful Shabbat dinner. He is too distracted by watching "the game" to notice. It's a telling scene because, while it is meant to be funny, it is also sad. Women should not be alone in carrying the emotional load of the family life and, for intermarriage to be successful, both partners need to be committed to doing this work.

Emotional load is a fairly new way people are conceptualizing gender roles in marriages and long-term relationships. We know that women are more likely to be the ones who organize the family calendar, keep family ties and celebrations going, keep track of which kid needs to be signed up for which program and when, stays on top of home organization, and more. These tasks are often invisible, and they do not seem like a big deal, but they end up taking a toll because (1) they take up a good deal of mental space and (2) they are rarely recognized.

It would be wonderful to imagine a world in which all genders share the emotional load equally. In addition to the obvious benefits for gender equality, my guess is that it would benefit Jewish society too; it could very well change the dynamic where predominately women convert or adopt Jewish practices. If men were to step into some of the work of this emotional load, it would not only make their homes happier and the world more just, it might just mean greater Jewish engagement overall.

Energy/Excitement

One of the things that sets this book apart from others is my approach as a rabbi. I believe there is tremendous energy and excitement that intermarriage brings to a relationship, and I notice that couples I work with who are excited and energetic about being intermarried (not just about being married but about the fact of the intermarriage itself) often do better. There is so much negativity around intermarriage, so it is easy to sometimes forget how exciting it is to get to learn about and experience new traditions. Many Jews are thrilled (I mean, thrilled!!) to finally get a Christmas tree. Many people marrying Jews are excited to get to celebrate Passover, with its beautiful ritual. Being excited about intermarriage is not only okay, it is awesome! This is one more terrific thing about this relationship and the family you'll create.

Equality/Equity

It's worth discussing how to go beyond "equality" and into "equity" in your relationship and home. Equality means everyone gets equal stuff. Equity means people get different stuff according to their needs to try to make things as fair as possible. For example, if you have a student who needs to wear glasses to see the teacher, they get glasses. Equality would mean the entire class gets glasses because it isn't fair for just one kid to get them. Equity means the goal isn't that everyone gets the glasses but that everyone can see the teacher. The kids who need glasses get them to level the playing field.

You're going to figure out for yourselves how you bring your cultures/religions into your home. I do suggest keeping equality and equity in mind. Rather than agreeing with your partner that "we will spend exactly equal time and dollars on each tradition," assess what is truly needed.

A lot of Jewish anxiety has been based on the idea that children will identify with the "dominant culture" if exposed to two traditions, and therefore Judaism will lose out. The anxiety here is that it's hard to swim upstream and easier to just celebrate something like Christmas if it's all around.

For this reason, a lot of intermarried folks take a lot of care to make sure that the Jewish holidays are given as much fanfare as Christmas, and sometimes more. It's an equity/equality decision. Don't do every-thing the same. Figure out what's needed and what will work for you according to your values and goals. And consider gender equality in who does the work to make all of that happen in terms of the emotional load (as discussed above).

The Everyday

Does your partner have a habit that drives you up the wall? One of the awesome things about marriage is we become witness to our partner's foibles, little habits, and everyday behaviors. People are totally bizarre,

E

if you think about it. It's amazing that we let others get close enough to let them see us when we're doing things like sleeping in our ancient and tattered favorite shirt, or trimming ear hair, or dancing around like a fool to our favorite song. Marriage is made up of many individual moments; tiny everyday encounters and experiences. When we think of our lives, we may think of big moments: milestones, trips we took, *simchas* (celebrations) we attended. But the real measure of our lives is in how we live the everyday.

Intermarriages, like all marriages, are a union of two different individuals who are, as all of us are, a little bit nuts. Culture and/or religion may influence your everyday actions and those of your partner. Maybe they avoid pork. Maybe they say prayers before bed. Maybe they have a habit of saying "thank God" after something good happens. My experience, however, is that most of the big challenges are not about what is going on in the everyday. You might disagree about how to celebrate holidays in December, but you don't disagree that it's nice to eat toast in the morning. You wouldn't have fallen in love if there wasn't some adoration (even when there's irritation) of how your partner moves through the world on a daily basis. When things get tough, focus on the little everyday things that make you love your partner. It's those things that count.

Sometimes marriage is defined in terms that signify entrapment: "ball and chain," "locked down," these types of things. But to have a happy marriage, one needs to feel a sense of freedom. Ideally, one's partner and relationship allows and enables them to pursue their own individual goals, pursuits, and interests. Many marriages have vows of fidelity in terms of romantic or sexual bonds. (Note: Not all marriages include this. Polyamory is becoming a more common feature of committed partnerships.) Still, freedom within the relationship is a necessary factor for a satisfying partnership. Frankness is tied in with freedom. If someone does not feel they can articulate their needs and desires, it is usually a sign of a problem not with the intermarriage but with the marriage itself. Fun is such an important part of cultural practice and also human relationships. In your marriage vows, you might talk about some important concepts and commitments you make to each other: a vow of fidelity, or friendship, or spending your future together. All of these delicious "F" words are included here.

Feelings/Fear

Like emotions (see "E"), big feelings may come up around some of your childhood traditions, or cultural teachings, or ways of approaching how you raise children (see "C"). You're entitled to your feelings. Remember that each person has their own feelings and you need to come to some kind of understanding of how to make things work for each of you. Honor your feelings, and honor those of your partner.

Some of the feelings that can come up in and around intermarriage have to do with fear. Fear can present in all kinds of ways: What if my culture gets eclipsed by that of my partner? What if I make a mistake about ritual or holiday norms? What if being intermarried is too challenging and the relationship doesn't work out? It isn't that these concerns aren't legitimate. It is reasonable to consider the "what ifs" and to plan for them. It's just that approaching a relationship from a place of fear is inevitably going to be more difficult and give rise to more conflict than if we approach from a place of love. Remember your loving feelings. If you have a concern, talk it out. If you are feeling nervous or fearful, address it head on. Try to come from an attitude of curiosity about what is possible, and problem solve from that place. The true antidote to fear is love. So really feel your feelings of love for your partner. Connecting to that feeling will always help you navigate fear and negativity.

Fellowship

Many Christian communities refer to their congregations as "fellowships." I like this term. Many of us think of a "fellowship" as some kind of scholarship or program we do for educational and career development. But think of the actual word: fellowship. There's a sense of brotherhood, sisterhood, and siblinghood there. There's a sense of connection and loyalty there.

If you think of books or films like *Lord of the Rings* that also speak of "fellowship," there is a sense of shared quest.

Your relationship should be one of fellowship: equals who are striving for the same goals. Not everyone in a fellowship is the same. In fact, fellowships work because people bring different backgrounds and skills. Create your own little fellowship to support each other as you move through life.

Festive Season

There is no time like December to bring out the big feelings. It's probably the time of year that requires the most negotiation. For more on my approach to the festive season, see "H" For "Holidays," and see my "December Delights: Creating and Crushing Chrismukkah" guide in the appendix.

But here I also want to note that what we think of as the "festive season" can be a really hard time for some people. Whether we are dealing with grief, family tension, personal stress, or other issues, seeing everyone walk around like they are on top of the world, seeing social media posts of "perfect" families, seeing chipper and cheerful decorations and music all around can actually make us feel worse.

There is no requirement to be festive at this time of year. Make the holidays your own (I know some people that hole up in a little cabin away from everything and everyone). Like all things cultural/religious, I'm encouraging you to do it your way.

Fidelity

If you have a commitment of fidelity with your partner, that often means you are not having sexual relations with anyone else. Some couples have open or polyamorous relationships, and these also have certain guidelines and understandings that should be adhered to. You make vows when you get married, so take those seriously.

One way of thinking about fidelity in intermarriage is abiding by the promises you make about religion/culture. Maybe when you got together you decided to celebrate Christmas. But now things are tense with the partner and you think, "Oh ya? See if we do Christmas this year!" Or perhaps you've agreed to raise children with a Jewish identity, and then the going gets tough in the marriage and, to spite your partner, you start to take your kid to church.

Marriage is no picnic, at least not all the time (but have picnics together!). There will be tough times. Just like the kind of fidelity around adultery or cheating that compels you to stay true to your promises even when you are annoyed with or sick of your spouse, you should consider the promises you make about religion and culture to be as iron-clad.

I'm not saying you can never change your mind. When my partner and I got married we were planning to have no Christmas tree or Christmas lights, but our circumstances changed (see "H" for "Holidays") and so I changed. But I don't make unilateral decisions and neither does my partner. We have to work it out together. That's the fidelity.

Forgiveness

You can plan stuff, and you can adhere to the principle of fidelity, but sometimes, I guarantee you, someone is going to mess up. Someone is going to make a mistake. Someone is going to be a pain during their partner's holiday dinner. Someone is going to say the wrong thing. (My partner took years to get the difference between *Shana tova* – happy new year, said at Rosh Hashanah, and *Chag sameach* – happy holiday, said at other holidays.) If you want a marriage to be successful, and I include intermarriage, you're going to have to forgive one another. That doesn't mean you sabotage things on purpose, expecting your partner's forgiveness. That means you try as much as possible to seek to understand your partner's motivations and actions, and treat them with compassion.

Frankness

Frankness matters because sometimes people harbor resentments over things they feel they have to do, or things they wish to do but feel they can't. In all relationships, but especially intermarriage, I encourage frankness. If you can't say what you want to say, why not? Does it have to do with sharing the emotional load (see "E")? This is something I work on with couples I'm marrying. Say what you want to say, always say what you mean, and listen respectfully. If you can do that you've done 80 per cent of the work.

Freedom

Freedom is important in any relationship. In an intermarriage, sometimes it's useful for the partners to discuss where a partner is free to do their own thing, culturally or religiously. Maybe one person attends church alone every now and then so they don't have to explain everything all the time. Maybe another will attend a synagogue's social action committee alone. Freedom enables both partners to have the aspects of their culture/religion that are meaningful to them, without everyone having to participate. Some families will have the Jewish partner abstain from decorating the home or the tree for the Christmas holidays.

Intermarriage is like choosing your own adventure. You can decide who is comfortable doing what. It's ideal when some things are done all together, but some things can be done alone and that is fine. Freedom!

Friendship

You've heard the classic line that one should marry their best friend? I'm here to disagree with that. I think too many people think their spouse should fill all roles for them, be all things, and I find that to be a killer to long-term fulfillment and happiness. In my life, there are plenty of things my partner and I do separately. It is important that I have a really good gal-pal or two so I have someone to see ballet with, or to talk through the TV shows I like with, or to have a real heart to heart with. These are things I can sometimes do with my partner but he hates ballet, doesn't like the same types of TV shows as I do, and though we have our own heart to hearts, sometimes I need a fresh perspective. You should absolutely have friends outside of your partner – good ones. If you don't have any, try to make some. I'm telling you that seeing these friends will be *good* for your marriage. You can't spend all your time together or you'll get sick of each other fast.

Having said that, you should feel like your partner is also your friend; like you would want to spend time with them even if they weren't your romantic partner. Get into their interests, including any cultural ones, at least enough that you know what they're talking about when they're pumped about something. My husband has even come to the ballet a few times.

Also remember how you treat and speak to your friends. You are unlikely to bring up grudges from five years ago. You are unlikely to nitpick tiny annoyances. Don't do that with a partner either.

Fun

F is also for fun. A successful intermarriage will use the partners' different cultures to create fun traditions. Maybe that looks like blending (see "B") and you create decorations for the December holidays that have both *dreidels* and Christmas trees. Maybe that looks like family trips to many different places of worship to learn about them. Maybe that is creating your own traditions, crafts, songs, Seder booklets, activities, and so on. Especially if there are children, a goal should be to make the cultural life of the home really fun!

In the Jewish world, we aren't always as good at the fun part. We have lots of holidays that reflect on our persecution. Some of us grew up with long and super boring sermons and services. A lot of Jews have been told they have an obligation to continue Judaism (including marrying someone Jewish) because of the Holocaust. Not fun! I'm not making light of the Holocaust here. But you can't guilt people into an identity and cultural/religious belief and practice. It has to be appealing for its own reasons. We need to bring the fun back into text study; let's get it out of a quiet and somber *beit midrash* (house of study) and host it in bars. Do it game-show-style. Make the prizes for the most interesting interpretation hilarious: giant stuffed animals, a wine tour, a comic book. Make it fun. The same goes for attending services. Services should include humor and stimulating discussion. They shouldn't be boring to attend. They don't have to be the kind of fun you have at an amusement park, but services should be fun in their own way.

Future Planning

Future planning is about the kinds of future-proofing you're doing. Let's say one of you dies – will the other continue the cultural traditions at home even if they aren't "theirs"? Let's say you get divorced – will you be seeking a *get* (Jewish divorce document; see "D" for "Divorce")? Let's say you want to plan a vacation together – does it matter if there's going to be a Christmas tree up at the all-inclusive resort? Think about what you need together and plan for it. The more you've decided on what to do in the event of something happening, the easier things will be.

Some people refer to intermarriage as "interfaith marriage," but for a large portion of the community faith really doesn't have much to do with it. Many couples are secular/atheist/spiritual but not religious and so God is not at the center of things. Blending cultures may be easier than blending faiths that contradict each other, so having "the God talk" is important for people building a life together. The God question often leads to questions of goodness. A common question I get is, "Can you be good without God?" The short answer is, "Of course!" This section discusses grandchildren, which is truly at the center of anxiety around intermarriage. People want their grandkids to experience the same richness and beauty in Judaism that they do. This is both possible and impossible, and we will talk about why. We also discuss guilt and how it works in religious/cultural life (yes, there is a stereotype about Jewish guilt; but there is also the same stereotype for Catholics and others). Guilt is rarely productive. What is productive? Giving. We'll talk about that too. *Gefilte fish*: What is it? Why do we eat it? What does it have to do with intermarriage? This is just a reminder that what is delicious to some is offensive to others. Everyone is entitled to their individual tastes.

Garbage

There is some understandable grief and worry in the religious world. Pews are emptier and emptier. Beloved churches and synagogues are closing. People are worried and sad. Sometimes they'll project those feelings.

The best recourse is to stop with the garbage. Stop blaming intermarriage for societal shifts that are sweeping and complicated, and stop listening to people who decry intermarriage. Jews tend to blame our lack of synagogue affiliation on intermarriage. Churches don't tend to, and they are experiencing the same decline. We are living in a world that is secularizing; a world in which community is more pluralistic than the traditional congregational structure; a world in which we often have kids later, work multiple jobs, and carry huge student debt – all of which are barriers to participation in religious institutional life. Stop with the blame and hate and fear-mongering around intermarriage. Surround yourself with people-building communities where that kind of garbage isn't tolerated and no one has time for it because they're too busy celebrating, building happy and thriving communal spaces, and trusting that more pluralism and diversity can only lead to more goodness.

Gefilte Fish

Gefilte fish is one of those things that are fun for intermarried people to explore. This is fish that is not cooked and often comes in scary-looking jars at the deli, and here's the secret revealed: it is gross. Sure, some people like it (hi, Mom!). But more people feel they "have to have it" at their holiday dinners even though it is gross! *Gefilte fish* is a reminder that some traditions are good to let go of. You decide which ones. Having said that, there will be people who throw this book across the room as they read this. Some people love *gefilte fish*. What's the lesson? No one is right! You can take something "Jewish" and have wildly diverging opinions on it. Same with something from any other culture. Some things you feel like you have to have, some things you are ready to let go of. You and your partner decide. And if your partner likes *gefilte fish*? Buy it. Set it out on the holiday table. But don't feel like you have to eat it!

Giving

Being in a partnership means you sometimes have to give. You may even have to give in, every now and then. Define your lines: What feels authentic to you? What feels fun and okay to give? What's too much? We shouldn't give with the expectation of getting. It shouldn't be "I'll celebrate your holidays, so you'll celebrate mine." It's better if it's "I celebrate your holidays because I love you and what matters to you matters to me." You're more likely to get happier (no guilt!) reciprocity that way and to feel better about what you're giving too.

God

One of the contentions of this book is that all marriages are intermarriages. As we were working on this book, my editor heard this doozy from someone: A couple was preparing for their child's B Mitzvah. The father was a Shabbat-keeping, Conservative Jew who wanted traditional liturgy. The mother was skeptical of the language of prayer and was raised Reform but was essentially a Humanist/Secular Jew. They couldn't agree on how to approach the B Mitzvah. Even in marriages in which both partners are Jewish, we still find intermarriages. Me as a secular Jew marrying a secular person who was raised without religion but with cultural traditions around Christmas is far less of an intermarriage than, say, me as a secular Jew marrying an Orthodox Jew who would expect synagogue attendance, daily prayer, keeping kosher, and so on. All marriages are intermarriages. One of the interesting factors that I find makes intermarriage work is belief. If both partners share some idea of cosmology, it is easier to traverse than if they have completely different faith systems. That can work too, of course, but presents different challenges. Do both partners believe in God? If so, which kind? A God who answers personal prayers? Some energy that is the source of life? No God at all?

These conversations really make the difference in terms of which rituals and practices will be included. For some people, agreeing about belief is much more important than celebrating certain holidays. For others, belief has nothing to do with their cultural expression. It is useful to discuss what the family believes, for everyone believes in something. If you are believers in a personal God, perhaps set aside time for family prayers. If you are a believer that there is no God who will solve the problems of the world, perhaps discuss what you do believe about humanity and its power to act. The God conversations often lead to conversations about goodness.

Goodness

A common question I get asked is, "Can you be good without God?" Of course! My colleague Greg Epstein has a whole book on the subject, which I recommend. So many non-believers are so ethical. So many "religious" people are so rotten. Think of where you locate your goodness and how you try to make a difference (see "T" for "*Tikkun Olam*," repairing the world). There is a prevalent belief in the world that goodness comes from religion. That's not my belief. Religion can inspire goodness in people, for sure, but it has also been the cause of wars, suffering, homophobia, hatred, and abuse. I don't think the religious have the corner on the goodness market at all.

For people in my communities, Oraynu Congregation in Toronto and the globally connected online community of SecularSynagogue.com, where most of us are atheist or agnostic, we talk about how we have to create it ourselves if we want to see an increase of goodness in the world. We don't believe in the efficacy of prayer, so we have to build networks, use human ingenuity, and work hard to fix the problems of our world. You may believe in some kind of God(s), in which case, more power to you. I still encourage you to think of goodness and how you define it, where you locate it, and how you plan to make it grow.

Google

Lots of Jews feel they don't have enough cultural capital – knowledge, Hebrew, Jewish literacy, experience – to walk into Jewish communal programs or spaces. It's not their fault! So many of us have been made to feel ashamed about something we don't know or don't do, myself included. I've been chastised for not knowing the right words, not knowing where we are in the prayer service, not knowing a certain religious idea. So many Jews say that they're a "bad" Jew or not a "real" Jew, largely because they internalized the idea that there is only one right way. This whole thing about who a "real" Jew is has caused a lot of destruction in the Jewish world (see "D" for "Definition"). As the Talmudic scholars say, "so much the more so" for someone who isn't Jewish and wants to accompany their Jewish partner to some service or holiday. It is very intimidating, and I really admire and applaud people who have bravely done this. It's not easy! If someone who isn't Jewish comes to a Jewish space and is jeered at, they are never going to return. We need to be truly welcoming and honor the courage it takes to show up.

For those who are wanting to connect Jewishly but feel like they are "bad" Jews or are not Jewish at all, you needn't feel like you don't know what's going on. Luckily, we live in a world in which Google exists! You can prep beforehand. Find out what the holiday is all about. Research the Torah portion of the week. Figure out a couple of key words to keep you hooked in. Google is your best friend if you are trying to figure out how to join in with Jewish stuff (whether you're Jewish or not).

Grandchildren

One of the reasons that in-laws get bent out of shape about intermarriage is their fears for the grandchildren. It's a big deal to become a grandparent! It makes sense that you want to have a say over how the child is being raised. You love and care about them so much. I understand. But I'm here to tell you: butt out! It's just not your place to give advice on the religious/cultural upbringing of your grandchild. Neither is it your place to comment about issues like circumcision, baptism, Sunday school, home-based celebrations the child is exposed to, or anything to do with what the parents of that child have chosen to do. I'm not dismissing how hard it is to butt out. It's the hardest thing. But it's the healthiest thing.

When I speak to grandparents who are struggling with accepting the choices their child has made, I remind them of what's really at stake and what really matters. Some Jewish parents sit *shiva* (the mourning rituals) for their children when they intermarry. They refuse to meet their grandchildren. What a tragic loss, not so much for the grandchildren, but for the grandparents! When you became a parent you had the choice of how to raise your kids. You hopefully did a good job and instilled some smarts and good values. So trust your parenting and let your kid figure out their own path once they are a parent.

What really matters here? I guarantee you will love a grandson regardless of whether he is circumcised. I also guarantee that if you make a big deal about circumcision (for or against) it will put pressure on your kid and their spouse and they will resent you. Don't muck up the joy of the birth of your grandchild with these hard feelings. It really does matter that they feel supported by you. You're going to get more access and happy feelings with your kid and grandkid if you can keep your cool. A lot is at stake.

I'm also going to gently tell you that it isn't fair to impose your views too strongly. It's hard enough to become a parent without a million people pressuring you to do it their way (see "C" for "Children"). For intermarried folks, they are often receiving this pressure from conflicting sides and different points of view. It's a lot to take. Don't create problems with these loved ones; it isn't worth it. You will love your grandkids no matter what. I promise.

Grief

Having said all that about grandparenting (see "Grandchildren" above), I do want to name and take seriously that, as the parent of adult children, when your kids convert or intermarry or raise kids unlike you'd have wanted, it can truly feel like a loss. Give yourself permission to feel that loss without projecting it onto your kids.

Those of us who are intermarried should remember that our parents need to grieve a little for the image and hopes of their family that were deeply held. This knowledge doesn't excuse bad behavior, but it can make it more understandable.

We all experience our own hurts and losses that require us to grieve. Some of us grieve family relationships that are irreparably damaged by the lack of acceptance of a partner. Some grieve holidays the way they used to be and no longer are. Some grieve an image of family life that hasn't come to fruition. Grieving is a healthy way to confront, integrate, and sometimes let go of loss.

Grudges/Grievances

My husband and I joke that we have a "grudge drawer" and when we do something to annoy the other, or we do something to make life harder for the other, it goes in the grudge drawer. Lose the car keys? Grudge drawer. Criticize my outfit? File it in the grudge drawer under "C" for "criticism" and "F" for "fashion." The grudge drawer deserves its own card catalogue system.

We need to learn how to forgive (see "F") and let things go! Here's the thing about that grudge drawer: things fester in there. Don't let deeply held and meaningful aspects of life find their way into the drawer. Don't stew in the way your partner is dismissive of your holidays or traditions. Don't file away your resentment over losing your sacred childhood customs. Keep the grudge drawer clean and deal with the important stuff. Be sure to clean out that grudge drawer every now and then. If your partner is working on a problem and is growing out of an annoying habit, let the grudge go.

Guilt

Jewish guilt is a thing. But then so is Catholic guilt. And I hear from a Sikh friend of mine that his parents know how to lay on the guilt real thick. So I suppose we can just agree that guilt is a real emotion. Here's the thing about it, though – it's not a productive emotion. When we do things out of guilt, we do them with resentment. Often, feeling guilty makes us actively avoid the very thing someone is trying to guilt us into doing. The more nagging we hear, the more we pull away.

We can't guilt our partners or kids into believing and being what they don't or aren't. If we feel guilty about our own beliefs and identities, we shouldn't. Part of intermarriage is getting people on the same team where possible and accepting difference where necessary. It's time to stop with all that guilt.

This letter explores how some of us need healing from past hurts inflicted on us by members of our family and community. In order to require less healing in the future, we need to look at "hurting." We are human and frail and full of foibles. We hurt each other. The goal is to avoid hurt and, especially, to be extra tender when it comes to issues of identity within your partnership. We'll also discuss hearing – as in, how to truly listen and hear one another in a relationship. "H" is also for helping, for holidays, for hosting, because if we do our best for our families, and if we work to make sure our holidays and celebrations are packed with joy, our spiritual and familial lives will be much richer. Finally, there is happiness: how to get it, how to keep it, how to create it for your partner.

Happiness

Here's something that'll blow the minds of all those people who have railed against intermarriage forever: intermarried folks tend to be happy. There is no current statistical information for divorce rates for intermarried folks versus in-married folks, but we do know from the 2013 Pew Research Center study on Jewish life in America that intermarriage rates are going up, with millennials being most likely to intermarry. We know from other population surveys like that conducted by Philip Cohen that the divorce rate in America is going down, with millennials being the least likely to divorce. In fact, for a lot of people, not only is intermarriage not a cause of a divorce, but finding a partner who is willing to share in one's traditions, who is open and communicative, and who is affirming, is likely to lead to longevity in marriage. There are other reasons why intermarried folks may, in fact, experience more happiness. I've said it before and I'm sure I'll say it again: intermarriage often compels people to decide, define, and discuss what really matters to them about their own culture. The result is often a more engaged and energized practice. Two Jews who get married but equally don't care about Judaism are not going to be as spiritually fulfilled as a couple from different cultures who work out all their stuff and walk the talk. If you decide and articulate what is culturally and spiritually significant, it'll go a long way in you being able to meaningfully engage with your identity. I have worked with so many intermarried folks who are living happy lives, have happy children, and are happy in their skin. If you're not feeling that way now, if doubt and negativity are bringing you down, please know that real happiness is achievable.

Healing

The truth is that there needs to be some healing from the horrific damage done by those who "spoke out" against intermarriage for generations. Some people do feel conflicted about their relationship. They are in love yet they have been taught that this love is bad. An anti-intermarriage narrative has inflicted real wounds on Jews and also on their partners who walk into families already unwelcome and treated with suspicion. It's necessary, and difficult, to work to try to heal from these wounds.

One of the couples I've worked with tried everything to talk through issues with the Jewish side of the family. An Orthodox family, the parents were extremely unwilling to welcome their new son-in-law.

The father threatened not to come to the wedding. The mother came along with her daughter and the non-Jewish almost-son-in-law, to their wedding meeting. I have never had a parent attend the wedding meeting before! I'm usually like, "Ignore your parents' wishes; this is your day!" (Sorry to all the parents of intermarried folks reading this. But, seriously, it's their day.) The mother had a lot to say about what should and shouldn't be included in the ceremony. This wasn't entirely her fault ... when I'd pose a question to the couple – for example, "Are you going to each break the glass or just one of you?" – they would look to her for the answer! She was, oddly, in charge of this wedding that she was opposed to.

One of the options I give for something to say when exchanging rings comes from the Song of Songs, "*Ani l'dodi v'dodi li*" – I am my beloved's and my beloved is mine. I like it for intermarriages because the Song of Songs is common to Christian and Jewish biblical canons. I also happen to have a thing for the Song of Songs because it is erotic poetry that somehow made its way into the Bible as a religious text. Mostly, I use it because the line is beautiful. I offered the option for this couple to say it to one another. When the mother of the bride heard her non-Jewish future-son-in-law repeat some Hebrew words, she went into hysterics. Happy ones. She laughed so hard she nearly fell off the chair (I'm not exaggerating; she actually bent over and almost tipped onto the floor). There was healing there. That family was one of the more oddball and quirky I've worked with. But, you know what? That wedding was full of joy. Everyone came! There was healing.

Sometimes healing comes from tough conversations. Sometimes from shared laughter. When we giggle together, we become co-conspirators in the sharing of an inside joke. We let go of tension. We stop taking ourselves so seriously. Sometimes people just get over their sh*t. If you're hurting right now, know that healing is possible. I've seen it.

Hearing

People suck at listening to one another. Very often we are distracted when our partners speak to us. Or we are thinking up the next thing we want to say (especially if we're in an argument). Once I was with an intermarried couple. The woman's mother had just died. The woman's partner was trying to be supportive but kept suggesting things she didn't want at the funeral. I'd say something like, "We can light memorial candles," and he'd say, "Oh, that's a nice idea," and she'd say, "Honey, I told you already, I don't want anything like that." This happened a few times until finally she turned to him and said emphatically: "Please. Heeeeeaaaaarrrr me." What a moment! This is so often what we are feeling inside: the need to be truly heard. Learning to hear each other is a real skill for married folks. Consider the different connotations of the words "listening" and "hearing." Which one suggests more intention and focus? Which one will enable both partners to feel best understood? Here's a therapist-recommended strategy: Each person gets to speak for three minutes (set a timer). Once one person concludes, the other has to repeat back the main points. There has to be agreement on what was said. Only then can the partner respond.

I've done this and it can be seriously annoying. But it works if the issue you have is needing to be heard. You might be explaining why certain holiday traditions are important to you. Or why you feel awkward with a particular ritual. Or why your partner's uncle makes you feel exhausted. It's important to be heard and to hear.

I asked some intermarried folks what advice they might have for other intermarrying folks. One of the responses I got back was this lovely quote:

> [Intermarriage] can be very rewarding, sharing cultures, and gives you a chance to choose/not choose certain aspects of your own culture, but it takes a lot of thought [and] faith in each other, and listening. And people often advise, do what suits you two and to heck with the family, but you know, they have thoughts and dreams and ideas that need to be honored (if not followed) too.

I love this because it advises folks to really listen to and hear each other, and to listen to and hear their respective families. And then this couple gets to do whatever they decide to do.

Helping

There is a Jewish tradition of helping others. This is familial and communal – it is considered a good deed to help others in the family. It is also how people get through life. The tradition is also about charity and justice (*tzedakah*) and repairing the world (*tikkun olam*). Some intermarried families volunteer at a church or non-denominational shelter during Thanksgiving. Doing this as a family is a reminder of the important things in any holiday and distracts from any "yours/mine" stuff that may be going on. Everyone is united in a higher purpose. I really believe that helping others is the best way to feel good about ourselves. It can be a part of healing and a way to avoid hurting one another as discussed above (see also "Hurting" below).

Holidays

Healing, hurting, and hearing really make their presence felt at the holidays. Many, many families fight about Christmas and Chanukah. Holidays can feel awfully loaded for people – tensions and expectations can run high and energy can begin to run low. Check out the Chrismukkah guide in the appendix for all things holiday-related. In it, I talk about how to have the best holiday ever – moving from the "December Dilemma" to "December Delights"! Many of these tips apply to any holiday, even if they are not from Jewish or Christian traditions. Hear all about why the holidays you're newly celebrating matter to your partner. Find resonances that work for you. Work together to make each and every holiday special in its own way. It doesn't have to be fancy. One Christmas Day, my partner and I huddled up on the couch with our kids, had some popcorn, and watched the Grinch and Rudolph movies we both remember fondly from childhood. It can be easy, but it has to be meaningful.

Honoring

People say different vows when they get married, but a pretty common one is that you will "honor" your partner. But what does this really mean? Some see it as a fidelity or commitment thing; that you won't cheat on them. I see it differently (fidelity is good too – see "F" for "Fidelity" – but I'm talking about something else right now). I see honoring your partner as recognizing them as a whole person. Your partner is full of wonderful qualities (or you wouldn't marry them). They are also full of foibles and flaws (or they wouldn't be human and, at the time of this writing, it is illegal to marry a non-human). Your partner has unique desires and dreams, loads of baggage, and some soft secrets of the heart. Honoring your partner is honoring their humanity. It's understanding that we are all, on some level, needing to be cared for and appreciated. We all want someone in our corner. If you're lucky enough to be in love, you often want your partner to be that person. Intermarriage is an aspect that requires honoring. Your partner's culture, heritage, beliefs, and practices need to be honored if you want to honor the whole person your partner is.

Hope

There's hope! There isn't just hope for you and your own happiness. There's hope for the Jewish community at large. There is hope in the ways in which clergy from other faiths are increasingly happy to work with us to co-officiate weddings. There is hope in a world that continues to grow in its acceptance of Jews, allowing for a trend in which people want to marry us, and then more people knowing Jews as family members and continuing to expand their acceptance and love (we hope). There's hope for a Jewish community that can move from the fear-based response to intermarriage and intermarried families and embrace a loving response where people are included and welcomed for who and what they are. There is hope that a book like this won't be necessary in a generation or two because a lot of the strife and stress I grew up with on this topic will be a thing of the past.

Hostility

Sometimes people won't play nice (see "A" for "A$$holes"). I remember once being at a Chanukah dinner with someone who wasn't Jewish. He tried to sing along to a song in Hebrew, which I thought was so vulnerable and brave and lovely. Someone else at the party laughed because he didn't know how to pronounce a word. In what world is it okay to laugh at someone who is trying their best to fit in? That laughter was a show of hostility. It was like a boundary marker: "You'll never be welcome here." I said to that person: "I think it takes much more courage to try something new than to always do what's comfortable." And then – and here's the hard part – I let it go. Well, I tried really hard to let it go, but it does seem to be surfacing here as I write this ... Anyway, the point is this: You don't have to take any crap. Don't let people be hostile to you and feel you just have to be polite and take it. However, try not to become hostile yourself. If you can keep calm and defend yourself, your partner, and your actions with a smile, you'll have won.

Hosting

One way to make holidays meaningful and to ensure they are inclusive is to host them yourselves! Invite the whole extended family, the mishmash of people and cultures. Get them to participate if they are willing. Non-Jews tend to dig playing with *dreidels* at Chanukah and celebrating the rituals of Passover. Jews can get into Easter egg hunts. If kids are involved (see "C" for "Children"), the grandparents may be willing to come. When you host, you can do it your way. Agree on how to make it meaningful and fun for you. Take back the holidays!

Hurting

It is a fact that any person will hurt and be hurt by their partner. Sometimes when trying to hurt the other, one partner might bring up issues of intermarriage: "Oh ya? Well, see who is making the Seder, then, because it ain't gonna be me!" Obviously the goal is to try not to hurt each other, but holidays, traditions, and values that have been agreed on should be given special honor and shouldn't be used to hurt. It does lasting damage to the health of the intermarriage and the family. Aim for hearing and healing where there has been hurting. It's amazing how much can be repaired when there is a serious commitment to kindness, empathy, giving, and trust in a relationship.

I

Inclusion is a big word in the fields of religion, education, and commerce. We'll explore how to create an inclusive home and create an inclusive family. Indivisibility is about presenting a united front to family members or friends who seek to sabotage a relationship or, under the guise of "just asking questions," project negativity. Insistence is about bottom lines: what it is you must keep in your home and life in order to feel authentic. Insist on that. In order to know what you'll insist on, you have to know what's important to you. Intermarriage is an invitation to explore your values and define for yourself and for/with your partner what is truly important. This section discusses "I" for "irritation." Let it be known henceforth and forever that you and your partner will irritate the heck out of each other. That's the nature of marriage – you are signing yourself up to be committed to someone who drives you bonkers. It's okay to get irritated. If you focus on the "I" for "important" and "I" for "insistence," you'll find your way through irritation.

Ignorant

There is a real difference between genuine ignorance and willful ignorance. Someone who is generally ignorant might say something offensive without realizing it. For example, they've bought into a stereotype they've heard many times. Perhaps some cousin says, "Hey, you're marrying a Jew? Great! Cha-ching!" This person has internalized a stereotype about Jews and money. It's possible they are genuinely ignorant that this is a stereotype. I suggest that if you are the non-Jewish spouse, you respond in a way that can help change this person's mind. You can dispel the myth by saying, "Actually, he's super broke. Not all Jews have money, you know!" Or you can address the antisemitism directly, "That stereotype we grew up with really reinforces some awful ideas people have had about Jews. I'm hoping now that I'm marrying X, our family will see that those stereotypes aren't true and are hurtful."

If you are marrying someone, it's your job to stick up for them. Sometimes the comment-making person is not actually ignorant but is willfully ignorant. This means that they have been told before that their ideas are bunk and they continue to spout them. Sometimes this person is "just asking questions" about a minority culture, but in a way that reinforces stereotypes or is meant to be insulting (these often start with "Is it true that Jews ... ?"). When someone is being willfully ignorant, you still should probably address the behavior in some way. You can explain that their behavior is hurtful. You can tell them they aren't welcome near you or your family if they keep it up. You can directly tell the person to lay off. There's a local program near me called "Shut It, Uncle Bob!" which is all about how to deal with a relative's racist or otherwise offensive comments at holiday dinners. Ignorance can be educated. Willful ignorance requires a different kind of response.

Important

Figure out what is important to you and do that. Conversely, figure out what is not important to you and don't do that. Sometimes we hold on to traditions or practices we were raised with but, when we think about it, they no longer serve our needs. Intermarriage can be a great opportunity to figure out what is really meaningful to you because you'll have to explain it to your partner and, in some cases, advocate for why your family should continue to do these things. In that process, you will likely crystallize what is important to you about your own cultural practices. Great! This is a sneaky side benefit of intermarriage. A lot of people marrying someone who grew up with the same religion and culture as them never examine their practices and can sometimes find themselves just going through the motions. It is my experience that intermarriage affords occasions and opportunities for some really deep and thoughtful reflection, examination, and explanation of what is important about identity and practice. Take these opportunities!

Inclusivity/Inclusion (Featuring InterfaithFamily.com)

When you think of the word "inclusion," what comes to mind? Many groups, communities, and organizations are coming up with ways to be more inclusive, to make everyone feel they belong. The Jewish community where I live has done tremendous work on inclusion, making sure we are taking steps towards meaningful inclusion of people with disabilities, Jews of color, expanding the roles of women, addressing homophobia in our texts and traditions, and more. I think we can apply some of the same principles to our own families. Are we making sure everyone feels they can participate fully? Are there barriers to address, such as language, knowledge, experience? Sometimes people do not *wish* to participate, and that's fine. Perhaps one parent is in charge of making Chanukah and the other in charge of decorating a Christmas tree. You get to decide. But sometimes someone wants to sing a holiday song or light a candle or do some other practice, but they are shy because they don't know the "rules" or the words. As much as possible, our families should be places of real belonging, where members fit in no matter what. If religion or culture is getting in the way of that, we need to figure out how to remove the barriers. It will make family life and each practice and celebration much more joyful to know that no one feels left out and everyone has a pathway to participation.

I believe one of the best resources out there to help folks create inclusive families is InterfaithFamily.com. This website will help you find an officiant, helps you talk about how to do holidays in a way that suits everyone, and offers really great information for folks who want to learn more about Judaism and other cultures. I highly recommend it and its resources.

Indivisibility

There will come a time when you have to explain your choices to extended family or friends. Perhaps you are having conflict around circumcision (see "C" for "Children"), or having a Christmas tree, or raising your kids "both," or the rituals you'll include in your wedding ceremony. In any and all situations, it's important that the intermarried couple be a united front. First you need to have the conversations to determine what you plan to do and why. Then you need to present your decisions completely and totally as a done deal, with complete and solid agreement and mutuality from the two of you. Perhaps there was some internal strife or discord – one of you wanted to circumcise and the other didn't; you wanted to get married by a rabbi but your partner didn't; you can't agree on how to handle the Passover/Easter conflict. Whatever hard conversations you have had, once you've decided and are explaining your choices to others, it's better if you can remain a united front. Be honest and authentic. You can explain that there were hard choices, but the more indivisible you can be in these moments, the more indivisible you are as a couple. Be bold.

Industriousness

Planning a wedding is hard work. Parenting is hard work. Juggling your religious, spiritual, and cultural life with all of the other responsibilities you shoulder is hard work. And, yes, sometimes the negotiations of intermarriage can feel like hard work. It's generally been my experience that worthy things are a little bit hard. It's easier to order pizza all the time and harder to cook balanced meals. It's easier to go on a Netflix binge than tackle that to-do list for work. It's also easier to let problems fester rather than dealing with them when they arise. It's easier to dismiss someone's point of view as "wrong" or "stupid" or "silly" when we disagree. All of these things happen sometimes. Sometimes we are just going to choose the path of least resistance. And, again, usually we are better off and happier having done the harder thing. This is not to say that life must be a misery. This is to say that we need to find the joy in doing hard work. Think of it as the kind of energy you get when you actually *do* tackle that to-do list and are getting somewhere. Think of how good you feel knowing your family is eating well and, actually, that recipe only took about thirty minutes, anyway. Think about that flow state of mind we can get when we find a good groove and are winning at life. That's the kind of industriousness I want you to apply to your marriage. Your marriage, in all aspects, requires some work or, if not work, some care, energy, and attention. Intermarriage is one more layer of that. Approach it with the attitude that there will be some work to do, but that you are totally up for it and excited to see how you learn and grow in the process. Who's afraid of a little hard work? Not you.

Insistence

Once you know what's important to you (see "Important" above), truly important, it's okay to be a little insistent about it. You need to express to your partner why something is very important. I always recommend that couples have some of these conversations before they get married. It'll be a hard road if someone determines it's really important to them to baptize a baby but it's really important to the other spouse that no church-based ritual be included in the life of the kids. Insist on the things that matter to you as early as possible so that you and your partner develop a roadmap for how things will work. If your partner insists on something that makes you uncomfortable, try to really hear them. Hear the "why" of the thing. See if you can live with it. If not, you need to insist right back. Again, it's better to know earlier if the things one person needs to insist on are impossible for the other.

Intensity

Marriage can be intense. Intermarriage can be intense. You probably have heard before of all the problems and *tsouris* (sorrows) and issues that intermarriage will bring up. Yep, life can be intense. You know what else is intense? Love. Love is the most intense feeling I have ever felt. When I think of how I felt falling in love with my partner, or at our wedding, when I think of my children, their infancy, their laughter, the brilliant things they say, I am overcome with powerful feelings of love. When there are challenges, things may feel intense. Try to meet that intensity with the intensity of your love; connect with the full force and power of the love you feel for your partner, family, and kids. Intensity can be a motivator for action and for moving through tough stuff. Find it when you need it.

Invitations

Sometimes when people put out invitations to weddings or baby namings or a *bris* (ritual circumcision), they give a little glossary or guide on what to expect. If a bunch of people won't know what a *chuppah* is, don't write "*chuppah* at 6:00 p.m." on the invitation. (A *chuppah* is the canopy that Jews get married under. It is symbolic of the marital home.) Sometimes people write about who is officiating, and explain their perspective and approach. Sometimes people note that this will be an intercultural celebration. Some will explain what a *bris* or baby naming is and what is involved. What do you want people to know about your celebration? Sometimes a little explanation goes a long way.

Irritation

Let me make you a solid 100 per cent guarantee: sometimes your partner is going to irritate the hell out of you. Welcome to marriage. The trick is to not let your irritation cloud your love for them. This applies whether you are intermarried or not. But for intermarried folks, some of the irritation might come from differences in cultural approaches – for example, is giving your partner the silent treatment a cultural norm that you grew up with in your family? Irritation can come from trying to make something happen without your partner's full participation (see above for "Inclusivity/Inclusion"). Irritation will happen. When it does, try to understand your partner's motivations, try to approach them with grace, and try to remember why you wanted to marry them in the first place.

Isolation

One challenge some intermarried folks have is if they live isolated from the community. One of the people in my online community, SecularSynagogue.com, lives in a small town in Europe. She is a secular Jew married to a practicing Christian. The Jewish and Christian communities where they live are all far too conservative to feel like a right fit. She was delighted to find our online community because she finally feels she has found "her people" (and when she announced her marriage in our group, she received nothing but cheers, congratulations, good wishes, and *mazel tov*, and a great conversation about how folks are making intermarriage work for them). It's going to be easier if you can find a way out of isolation and talk to others about how they navigate intermarriage. Isolation isn't usually a good thing for humans. It turns out we need each other, even if we annoy each other.

Intermarriage is a journey; we learn, we grow, we change. In partnerships, we are changed by our relationship and we work to keep making changes in the relationship so that everyone has their needs met. This is how we create peace and justice in the home. Justice is an important Jewish concept. The word *tzedakah* means both charity and justice, and this section considers how we apply it to our lives. Do you feel like you have to juggle many balls in the air? Juggling is the idea that we have to find a way to stay balanced when there is a lot going on. And today, people really do have a lot going on. Juggling is an art and, in my experience, you get better at it with practice. "J" is also for joy and, truly, this is at the center of things here. All of us need to find and experience true joy in our partnerships, families, celebrations, cultural experiences, and communities. If it isn't joyful, it isn't working. Lastly, jazz is a great metaphor for marriage and intermarriage. We improvise, we harmonize, we make music together.

Jazz

Jazz is a type of music, of course, but I see it as a metaphor. Just like the jazzy klezmer traditions that blended various types of music from the cultures that surrounded it, intermarriage is a mélange of styles. Jazz is improvisational: you get to create your own sound; you get to break the rules. Intermarriage can be like that too.

Jealousy

Jealousy is an interesting emotion. It is very natural and yet also quite a destructive, unproductive emotion. In marriage, one sometimes assumes jealousy is over another love interest, a crush, or perhaps even an extramarital romantic or sexual liaison. Unlike many rabbis/officiants, I have very few rules about whom I will marry. I don't require that couples pledge to raise Jewish children or have a Jewish home (and I certainly would never ask for that home to be exclusively Jewish). I don't require couples to attend counseling or marital classes with me. I don't require they do or say anything particular in their ceremony (besides what is legally required). What I do insist on is an equal partnership. I will say no to couples if I believe there to be an unhealthy or abusive dynamic. I emphasize with couples that I support relationships that are equal in nature. Jealousy is often a warning sign; it can mean one person is possessive or controlling. I watch out for jealousy in relationships.

Perhaps this is why I'm sensitive to another form of jealousy – the "but what about me/mine" kind of jealousy. This has nothing to do with cheating but everything to do with feeling cheated. Sometimes people can't ever enjoy their partner's traditions or celebrations because, regardless of how inclusive their partner or their partner's family tries to be, they don't have the generosity of spirit to try to adapt to or adopt their partner's traditions. I'm talking about people who are unduly jealous over time, family, and occasions that aren't "theirs" or from "their side."

Rather than feeling sad or defensive at moments or occasions that are foreign to you, try to experience joy when your partner is experiencing joy; make it familial and festive. Often in marriage, the more we give, the more we get. Our partner will see us giving over to joy and celebration for them, and they will be more likely to do the same in turn.

Jerks

See "A" for "A$$holes."

Jesus

For many Christians, Jesus is the son of God; a prophet who sacrificed himself to save those who believe in him. For many Christians and non-Christians, Jesus was an influential leader who believed in alleviating poverty, doing good, helping others. Sometimes it's an issue for a Jewish-Christian relationship when there are different beliefs about religion or cosmology. Sometimes it's no issue at all: you believe what you want and I'll believe what I want and if we have kids we'll teach them what we each believe and they can decide what they believe. It's a nice and pluralistic approach for a messy world. With cultural traditions, it can be easier to blend/mix/share. But with religious beliefs, it can be trickier: Is Jesus the son of God or isn't he? Interestingly, if you go back in history, there were a number of Jews who believed that Jesus was a prophet, if not the messiah. While I believe that the contemporary Jews for Jesus movement is nothing more than deceptive missionary tactics, there was a time when one could be fully Jewish in identity and practice but also be something of a follower of Jesus. It was something like the "Jesus Movement" of Judaism. Of course, as time went on and a whole other religion developed, including new biblical texts, lines got drawn.

All of this serves as a reminder that the way things are is never the way things always were. There is no original or authentic truth to any of our beliefs or practices, really. There has always been diversity in Judaism in terms of who we are and what we do. Whatever your beliefs about Jesus, take the true lessons from his life: do and be good.

Jokes

Jokes are joyful. There is a whole catalogue of Jewish jokes; that is, jokes by Jews and jokes about Jews and our issues. Many people believe that Jews developed a good sense of humor to be able to handle the difficult circumstances of their lives and antisemitism. Humor was and is a survival strategy. Some people think that being Jewish comes with a cultural legacy of critical thinking and questioning, and through those processes life in its beautiful absurdity can make us laugh. Being funny is a very good thing. What isn't funny is when the humor in which we delight makes someone or someone's values or beliefs the butt of the joke. I've seen people get made fun of for their lack of Jewish literacy. That's not funny. Anyone, Jewish or not, who is in a Jewish space or doing something Jewish with family deserves to feel included and respected. It is a serious concern in Judaism that we avoid making others feel shame. We must always endeavor to laugh with, not at, those around us, and this is particularly true if people are trying their best to blend in with family and traditions that are new for them. Make jokes to make them feel comfortable and bring them in. Never joke in a way that shuts someone out.

Journey

Intermarriage is a journey you go on together. At first, I insisted on having no Christmas tree in our home (see "C" for "Communication/ Chrismukkah"). My husband's family has a tree and I thought we'd go there and decorate it with our kids so they get the tradition and experience but our home would be kept "just Jewish." But then my husband's family moved away and so things changed. I learned to be flexible on the tree (we get a little one that we decorate with homemade crafts and plant later on). Our intermarriage is a journey. We learn, we grow, we change.

All marriages are a journey of one sort or another. Everyone is constantly evolving and the real leap of faith of marriage is pledging to stay with someone through those changes. People can become more or less religious and observant, can determine that culture is more or less important to them, can explore becoming something new via conversion, or can explore doing something different like a new holiday tradition. There are lots of ways that the journey of marriage can present challenges and obstacles, yet there are so many ways that marriage forces us to reckon with who we are and who it is we wish to become. Doing this with a supportive partner can create meaning and growth in so many unexpected ways. Enjoy the journey!

Joy

Many of us are living some pretty spectacular lives. Not all of us, of course. We have real challenges and certainly don't all have the same resources and opportunities. But, overall, I'd say we are living in a time when people are experiencing life in thrilling ways. We are really conscious about how to live, more than perhaps ever before. We have more choices, more freedom, and more insight into how to build a meaningful life. We are living longer, in better health. And we are figuring out this thing called "work/life balance."

Please welcome joy into your hearts and homes. Don't let the a$$holes (see "A") get you down. I experience so much joy when I do Shabbat with my partner and our kids. And it fills me with joy to know that he continues this even when I'm away. I delight in the joy of his family celebrations too. They don't have to be originally "mine" in order for them to bring me joy. But sometimes joy is hard to come by for many Jews. A lot of Jews grew up with a lot of negativity. It's telling that in the Yiddish culture the common answer to "How are you?" is "How should I be?" We are, and this is a huge generalization, a *kvetchy*, complainy people. Sometimes we need to experience a little less *oy* and a lot more joy!

Judaism/Jewishness

You might have thought I'd put this first in the "J" section but, frankly, we are too used to centering Judaism/Jewishness in the Jewish world. Hello?! We are, like, 3 per cent of the population. It's a big wide world out there and lots of different kinds of folks are marrying lots more different kinds of folks. Why do we think we should be the exception? Why do we fret about it so very much? Anyway, in a move to de-center us a little and offer a touch of humility, I put Judaism eighth in this section.

Judaism is an ancient religion and culture. According to the 2013 Pew Research Center report on American Judaism, most Jews, whether self-identified as religious or not, define Judaism as an ancestry or an inherited culture over a religion. So Judaism is a nation, a people. Judaism is also a set of beliefs and practices. Yet it is shared with people who have differing and contrary beliefs and very different practices. Who and what are we? Well, that is the question and anxiety that has been at the heart of much of Jewish life for centuries now. Guess what? It's complicated.

Here's what I know for sure: Some people feel strongly that they have a Jewish identity. Jewish is something they *are*. Conversely, some people feel pretty much the same as any Canadian, American, Australian, and German Jews feel – Judaism is more something they *do*.

Much of the Jewish world has been obsessed with instilling Jewish identity. I don't disagree with the importance of identity. But, at the same time, I believe that people are made up of multiple identities. For some, being Jewish is crucial and for others that is not the case. To be or to do? These are some of the questions intermarried folks grapple with. Will all partners "be" the same or can they "do" some of the same things together? Will child-rearing center on instilling identity (and, if so, which one, or both?), or will it center on instilling modes of cultural practice? These have always been questions for Jews, the Jewish culture, and the Jewish religion, but perhaps more so now that we have many people who aren't Jewish joining our families. How do you see Judaism/Jewishness? How does it work in your life and home? These are great questions to ponder and discuss as you chart your intermarried course together.

Juggling

People today juggle lots of different priorities and responsibilities. We don't just throw birthday parties for our kids – our parties must be "Pinterest-perfect" or "Instaworthy," with both enough food for a crowd and also adherence to standards of local and organic, gluten-free, and allergen-conscious eating. Dude. I just want to have kids go on a scavenger hunt and eat pizza. While planning these parties, we are working a lot more than people used to work. We are often having kids later in life, which means we end up caring for aging parents along with our young children. We have debt loads and stresses that previous generations simply wouldn't have understood. We also want to enjoy our lives (imagine that!) and so we spend time and money on personal betterment, travel, and a host of other activities. Life is tiring and full of juggling. Although I'm generally celebratory of intermarriage, sometimes it can feel like one more thing to juggle – one more conversation to have, or an in-law who won't understand something, or a tradition to try to massage. So I want to say this: I see you and all those balls you're valiantly keeping up in the air. Good job. Yes, intermarriage takes a little work (all marriages take work!), but you've got this.

Justice

Justice is an important Jewish concept. The Hebrew word *tzedakah* means both charity and justice. Any family should consider how to be charitable and, more importantly, foster justice both in and outside the home. I was ordained in the Humanistic Jewish movement, which makes human concerns and needs central to Jewish practice and experience. We take Jewish ethics seriously (this is not to say that we are the only Jewish movement that takes Jewish ethics seriously, nor that we subscribe to all that is sometimes called "Jewish ethics," some of which can be deeply unethical). Nevertheless, for my partner, the notions of *tzedakah* and *tikkun olam* (repairing the world) are a real draw to the Jewish practice he has come to participate in. These are universal human values, caring for others and the earth, through a Jewish lens. The lens is new to him but the values are his own. Intermarriages built on a shared value system promoting justice and goodness are certainly positive and wonderful unions.

Part of the mission of Judaism, I believe, is to improve the world. As such, we should take seriously the idea that intermarriages of all kinds help break down barriers, and they promote dialogue and love between people who come from different ancestries and communities. This is a wonderful thing! I understand that a lot of the arguments against intermarriage are not intentionally racist or tribalist, but their impacts sometimes are. I do not believe people should only hang out with people who are "like" them. We learn and grow from encountering and embracing difference. Intermarriage, then, is itself a force for justice, even the Jewish promotion of justice, in the world.

There is tension between the Jewish concepts of *keva* and *kavannah*, adhering to the letter of Jewish law or to the spirit of Jewish law. It's a fairly fascinating conversation to have about meaning: Do we do things because we are "commanded," because that's how others do them, because that's what authorities dictate? Or do we do things because of their inherent spiritual value, their impact on us and the world, their intrinsic goodness? How much can rules be changed without sacrificing their value? In order to have this conversation, people need another "K": knowledge. A healthy intermarriage means that both partners acquire knowledge about the cultures they're bringing to their home. Often Jewish people learn much more about Judaism when they have a partner who starts learning about it. Intermarriage can deepen knowledge and connection to one's own culture – a hidden benefit that is rarely discussed! Kosher laws are the dietary laws of the Jews. Many, many Jews do not keep kosher at all. It is a discussion to have that can lead to other discussions: how you eat is going to be a daily reminder of who you are. The letter "K" discusses the klunkiness of relationships, how sometimes we stumble along but, actually, we're still getting somewhere. Finally, kindness goes a long way in creating a healthy dynamic. Sometimes we are stuck in our anxiety or worry about getting things wrong. Be kind to yourself and your partner as you go on this journey together.

Kaleidoscope

Culture is like a kaleidoscope. It isn't unitary or uniform. It is a constellation of many different parts moving all at once. What I consider culturally important to me might differ significantly from the next person. Same culture; same identity; different expression. If you can remember being a kid and looking though a kaleidoscope, you might remember a feeling of awe at the beauty of it. When we look at the kaleidoscope of culture, we can appreciate a similar sense of awe. There are Jews from the Ashkenazi, Sephardic, Ladino traditions; Jews from Latin America and the Middle East, from Arabic and Mizrahi traditions; Jews from China, India, and Ethiopia; and Jews from everywhere else – we all have different cultural traditions and practices. Being "Jewish" means different things to different people. Being Jewish can mean so many disparate things that it can sometimes seem like it means almost nothing specific. To some, it is to read Torah and pray every day. To some, those things never ever feature in their Jewish lives, but they still feel and do Jewish in their own way, via Jewish art and film, food and literature, and family. To some, they have no Jewish family, but they do holiday celebrations and study. To some, there is nothing more Jewish than *gefilte fish*, to some it's getting a henna tattoo on *Mimouna* (a traditionally Sephardic holiday at the end of Passover), for some it's a bagel and *The New York Times*. No one is right or wrong, although many of us have been told we are "Jewing it wrong" in some way or the other. Culture is a kaleidoscope, and in the various configurations of culture, there is a lot of beauty.

Kaput

If you've ever said the word *kaput* (finished, finito, done), you've spoken Yiddish. If you've ever said words like *schlep* (drag, lug) or *tuchus* (bum), you've spoken Yiddish. There are a lot of people who use these words not knowing their Ashkenazi origins. Why does that matter? Intermarriage is the continuation and culmination of centuries of us living with others. Not only have Jews acquired cultural practices from the global communities in which we've lived, but we've contributed to the global community as well. In societies where Jews and Jewish cultures are completely interwoven into the fabric of the larger Jewish culture, how could there not be intermarriage?

For example, there are more Jews living in New York City than in any other city in the world. I've heard it said that all Jews are, in a sense, like New Yorkers, and all New Yorkers are, in a sense, like Jews. These are cultural stereotypes and I'm sure there are throngs of people who would object, but I sort of get it. New York, a place constructed and largely defined by the immigrant experience that also somehow represents the American experience, a place that is cosmopolitan and gritty, where you can and sometimes need to be pushy but also live with a real sense of community and heart, seems very Jewish to me. Did New York create the diasporic Jew or did the Jew create New York? Look, there's no way to parse out how and who affected what and how. Cultures blend; we enrich each other. Intermarriage is part of that dynamic. End of story. *Kaput*!

Karma

Karma is a great example of a seriously unJewish concept that lots of Jewish people like. There are a number of "JewBus": Jewish Buddhist types. Although the concept of karma is shared by, and has different resonances in, many Eastern religions, we tend to be familiar with the Buddhist version. I'm not a Buddhist, so I am speaking somewhat out of turn here, but I believe that most of our Western understanding of karma seriously misses the mark. In Buddhism, karma is related to the concept of work and action. The idea is that we reap what we sow; the good we put into the world comes back to us and so does the negativity we put into the world. In the West, we often talk about someone "having bad karma" because they have bad luck. Does the biblical Job have bad karma? How would I know? It's notable that concepts from Eastern religion have made their way into the vocabularies and beliefs of Jews. Karma is only one example. Lots of people have learned Sanskrit words and yogic concepts from yoga studios or meditation classes. You can find Jewish yoga, Jewish meditation, Jewish-Buddhist courses and temples. I'm wary of issues of cultural appropriation, but I understand that we can benefit from sharing with and learning from others, particularly when we are in loving relationships with those others. Then the other becomes the self, or at least deeply connected to the self in new ways. If you have ever talked about "karma" or "chakras" or any other concept that isn't your own, let that give you pause the next time you hear about some idealized "pure" version of Judaism. It has never existed. It never will.

Keva/Kavannah

One of the central tensions, rarely discussed, in Jewish life is the weighing of practice on the side of either *keva* or *kavannah*. *Keva* gets translated in different ways but it means something like fixity or structure. It's when people follow, as closely as possible, the letter of Jewish law. There are advantages to this, to be sure. People appreciate the discipline that a set of rules and a daily routine provides. There is lots of research on habits and their power for people. My favorite author on the topic is Gretchen Rubin, whose books focus on creating positive and happy-making habits. Rather than struggling to find time to light Shabbat candles or remember which holiday is when; rather than figuring out a time to pray, meditate, or connect with Jewish learning; or rather than struggling to fit Jewishness into life, people prefer to simply have the timing, the set of rules and practices, and the modes to follow all laid out for them. For some people, this provides a healthy and happy structure to their lives.

Other people (those more like me, if I'm honest), rebel a little against pre-fixed rules. I appreciate structure in some ways but I also want to have the freedom to figure out what I want to do and what my reasons are for doing it. I am not the kind of person who does something just because I'm told. This certainly has to do with cosmological belief. I can appreciate that if you believe Jewish law is God-given, and you believe in that God, you are more likely to want to follow the rules. Those aren't my beliefs; I believe humans created the rules to serve human needs, and that human needs change over time, necessitating a change in the rules, or at least how we adhere to those rules.

Enter the concept *kavannah*. *Kavannah* means something like intention. So, rather than following the rules, the fixity of the law, we take what we think is the meaning behind the law. It's an approach that honors the spirit of the law rather than the letter of the law.

Why do I bring this up in the context of intermarriage? A few reasons. First, most people willing to intermarry are willing to break Jewish law. We are *kavannah*-types. But sometimes the *keva*-types give us a hard time. It can be useful to have Jewish framing to explain our choices (we don't have to explain or justify if we don't want to, of course). We can talk about how we are rooting our relationships and lives in Jewish practice and beliefs, but our practices and beliefs are based on what we find to be good in our tradition and culture.

The concept of *kavannah* has gained a lot of traction in Judaism via Jewish mysticism. You can find a *kavannah* (intention, deeper meaning, meditation, reflection) for verses of the Torah, for everyday practices, and so on. The idea is not to simply go through the motions, but to dwell on why you're doing what you're doing. It's similar to yoga practices when we set an intention for the practice, or sometimes if you choose an intention or word to focus on for the month or year ... a theme of sorts. I'm all for doing Jewish in a purposeful, meaning-driven way. So figure out your intentions, in all senses of the word, and communicate with each other. What will you do from your cultural background and why?

Kids

I don't think that any kid should have to justify their connection to their people. My own kids, children of a rabbi, hopefully won't have to. But it sucks that so many kids get told they're not a "real" Jew. Seriously? What even is a "real" Jew? The kid of Moses or Solomon? (See "Kings" below.) A kid who does nothing Jewish, has a Christmas tree and loves it, but happens to have a Jewish mom? A kid who practices and does a ton of cool Jewish stuff but has never converted and has a Jewish dad? A kid whose parents feel connected to Judaism based on an ancestry.com search that found their great-great-great-grandparent was Jewish? If you find yourself deciding who "counts" as Jewish as you read these examples, here's my solemn and loving suggestion: Stop that right now. Entertain the idea that it isn't for you or for me to determine who's in and who's out. That whole dynamic is tired and has caused a lot of problems. Your kid = your problem (I don't mean the kid is a problem; I mean it's up to you to figure out issues of identity and education). Not your kid = not your problem! Leave it alone. You do you. For more on raising kids in intermarried homes, see "C" for "Children."

Kindness

Public service announcement for everyone: At almost any Jewish gathering of any kind, there are people who aren't Jewish and people who are Jewish but didn't grow up doing much that was Jewish. As such, we should expect to experience a sense of klunkiness (see below). I disagree strongly with the cultish, in-group mentality that is promoted in so many Jewish spaces and communities, the one that says if you don't know the order of the prayer service or the right blessing or tune or ritual then you are somehow less-than. You are putting yourself in a new space, which requires vulnerability and courage: you are so not less-than! If I had one wish for the Jewish community as a whole, it would be that we make kindness the center of our spaces and practices. Kindness and love are ultimately what it's all about (that's a real *kavannah* approach). We all deserve kindness and we all grow from being kind. So if you see someone struggling to keep up in *shul*, whisper the page number and maybe also a sentence or two about what this part of the service is all about. Or show someone how to light the *menorah* using the *Shamash* and explain what *Shamash* symbolizes as the leader candle. Or be brave and ask a question, assuming that someone else near you shares your question but is too intimidated to ask it. Let's remember to be kind to everyone we are in community with. That's the point of community in the first place.

Kings

Judaism no longer has a monarchy, but our tradition comes with stories of important kings. You've likely heard of King David, a central figure in the Jewish text. He kills that large Goliath dude. He becomes the King of the United Kingdom of Israel and Judah. (Without getting into issues of historical accuracy too much, I do feel it's important to note here that much of this isn't historically or archaeologically verified. These are central stories and they may lend "truths" without necessarily being "true.") It is said that the messiah will be descended from the line of David. He's a big deal. If you remember anything from Sunday school, it might be that David spied on Bathsheba bathing and lusted after her, summoning her, and ultimately stealing her from her husband Uriah, whom he orders killed. There are a few lessons we can draw from this: First, wow, the mistreatment of women by powerful men goes way, way back. Second, the story suggests intermarriage was no big deal. It is thought that Bathsheba was from the tribe of Judah (some believe she was descended from Ham, which introduces an interesting racial narrative). But she was married to a Hittite (the dude David has killed). David had eight wives, most of whose names you don't know. We know Bathsheba. She becomes the mother of King Solomon, the Queen Mother. She was intermarried. We also have Ruth from the Book of Ruth, Joseph (of the raincoat), Moses, and others. Some of the big names in the biblical text are intermarried.

In the Book of Samuel where we find these stories, the Kingdom is doing well. Under Solomon, detailed in the Book of Kings (2 Kings is where the history starts being a bit more verifiable), things aren't going so well. Things fall apart; the center cannot hold (to borrow from "The Second Coming" by William Yeats). In 1 Kings 11:2, the text notes that Solomon has wives from some of the forbidden tribes, but he loves them and won't let them go. Interesting! Why does the Bible sometimes say intermarriage is cool and sometimes not? Why mention Solomon's intermarriage here? Well, we can surmise that intermarriage was fairly common. Some of the biblical writers were like, "Okay, cool. People are doing this so let's write about realistic relationships." Other biblical writers were like, "People are doing this and it's not cool so let's write stories that show the connection between intermarrying and the whole peoplehood falling apart. We will save Judaism by discouraging intermarriage." Is this familiar? Even today you have some who see that intermarriage is happening and inevitable and so want to shape communal narratives around acceptance and expansion, and others who fear intermarriage and try to shut it down. Our stories, ourselves.

Klunkiness

I want to acknowledge that not all knowledge gets acquired quickly and completely. There will definitely be times when one or both of you will feel like you don't know what's up. I see this sometimes at funerals and *shivas* (houses of mourning). Someone who isn't Jewish might show up at the *shiva* with flowers, which is traditional for them but not for many Jews. Or they show up and prayers start and they feel like a fish out of water. You should know that many Jews have these experiences if they weren't raised with much Jewish knowledge or practice. This isn't the exclusive experience of the non-Jewish partner. Sometimes connecting with a culture that isn't your own feels klunky. I want to tell you that this is okay! All of us are awkward and lacking in experience in some parts of life. The bar shouldn't be so high that you feel you have to be perfect. You're learning. We're all learning. Welcome to the human experience.

A Jewish partner who is trying to connect with their partner's culture has to be open to acquiring knowledge and experiencing klunkiness. Maybe you don't know what goes on during *Eid*. Maybe you haven't really experienced Chinese New Year and you're not sure what colors to wear or what gifts are appropriate to bring. Figure it out, let yourself experience klunkiness, and remind yourself that the cost of avoiding participating with your partner is much higher than the cost of feeling foolish.

Knowledge

Here's the thing – you can't figure out stuff about *keva* or *kavannah* or about kosher laws or about anything, really, without first acquiring a little knowledge. This book is a great start! It's an introduction, a primer of sorts, to the kinds of questions you might ask. A healthy intermarriage means that both partners acquire knowledge about the cultures they're bringing into their home. I was so excited to learn more about the order of a church service, Scottish history, and Thanksgiving traditions when I started exploring these with my partner. We go to church because I want to see the kinds of things he grew up with! It was fun when we attended the church where he was christened (baptized), for example. Many Jews receive a terrible Jewish education and aren't particularly knowledgeable about Judaism themselves. So it can be difficult to explain to one's partner what the traditions are, what they mean, without figuring out your own *keva* and *kavannah* balance. The wonderful thing about intermarriage is that often Jewish people learn much more about Judaism when they have a partner who starts learning about it. This can be a journey of learning that really brings you closer together. Intermarriage can deepen one's knowledge and connections to one's own culture – a hidden benefit that is rarely discussed but that I've seen play out in countless couples' lives.

One such couple were Alana and Joseph (not their real names), who went on a beautiful exploration of stories and music together. Alana wasn't Jewish, Joseph was. But Alana was really interested in literature. They started reading a Jewish story that had some biblical allusions. So they read that story in the Bible. Then they realized it was fascinating and so they read more stories with that biblical allusion. And so it went, following thread after thread. They read these stories and books together *out loud*. It's so romantic and sweet! They did something similar with Jewish music – first learning about klezmer, and then some similar musical traditions like gypsy funk, and then that led to jazz, which led back to Jewish jazz, and then they got into exploring Ladino music and so on. These people are awesome and I want them to be my friends. The point is that Joseph would have never explored Jewish literature and music with that kind of depth if it weren't for Alana trying to learn. His intermarriage deepened his connection to Jewish culture. Not everyone does a deep dive into literary and music archives, but this trend is something I see all the time. Knowledge is power, they say. So, too, in a marriage – it can serve as the glue that keeps you connected to tradition and connected to each other.

Kosher

Kosher laws, the Jewish dietary laws, are a perfect example of *keva* and *kavannah* and how these work in everyday life. Many, many Jews do not keep kosher at all. This is, in many cases, because they're not *keva* people; they have no interest in following what seems to be an arbitrary set of rules. Sometimes, however, we throw the baby out with the bathwater. You don't have to keep fully kosher to take the *kavannah* of the kosher laws and apply it to your own food choices. One of the *kavannot* (the plural of *kavannah*) is to treat animals with as little cruelty as possible. Another is to prioritize your health. These are worthwhile intentions, even if we find that the actual rules around what to eat no longer serve those intentions. Many Jews are concerned that the rules for slaughtering animals are actually no longer the least painful for and least cruel towards animals (there have been just a few technological innovations in the many centuries since the rules were written). Many Jews would rather eat organic, local, vegetarian, or in some other way that they feel fulfills the *kavannah* of kosher. You can live a life eating kosher cakes and soft drinks, but your body will not be as nourished as if you eat locally raised pork. You can choose to stick to the letter of the law – *keva* – and eat *matzah* bagels at Passover, but you wouldn't be honoring the symbolism of avoiding bread at Passover. I prefer to eat chickpeas and corn (still not allowed for some Jewish movements) and avoid *matzah* bread and cakes. Your way doesn't have to be my way. The *keva* versus *kavannah* debate is an invitation for you to determine what you want to do and why.

Eating is important; we do it daily. Some people like keeping kosher because it means they are practicing their Judaism and feeling connected to it all day, every day. So, discussing how you want to eat with your partner is a discussion to have that can lead to other discussions. How you eat is going to be a daily reminder of who you are. For me, it is more important to be vegetarian, support local food growers, and eat ethically than it is to follow kosher laws. My husband is not a vegetarian, but we do share concerns of environmental sustainability, and we shop, cook, and eat accordingly. Each couple needs to determine how their identity affects their daily choices. You are what you eat! And you are somewhere on the spectrum of *keva* and *kavannah*. It's useful to figure out where and what that means for you.

I encourage people to read widely in the literature of their partner's culture because it's a great way to get to know the feeling and some of the customs of the culture. It's a nice way to learn together (another "L" we'll discuss). What's love got to do with it? When it comes to marriage, hopefully a lot! Intermarriage expands love from within Jewish couples and communities into other families and communities. When we fall in love with someone unlike ourselves, we expand love between and across difference. That is something the world needs much more of! Marriages are, of course, based on love but they are also legal contracts. Intermarriage might have an impact on some of the legal considerations of marriage, particularly if custody issues arise later on. Legalities are something to consider for any marriage, unromantic as they may be. Luggage or baggage is also important to consider. Everyone who is with someone long term must negotiate their relationship in the context of the baggage they bring to the relationship. What are you lugging around? And, as this section asks, can we let go of some of it? Sometimes we're holding on to an idea or a practice that is just no longer serving us. If we can let go of the things that are holding us back, we pave the way for much more joy.

Lean In

Facebook COO Sheryl Sandberg's famous 2013 book *Lean In* advises women to "lean in" to work when they become pregnant and begin the role of parenting. The argument is that workplace culture often excludes women from important professional roles and access to information, even when women might wish to participate. The idea is that women tend to "lean out" when on the mommy-track, but they can lean in instead, and have both their children and their careers flourish at the same time. I think the advice is good for many women, and not practical or relatable to many others (a lot of marginalized working women responded that they would love a world in which "leaning in" was a choice). "Leaning in" can also serve as a great metaphor for intermarriage. Lean in to listen to your partner. Lean in to their holidays and other cultural moments. Lean in to making the relationship sound even when parenting takes a lot of the focus.

Learning

Sometimes learning about your partner's culture can be helpful. I saw things in a new light when I learned about earlier followers of Jesus, before there was something called Christianity, and how many of them were Jewish in identity and practice. It made me think about the lines in the sand we draw and how, perhaps, they are arbitrary. Perhaps, sometimes, they can shift. I am not saying I've accepted Jesus as the messiah. I'm saying that learning can broaden our perspectives. A great way to learn about culture is through reading (see "Literature" below).

Legalities

It is sad but true that some marriages don't last. The stereotype is that intermarriages are doomed from the start because the partners are just "too different." I don't believe there is a higher rate of divorce amongst intermarried folks (I'd love to know for sure but I can't find that information anywhere). I think bridging differences is great for a relationship. All of us will experience differences of opinion with partners, so we might as well get good at navigating them. However, in the event that a relationship dissolves, there can be a problematic aftermath in terms of intermarriage.

What I say to couples who are divorcing is that you should do your best to remember why you got married and try to end the relationship the same way it started – with a sense of respect for your partner and a desire for a better future. Perhaps that better future is best fostered apart than together but, ideally, you want happiness for yourself and the other person.

What is really sad and harmful is when people use religion or culture as punishment in a divorce. I've seen folks forbid their kids from attending Jewish Sunday school when that had previously been the arrangement. I've seen folks threaten to forcibly baptize their kids. I'm sure it has gone the other way when Christmas or other family holidays and traditions are taken away.

Try to remember that if you've got kids, these are really harmful things to inflict on them. You are messing with their sense of home, tradition, identity, and culture. It's not a good modeling of values, nor is it a healthy way to resolve conflict with your current or ex-spouse. Avoid the legalities of stipulating who gets to go to Sunday school and when; who gets Christmas and how. This isn't the place for lawyers. This is the place to lead with some heart and courage.

I think of Charlotte, a character on the HBO show *Sex and the City*. She converted when she decided to marry her husband. At one point, they separate and she maintains her Jewish practice declaring, "I'm not a fair-weather Jew!" I'm not saying you have to convert or keep up a Jewish identity and practice after divorce. But I do like the idea of remaining committed to the values you developed as an intermarried family even in times of divorce.

Legalities can also mean referring to *halachah*, or Jewish law. In Jewish law there are rules for many things, and it is up to each person or couple to decide how much of the law they practice. For observant, orthodox people, many or most of the laws are part of the daily rhythm of the house. Most people who choose intermarriage are not so observant or orthodox, which means they selectively apply to their lives those laws they deem meaningful. Some feel this is a "watered-down" approach. I think it is a sensible one – decide what you want to practice and why. See "K" for "*Keva/Kavannah*" for more on this. All of us have to live within the boundaries of what is legal but, for most of us, it is our morality and ethics that guide how we live, much more than written codes of law.

Listening

See "C" for "Communication" and "H" for "Hearing." The most important part of communicating is being able to truly hear your partner.

Literature

I often teach students about literature and about how literature can be a tool to gain cultural enrichment, to foster empathy for someone different from you, and to experience the richness of traditions that may not belong to you. For non-Jews, you'll learn a lot about your partner by reading Mordecai Richler, Chaim Potok, Amos Oz, and Rebecca Goldstein. This type of literature can create fantastic discussions amongst intermarried people. Also good to note is that many Jews do not relate to some characters in "Jewish literature" (Philip Roth comes to mind). Literature can build on and perpetuate stereotypes, and it can also shatter them. Reading together can be an entry point into having these conversations together. I think one of the most romantic things a couple can do is read aloud to each other (I'm a nerd and that's okay! I'll take prose over presents any day). So cozy up and get your learnin' on.

Losing It

As I write this book on marriage and intermarriage, I feel a little disingenuous, as though I'm some kind of expert. I have worked with many couples on their intermarriages, so I'm an expert in that respect. But in my own marriage there are ups and downs, just like everyone else experiences. I will admit that sometimes I simply lose it. I get frustrated and feel like I haven't been seen by my partner. This is part of all marriages, and some of the iterations are unique to intermarriages. Here's an example: One year my husband, a teacher, had his school's curriculum night on the first night of Rosh Hashanah. Curriculum night is when parents come to find out what their kids will be learning that year. It's a big deal and teachers are definitely expected to show up. Rosh Hashanah is one of the most important holidays of the year, and, bonus, if you're a rabbi, comes with its particular sense of importance and, yes, stress. I told him I really didn't want him to go to curriculum night; that it was unfair that such a thing would be planned on such an important religious holiday. He spoke to his principal who recognized her mistake, apologized, but still pretty much insisted he show up. I had that feeling rise up, that sense of being a minority and experiencing a lack of cultural privilege. (I kept ruminating, "No such work event would happen on Christmas Eve!") And, I admit, I lost it. I was sad and angry and stomped around and let my frustration get the better of me. Then, later, my husband promised he'd never attend a work event on an important holiday again. I promised I'd try to keep in mind how generous he is with bringing Judaism into our lives and how he celebrates our holidays with genuine interest and joy. We made up. I wasn't wrong to think about my lack of cultural privilege, but nor is it productive to continue ruminating and to stay stuck in that frustrated place. I had to let it go and figure out how to have a meaningful and happy Rosh Hashanah anyway.

Loss and Letting Go

You gain a lot by making your life with someone: support, a witness to your life, a co-parent, perhaps a best friend. But it's important to say that there is some loss too. Dealing with loss and learning how to let go are important because people aren't built to simply move from one family to another without acknowledging the differences. Sometimes we want our home to be "just like" the home we grew up in. I've seen people lose their minds over Christmas dinners that just don't "feel right." The challenge of keeping certain traditions is that it can make us feel like things should always be the same as they were. But things are never the same. My Passover dinner will never be how it was when I was a child. The people around the table are different, the Jewish resonances of the holiday are different, and I am different. We all need to decide what we will keep from our traditions and what we can let go. Yes, there can be a sense of loss for what is no longer the way we remember it being or would like it to be. It is therefore essential to consider what is gained. I have gained so much by being with my partner. I have gained new holiday traditions as we do Christmas with his family. But well beyond that, I have gained a source of support, a great co-parent, a wonderful partner to go on adventures with, and much more. It is easier to work on letting go and to take our focus off loss when we cultivate an attitude of gratitude for what we have. For most of us, our marriages bring us much more than they cost us – which is why we chose this partnership to begin with. So we might as well enjoy what they are and worry less about what they're not.

Love

"L" is for "love" because that is at the heart of things (excuse the pun). Remember the love when things get challenging! Love your partner wholly and fully for who they are, including their religion/culture. That's all I'm going to say about love right here but this whole book is really all about loving your partner and partnership. I wouldn't say "love is all you need"; love is a necessary but insufficient condition for a successful marriage. Marriage also takes commitment, compromise, communication, and kindness. But love should fuel it all.

Luggage/Baggage

Unless you married your high school sweetheart, chances are you have some relationship luggage/baggage you are carrying around with you. And if you've married your high school sweetheart, your luggage/baggage is likely that you didn't get to date widely before committing. We're all messed up in our own way! Or, put differently, we all come to any relationship bringing things with us from the past. This can include dynamics from our families of origin, previous romantic relationships, and our own personal stuff. You're never going to be entirely free from your luggage/baggage, but you can learn to lighten the load. Sometimes this takes therapy. Is there something in the way of marital bliss that comes from someone's luggage/baggage? Can you identify it? Sometimes intermarriage is part of someone's luggage/baggage because there was family drama around the partner of choice, or they carry some guilt about whom they chose to love. Sometimes the luggage/baggage is about how others have made a partner or the couple feel excluded or unworthy of support, community, an officiant, and son. So, lighten the load and let some of it go (see "Loss and Letting Go" above).

Not all intercultural relationships result in marriage, but given that the word "marriage" appears in the title of this book, I spend some time talking about it. I always tell my couples not to focus so much on the wedding, but on the marriage itself. I'll give examples of vows that can be used to center and ground a marriage, and tips and tricks for healthy marriages. (Note: "Never go to bed angry" isn't one of them. That is ridiculous. Every couple I know has gone to bed angry.) Mindfulness is a concept that has a certain cultural cachet right now. But there's a reason for that: being able to focus on the present moment really does make life better. The more mindfully we approach our partner's culture/religion, the more meaning we will experience. And meaning, also discussed here, is what it's all about. Moses is likely the most revered character in Jewish literature. Guess what? He was intermarried. We're going to talk about it. The word "mixed," as in "mixed marriage" or as in kids who identify as "mixed," is interesting. Some people like it as it evokes a sense of blending or a mélange. Some don't as it evokes being "mixed up." Here I'll talk about some people who call their family "mixed" as well as some who choose to avoid the word.

Marriage

All marriages are intermarriages. Not all marriages involve partners who come from different religions/cultures, but all marriages involve two people who are fundamentally different from each other in many ways. We all have to figure out the differences that are dealbreakers for us and those we can work with.

For me, I had some political dealbreakers. I don't think I could have married someone who was anti-choice/pro-life, for example. It just suggests to me someone whose values are so different from my feminist ones. I also have some religious dealbreakers. The truth is, my "intermarriage" is much less of a coming together of difference than it would have been for me to marry an Orthodox Jew or a practicing Sikh, Muslim, or Christian.

My husband and I are very similar in terms of our beliefs around cosmology (pretty much atheist), politics (lefty-types but with a sense of realism), child-rearing (lots of play and humor, with a healthy dose of structure and discipline). We agree on most things in terms of how to share household tasks, manage money, and more. We are both very independent, valuing our personal friendships and freedom, while we work towards a solid partnership.

So, yes, we are "intermarried," but our marriage would have similar clashes or conversations if the difference between us had more to do with any of these other important aspects of relational life. Our cultural life is actually not that hard to sort out. He likes the Jewish traditions and values our family participates in and, because we do them in a fairly secular way, he feels included and that he can benefit too. He'd find it hard if I were insisting on prayer at home, but I don't. I'd find it hard if he wanted us to attend church regularly, but he doesn't. It's not as hard as some would make it out to be!

Whatever your relationship and arrangement, consider all the things that you have to negotiate. Is religion/culture a major factor? Maybe yes and maybe no. What's certain is that all of us have to find our way through those points of negotiation because we never marry someone exactly like us. If you have married someone exactly like you, then wow, congratulations! But, also, I bet your spouse drives you crazy!

So, what makes a strong marriage? Different folks have different ideas about this and here are mine: A strong marriage is a partnership in which you feel like yourself, so does your partner, and you share the experience of life with each other. A strong marriage is built on witnessing one another's joys, successes, and challenges. It's offering support without offering to fix or take over. It's experiencing a lot of life together, and making sure those experiences are as joyful, as meaningful, and as enriching as possible.

When I meet with couples to discuss officiating their wedding, I tell them that folks often work so hard to create the perfect wedding that they forget to work on the marriage. The wedding is just one day and if what you're after is a fairy-tale day, you might just be setting yourself up for disappointment for the rest of the days that follow because marriage isn't a fairy tale. There's rarely a "happily ever after" without a whole ton of sweat, talk, and (sometimes) vodka. I want you to be happy but not in the sense that you'll be blissful and carefree forever. True happiness requires struggle, grit, perseverance, and challenge. To be happy in your life and marriage, there will be hard times that make you stronger. Have the fairy-tale day if that's your thing and then buckle up for some work. But it's the good kind of work; the kind where you find your flow, accomplish a lot, delight in how far you've come, and then keep on striving.

Am I going to tell you to never go to bed angry? Of course not. That's ridiculous. Sometimes when you're in the thick of it, it will take longer than a day to sort out. This isn't a sitcom where all problems are easily resolved in twenty-two minutes. There's no sappy music at the moment of resolution and revelation. I guarantee that you *will* sometimes go to bed angry. I just hope that more often you go to bed feeling snuggly and close to each other.

The traditional Jewish marital vow spoken at the wedding ceremony is "You are consecrated to me according to the laws of Moses and Israel." Only the groom says it (brides say nothing in traditional Jewish ceremonies). To be clear, my couples don't say this because it simply isn't true. The laws of Moses and Israel are rarely if ever the most important consideration in this union. We sign both the Jewish wedding contract, the *ketubah,* and a civil one. We bring in Jewish culture, but the couples are almost never intending to keep most of the "laws of Moses and Israel" in their homes. What are they intending? Some cultural practice, not because it is commanded but because it is chosen. We make marriages out of what is meaningful to us.

Meaning

What is the reason for being Jewish or, as some say, "doing Jewish" at all? In my view, it is two-directional. I love that this is just about the middle of the book because the next thing I'm going to say is pretty much the crux of it all: *Judaism is a way to enrich your life and make you a better person in the world.* That's what it's for. It's always two-directional if it's really meaningful. Some Jews only care about the first part: their own lives and enriching them. Some Jews care an awful lot about the second part: being good people in the world. Both are worthwhile but carry risks. If we are too focused on ourselves, we risk a kind of chauvinism whereby we think being Jewish makes us unduly special. Jews are special the way all people(s) are special; each unique with their own beauty and gifts but no more so than anyone else. If we are too focused on others, we risk losing ourselves, losing our grounding in our peoplehood, cultural traditions and values, and sense of making sacred the experience of our own lives. Judaism works in my life because it brings beauty and joy to me. It helps me raise my children with a sense of identity, history, rootedness, and values. It brings me practices like Shabbat that connect me to my culture and remind me to pause and take in the beauty of my life. It gives me a calendar, a way to mark time meaningfully, including holidays for each season and celebrations for new weeks, months, and years. Doing Jewish makes my life better.

It also gives me language and practices for values like *bikkur cholim* (caring for the sick) and like *shalom bayit* (peace in the home). I know about *tikkun olam* (repairing the world) and *tzedakah* (charity and justice), and I have communities through which I can pursue them. I have a textual tradition that compels me to honor and love the stranger.

Here's the thing: people don't have to be Jewish to experience this two-directional goodness. My husband experiences it and so do countless people who aren't Jewish. Judaism can potentially enrich the home and family life for everyone, even those who aren't Jewish and don't plan to be. It's all about figuring out which practices are meaningful for you. There are some I do alone, some I do with my kids, and some we all do together. Keep your eye on the meaningful prize to figure out what to do.

Mentsch

There's a Jewish concept of a *"mentsch."* The Yiddish word literally refers to "man" but its meaning and usage more clearly describe someone, regardless of gender, who is decent, kind, giving, good. So, regardless of where you fit in to a family with an intermarriage, be a *mentsch*. If you're Jewish, be kind and generous in explaining Jewish terms and concepts to your family. If you're not Jewish, be open to learning about it and working on any antisemitic attitudes you may have picked up along the way in life. If you're a parent and unsure about your child's marriage, support them, embrace your new kid-in-law, and learn to get comfortable with your kids making choices you may not have made (all kids do this; it's the mark of them becoming adults). We will all get much further and do much better if we remember to be a *mentsch*.

Mindfulness

Because life is an accrual and accretion of moments, it's worthwhile to be mindful during those moments. It's easy to let stress or strife get in the way but, truly, you can miss a lot of life that way. Judaism creates a practice of mindfulness via blessings that remind us to be grateful (there are versions for folks who'd rather not pray too), via practices like Shabbat that get us to slow down, and via instituted practices around respecting and blessing parents, children, and the sick or suffering. Other cultures also have mindfulness practices like meditation, prayer, blessings, and silence.

We are living in a cultural moment in which mindfulness is touted everywhere. Sometimes it can feel like one more thing on the to-do list. Ironically, trying to be mindful is creating a lot of stress for some people! All it really means is to work on being present and focused in a moment and then another moment. All it really means is to take stock of what is going on right now. If culture/religion can help you with that, great! If mindfulness helps you enjoy your culture/religion more, also great!

Mistakes/Messes

Hey! Guess what? You're going to step in it at some point. If you're not Jewish and trying to figure it out; if you're Jewish and trying to explain a new concept or practice to your partner; if you're negotiating how to do holidays or deciding on family traditions and gatherings – no matter what is going on in your marriage, there will be times when you make a mistake. Someone will say something hurtful. Some misunderstanding will cause tension or even a rift. It happens. If you are a mistake-free human, you are doing life in a way that is much too safe – which is a mistake in itself!

Try to learn from mistakes. Try to be humble and open. Try to work through problems. Try to forgive. It'd be easy to go through life keeping score of all the wrongs done to us by our loved ones, but it wouldn't be a whole lot of fun. If you have a partner willing to create an intermarriage that is meaningful and rich, you've got a good thing going. Expect mistakes from yourself and from them, and work to fix them.

Mixed

The word "mixed," as in "mixed marriage" or kids who identify as "mixed," is interesting. Some people like it as it evokes a sense of blending or a mélange. When I was a scholar of postcolonial theory and literature, I spent a lot of time thinking about concepts like hybridity, creolization, crossing borders/boundaries, and cultural influence. I think it can be quite empowering to acknowledge that culture is always the product of mixing with others. What we consider "Jewish" has often been influenced by the places Jews have lived and the peoples we've encountered.

Some families don't identify as "mixed" as it evokes for them a sense of being "mixed up." At the Sunday school run by the congregation I serve, most of our families are intermarried. Some of the kids have told me that they're "mixed" and have no problem with putting a Christmas tree on their Chanukah *menorah* decoration. Some parents tell me they want to raise their kids by "being both" (this term is often used by Susan Katz Miller, who has a book by that name; she has lots of experience in her own life and works with others who are "both"). For some people, being both means doing separate holidays and educating kids about the two religions present in their home. For some people, mixing means blending – having a painted Easter egg as the egg on the Passover Seder plate, for example. Mixed can mean all kinds of things.

For my kids, we decided that we'd inculcate a sense of Jewish identity. They wouldn't call themselves "mixed." They'd say something more like, "I'm Jewish but I also get Christmas presents." They feel perfectly fine with it – not confused or conflicted at all. When we hear "mixed up" instead of "mixed," chances are we are imposing our own internalized sense that intermarriage is confusing for kids. I grew up hearing this all the time. So far, my kids aren't confused about their cultural identity. They are also not confused about me being their mom even though I have a different last name than they have. Families are both mixed and mixed up in all kinds of ways. Most of the time, the kids are alright.

Moments

Sometimes when I speak about the two-directional goodness Judaism can bring to your life (see "Meaning" above) – enriching the self and empowering you to be better in the world – people feel overwhelmed. It's not like you have to stress about pursuing your highest self all the damn time. No one can sustain that! I like to think of Jewish practice as a series of moments. Yes, identity is something of a constant for some people. I might *be* Jewish all the time but I don't think about it all the time! Judaism functions largely through practice. So do other religions/cultures! Sometimes figuring out how you want to run your house is deciding on a series of moments. For some families, the custom is "Friday nights we light Shabbat candles"; for some, "Our Buddhism gives rise to a gratitude practice"; for others, "We do Easter egg hunts on Easter"; and still others, "We do fireworks for Diwali." Whatever your practices are, they are likely driven and defined by a series of moments. The moments both lead to and create memories. Your cultural life doesn't have to be complicated. Be intentional about certain moments and those will lead to and add up to a life that is of your own choosing.

Money

See "C" for "Cost."

Moses

Moses is likely the most revered character in Jewish literature. Guess what? He was intermarried. Tziporah is a Midianite. Their relationship is one of mutual support. She empowers him to lead his people to freedom. She saves him in some really difficult moments. She uses the leadership lessons she learned from her father, Jethrow, a Midianite priest (who also helps Moses). Being intermarried doesn't hinder Moses from being part of his people. On the contrary, it helps him become a great leader.

Later in the Exodus narrative, Miriam and Aaron, Moses' brother and sister, are upset that he marries a "Cushite" woman. Some people think this again refers to Tziporah, but the simplest explanation is that Moses took another wife (it was kosher then). Cushite is understood to mean darker skinned, and a lot of interesting racial narratives come through in interpretations of this bit of the Torah. Are Miriam and Aaron mad that Moses has found a woman besides Tziporah? Mad because she is a person of color? What's going on here?

There are many ways to understand this text. Some take a more literal approach. I believe the Torah was written by people for people and that these stories are meant to be instructive, without being "true" necessarily. So, what is instructive here?

First, intermarriage has always been a thing. Second, people have always squabbled over various aspects of it. Third, in many cases, the

Jewish people have been strengthened by the folks from other cultures and places who come into our tents, our people, and our culture.

Lots of intermarried people have been told that "Judaism forbids intermarriage." What is even truer is to say that rabbis over the last while forbade intermarriage (and some are now reconsidering). Intermarriage has always been part of our people. If it was good enough for *Moshe Rabbeinu* – Moses the great teacher of us all, leader of the people, deliverer of freedom, patriarch to the future messiah – and if he was intermarried, I'm going to say it's good enough for us! (Note: I don't recommend the bigamy part.)[5]

Mystery

For some people who haven't encountered a lot of Jews or don't know much about Judaism, our practices can be something of a mystery. Look, if all you know about us is circumcision and *matzah*, I get that it can seem a little funky. Judaism doesn't have to be mysterious. Every single text, practice, and holiday is searchable on Google today, and there are fantastic and trustworthy sites like My Jewish Learning to answer questions. Not only that, the Jewish partner can offer insight into what they do and why it's meaningful. There's no reason why there should be a barrier to participation for the partner of a Jewish person over lack of knowledge. We all need to demystify what we do and why. This makes Judaism accessible not only for the non-Jews who are part of our families but for the many, many Jews who are themselves not Jewishly educated and who have a limited Jewish literacy. Have a question about Judaism? Ask! And if you're too shy to ask, google it.

N

It makes sense that all intermarriages (like all marriages generally) involve negotiation. I'm going to give step-by-step discussion questions and negotiation techniques – set a timer, active listening, never say never – to help couples with this practice. Negativity is about changing one's mindset. Rather than seeing all of the problems of intermarriage, this is about focusing on the positive; going from "no, but" to "yes, and." Having said that, we will also cover some "no-nos" and even the point at which we simply say "nope" to someone's judgment or attitude. Normal is a concept that should always be in scare quotes. A lot of people are opposed to intermarriage because it isn't "normal" for them. But those people do things that are not "normal" for me! Truth: There is no normal. Every marriage is unique. To find what works for you, consider what you and your partner really need. As in, need versus want. Not everyone gets everything they want, but hopefully everyone gets everything they need.

Nag

Try not to be a nag about stuff. Try to hear your partner out so they don't feel like they have to nag about stuff. That's it.

Nationhood

Related to culture (see "C"), nationhood is an important and really complex idea. On the one hand, Jews are undeniably a nation – we are a people with a particular set of histories, practices, and beliefs. And yet we are made up of many other nations and cultures. We speak so many languages, some of them "Jewish" (Hebrew, Yiddish, Ladino) and some of them not specifically Jewish but used, in our lives, to express Jewish ideas and practices. We actually span such a spectrum of beliefs and values that it's difficult to name one that would apply to all or even most Jews. And the "Jewish values" we could name are not exclusively Jewish. Non-Jews also believe in things like education, justice, and family.

It's precisely because of this complexity that some folks feel so strongly about intermarriage. Being a part of the Jewish nation is of such importance to folks, and yet the nationhood aspect always feels a little bit precarious. Our feelings on this can be delicate: we know we are part of a people we can't adequately define.

I feel a familial connection to all Jews, and yet I disagree so strongly with some of what is deemed to be Jewish practice, values, and beliefs and how people use their Judaism as a force in community and the world. Often there is much more that separates me from other Jews than unites me to them. And yet nationhood is something we feel in our bones.

In the world in which we currently find ourselves, where globalization threatens any real sense of nationhood for anyone, or at least complicates it, Jews can sometimes feel particularly at risk of being assimilated. This is why many Jews fear intermarriage: it's one more threat to the perceived continuity of the peoplehood. I don't agree with their fear nor do I find it to be productive, but it does help me understand where folks are coming from. The truth is that the institutional forms of Judaism that exist now *are* changing. Our structures have *always* changed in order to keep up with the times. At one point, being Jewish meant hauling an animal for sacrifice to the central temple in Jerusalem. Synagogue-style Judaism would have been unimaginable to those people. The future of Judaism may very well be unimaginable to us today. Every generation must find the forms of

Jewish practice that are meaningful *to them*. Intermarriage may very well have an impact on what Jewish culture and practice look like, but that is completely in keeping with the ways in which social forces have always shaped what we do. If there is one thing that is truly traditional in Judaism, it's change.

If you're joining a Jewish family through marriage, welcome! Whether or not you're choosing to be Jewish yourself, you are joining a complicated and messy, wonderful and strange, deeply flawed and very beautiful nation, people, and community.

Needs versus Wants

When you or your partner truly need something, it is worth paying attention to that need. I've heard it said that the fight you most commonly have with your partner is reflective of your greatest need going unmet. Sometimes our needs are different from those of our partner and so it can be hard to understand why they aren't obvious. The other person might find it hard to understand why this need is such a big deal. For a relationship to be fulfilling, both parties need to work on ensuring their partner's needs are met. Having said that, there is a difference between "need" and "want." Most of us might want certain things of our partner but they are not genuine needs and, truly, we can't always get everything we want. I *want* my partner to get up with the kids when they wake up at 5:30 a.m. I'm sure he also wants me to do that. We have to compromise. There are times, however, when that want becomes a need: I have a big service to lead that night or I'm feeling really depleted. If I can communicate that I *need* a sleep-in then I'm more likely to get it.

This all has to do with intermarriage because we all need to figure out what we want to retain from our cultural and religious heritages and what we absolutely need to retain in order to feel spiritually or emotionally whole. Our partner will have their own needs too. Part of negotiation is figuring out what is a want, what is a need, and how everyone can get their needs met.

Negativity/Naysaying

Sometimes I think people confuse saying no with being negative. Oh, how the opposite is true. Sometimes saying no is the most joyful, wonderful act. It is an act of setting boundaries, of putting yourself first. Say no to lots of stuff: pressure on how to practice your culture/ religion, exclusionary attitudes from others, doing more than you're comfortable with, prayers and rituals in which you don't believe. I'm such a believer in being your authentic self. Saying no when appropriate can provide space for that. Say no as needed.

Negativity is different than saying no. It's naysaying for the sake of it. It's the attitude that says "this is going to be hard"; "I am alone in this/these feelings"; "my partner will never get it/me"; "I might as well not even try because I'll never get it right." Don't be a downer at the holiday dinner. Don't avoid learning about your partner's culture because you're afraid you'll get something wrong. You will get something wrong! Go anyway. If you're finding things really hard, it might be time to work on changing your mindset. Rather than seeing all of the problems of intermarriage, focus on the positive; going from "no, but" to "yes, and." Remember the good your partner, kid, or family member brings to your life, and work through problems with the attitude that all will be well, because you'll make sure it is well. Remember, be a *mentsch* (see "M").

Negotiation

All relationships involve some kind of negotiation and intermarriages are no different. In an intermarriage you may need to sort through some particular stuff. It comes up a lot when folks discuss the "December Dilemma" – or how to do Christmas/Kwanzaa/Judaism/Diwali/ Solstice, whatever combination of holidays matter to your family, in an equitable way that feels good and celebratory for all.

Whatever your particulars of negotiation, here are some practical tips I've used with couples.

- Practice active listening. Listen to your partner and then repeat back what they've said, making sure you got it right before replying. Sometimes all we need is to be fully heard.
- It's hard to actively listen for a really long time. Set a timer for three minutes. That's how long the first person speaks. The other person will get their three minutes when the first person says their partner understood what they said.
- Schedule fun stuff after hard stuff. If you know you're going to have it out about an issue, or talk through a decision you have to make when you don't agree, schedule the time to have the full discussion and then schedule a date night or something fun afterwards. It's

nice to know you are going to resolve things enough that you can head to the movies together and feel good about it.

- Make lists. I love lists for pretty much all things. When deciding on something together, it can help to have lists. If this is a "December Dilemma" thing, make a list separately of all the traditions you like or want to celebrate. Then rate their importance from one to ten. As you exchange lists, note the really important ones for your partner. These would be good to be flexible on. If your partner rates having a Christmas tree as a "ten" in importance and it's an absolute deal-breaker for you, it might be good to figure that all out before the wedding. Sometimes my clients make lists about the pros and cons of a decision they have to make (circumcision/baptism, sending kids to religious/cultural school, having a B Mitzvah). As you look at the list, again, rate the items. Sometimes there are twelve "pros" to a decision but the one "con" is so important to you it outweighs the others. It's not pure math, but sometimes people like these visuals as a way of approaching a subject to better understand one another.
- Be kind. Try to be kind to each other. This is your person you are building a life with. Even and especially when you are in the thick of something, if you can show each other kindness, it will go a long way.

Never Say Never

Here's a secret: there are people who vow they'll never intermarry and then they fall in love with someone and then they intermarry. Here's another: there are parents who say they'll disown a child if they inter-marry but then end up dancing joyfully at their kid's Hindu/Jewish wedding. Here's another: if you had told the Jews living in Spain in the mid-1400s that Spanish Jewry was about to be decimated and scattered, they'd have thought you crazy. The same applies for Jews living in Berlin and for German Jewry overall in 1929. Who could have imagined even three decades ago that I'd be a rabbi (a woman!), writing this book about intermarriage in a cafe in Toronto (I was born in South Africa to Jews from Polish and Lithuanian roots), with my non-Jewish spouse and fully Jewish kids down the block? Things change. They change for us personally, for us culturally, for us globally. We all think we know our lines and dealbreakers and must-haves and will-nevers and all that. My advice is to be flexible. Things change! Check out my "December Delights: Creating and Crushing Chrismukkah" guide in the appendix for a story about how I ended up with a Charlie Brown Christmas tree despite saying I'd never.

No-Nos

In general, my goal is not to give a lot of "must-dos" and "absolute nos" when it comes to intermarriage. Everyone figures out their own path. A lot of rabbis will officiate a wedding of an intermarrying couple, for example, only if the couple agrees to a whole host of rules. The couple must commit to raising a child with a Jewish identity (and no other cultural identity or affiliation). The couple must agree to do holidays at home, to educate kids Jewishly. Sometimes rabbis force conversion on folks which, frankly, has always seemed bananas to me. Why would you compel people to join a people instead of showing them how awesome it is to be part of the people and welcoming them in if and when they're ready? My husband has no interest in conversion but participates actively in Jewish life. That's much more meaningful than a conversion of convenience between a non-practicing and non-engaged Jew and their spouse. Our goal should be making Jewish life *more* accessible; not throwing barriers up and hoops to jump through for folks wanting to connect.

Anyway, all of that is to say that I'm not really interested in telling you what to do and how to do it. However, there are a few things I've seen that tend to get in the way of folks finding a path to happy partnerships in intermarriages. So there are just a few "no-nos" I'll dole out now:

• Don't use culture/religion as a weapon of war.

By this one I mean, don't threaten to take away Christmas, or threaten to start taking the kids to church, or threaten to introduce new identities not agreed upon. Once you've decided how you're running your home and raising your kids, don't change it up in moments of anger. These kinds of threats are super destructive.

• Don't let your partner feel alone in the practicing of their culture.

I'm not saying a partner should never *do* stuff alone. I do Jewish stuff alone or with friends all the time. I don't expect my husband to always come along. Having said that, there is nothing worse than feeling lonely in your relationship. Sometimes you've got to be a buddy and come to that Jewish film festival, go to the *Iftar* dinner, attend the church bazaar that your in-laws really care about. You don't have to convert or do stuff all the time to, once in a while, accompany your spouse to something so they feel supported by you. The company we give each other in marriage is an important part of being married.

- Don't let your in-laws or parents ruin your wedding.

This is a big one. People have strong opinions about the person their kid is marrying; about how that marriage should be; and, in particular, about how the wedding should go. I've met with many couples intermarrying who have parents and in-laws who are imposing a lot of their own ideas. My least favourite couple to meet with for a wedding is the couple that is only meeting with me, a rabbi, to please the parent. More than once I've declined doing their wedding, encouraging them to find an officiant who is reflective of their own beliefs and values. I've also had parents of more traditionally Jewish folks balk at me as officiant when I am the choice of their child. They're not used to a female rabbi. Or a rabbi who doesn't lead traditional prayer. Or a rabbi who will officiate a wedding on a Saturday before sundown (in their eyes, breaking the rules of Shabbat – rules the family almost never follows, anyway). For more on weddings, see "W."

- Don't let your in-laws or parents ruin other stuff either.

This applies beyond intermarrying families, but sometimes the strong opinions of our parents and in-laws can really poison some joyful moments. I serve many intermarried couples who choose not to circumcise their children (I serve Jewish/Jewish couples who also make this choice). Sometimes the Jewish side of the family sees the choice not to circumcise as the spouse who isn't Jewish "winning." Don't fall victim to the trap of thinking this way. It's so negative and destructive. Be a united front. Tell your in-laws or parents that they did a great job parenting, thank you, but now it's your turn. You are in charge of the decisions of your house and kids. And while you so want them to be part of your joy, you don't want them to bring their negativity with them (see "G" for "Grandchildren").

Nope

You know that feeling you get sometimes when you just have to say "NOPE!" I had that moment when folks were telling me what to do about circumcising my son. I was like, "Nope, I don't want to listen to anyone on this. Not your business." Sometimes people get that feeling when their parents accuse them of "marrying out" or when they say something like "If you intermarry, then Hitler won." Nope, nope, nopity, nope, nope. Here's what's going on with that feeling: if your goal is to try to convince someone of something like not to marry their beloved or not to circumcise their kid, and you're trying because you care so much and feel so strongly about these issues, pushing someone to the point of "nope" is always going to counter your aims. I said to someone I love, "You know, the more you try to compel me to do things your way, the less likely I am to actually do things your way." I was in the land of nope. What can I say? I'm rebellious by nature. I also think people need to stay out of each other's sh*t a little more.

A lot of folks have been pushed to the point of "nope" by hearing exclusionary and rude statements about intermarriage. That's the person we love you're talking about! Or our kids! As soon as you say bad stuff about the people I love most, I'm going to be out of there super fast. To all those who have felt "nope" in Jewish spaces, this is for you: Find a space that makes you say and feel "Yes!" That sees you and your family for the beautiful, complicated, messy, glorious bunch of people you are. That makes you feel welcome in the way you need. We are lucky to be living in a time when we needn't feel "nope" no more.

Normal

Look, we all want to be "normal" and none of us are. There is no normal family, no normal way to do intermarriage, no normal life. We are all unique. That's a good thing! Sometimes when we can embrace the idea that we aren't going to fit in, or fit a mold, or do things the way others do, we can feel freer. Many years ago, I was a summer camp director and I went to a training on how to promote a cohesive community at camp. The lesson was to "take expectations and then mess them up." In the camp context, that meant have the kids be the "counsellors" for the day or have everyone eat dessert first. Pretend you're going to have a really important and serious discussion about something and then introduce a water fight instead. You know, keep things interesting and keep kids on their toes. I love this idea for disrupting "normal" in family life too. Can you have a carpet picnic? Can you hunt for *chametz* (bread products that some families remove from their home prior to Passover) in the house Nancy Drew–style, with a flashlight and a map? Can you host a baby-naming ceremony where each person discusses the significance of their own name? How can you take expectations and mess them up? Create a new normal for you?

Nuptials

See "W" for "Weddings."

Optimism is about adopting an outlook that understands that things will be okay. Having a fight over the holidays? They'll turn out beautifully, don't worry. Someone's parent is horrified about this upcoming marriage? People usually behave themselves at weddings. Optimism comes to me naturally, in spite of my tendency to worry. I think it's a useful habit of mind that I teach and talk about. Oppression is tied to systemic and structural practices that are harmful to minority groups. Jews have historically been one such group. Intermarriage can be a tool to fight oppression, for it shows that people can learn to love across difference. It can also be a tool to understand oppression: when you learn about the history and beliefs of your partner, remind yourself that there are so many other cultures and practices out there that we can all better seek to understand. Those of us in intercultural partnerships also need to approach our relationship with openness. This openness makes space to go well beyond any challenges that the coming together of cultures produces. Indeed, one may even find oneself seeking and finding opportunities instead of challenges. The usual narrative is that intermarriage is a threat to Judaism. But I disagree. I think intermarriage is an opportunity for Judaism to be enlivened and enriched.

Officiating

While it can be stressful to find the right officiant for you, the good news is that it is getting easier and easier as more rabbis and clergy open up to officiating intermarriages. There are many benefits to working with someone who has received training and grounding in the religion/culture and practices of cultural leadership. Have you ever been at a wedding and had to fight the desire to roll your eyes when the officiant says something that doesn't reflect the couple at all? When I serve families, my goal is that every word I say reflects them and their values. This is an important milestone in their lives and they deserve to have it truly reflect them. They also deserve for it to be beautiful and meaningful. Sometimes you'll get more of that beauty and meaning with an officiant who has been trained to do ceremonies.

Having said that, if you can't find an officiant that checks all those boxes, you've got other options! Some folks get married by a justice of the peace. Some get a friend to marry them (not all jurisdictions allow this, but many do). You've got choices. If you're having a wedding, or baby naming, or B Mitzvah, or funeral, or other ceremony presided over by someone, find an officiant who truly reflects your values.

I am a very busy rabbi when it comes to life-cycle services, particularly weddings. I am always delighted to serve a couple, but I prefer if they choose me because they like me and because our values align, rather than because they need a rabbi and very few will perform intermarriages. I'd so much rather be able to refer to rabbinic colleagues if the religious, theological, and stylistic fit is better. We're not quite there yet. Many Jewish movements still prohibit rabbis from officiating at an intermarriage. But it's changing. I look forward to the day when my colleagues and I are referring couples to one another all the time because we all have an investment in finding the perfect fit for each couple that approaches us.

Okay

Here's the optimist in me: You'll be okay. You really will. People work out their stuff and grow and change and sometimes it's hard but, for real, they're almost always okay. You're okay right now and you're going to be even more okay tomorrow.

Openness

I see intermarriage as an opportunity (see below). People thrive in intermarriages when they approach their partner and their partner's culture with an attitude and air of openness. We are living in a time when there is a lot of focus on mindfulness, on having an abundant mindset, on trusting that things are okay. Sometimes I love that stuff. I really do believe that we can almost always look for the awesome in any situation and find it. Many of us have so much good in our lives, and we always will live better if we focus on that good instead of whatever is wrong or lacking. As I write this, I want to acknowledge that this is true despite huge amounts of pain. There is abundance. There is also hurt, pain, trauma, poverty, sickness, suffering. All of these are happening at once. The more privileged someone is, the easier it is to focus on the abundance in their life (this needs saying because sometimes people without a whole lot are told they just need to fix their mindset to fix all their problems, and that's BS). With those caveats, consider your own life as it is right now. What is awesome about it? I bet you can think of lots of things. Now, what is hard about it? I bet you can think of a few things there too. What can be done about the hard things; that is, what is within your control to change or fix? Sometimes our attitude about a problem only compounds the problem. Rather than seeing challenges as insurmountable, we do better if we consider accepting what is and embracing imperfection while doing our best to improve things.

What am I on about? Well, this is a real process when it comes to intermarriage. Let's say you're the parent of someone who is intermarrying and you aren't comfortable. This could be because you are worried about Jewish continuity, worried about your kid engaging in cultural traditions that are foreign to you, worried about whether holidays will feel different, and so on. Plenty of folks have plenty of worries when it comes to their kids intermarrying, so insert your own examples here as needed. It's possible to focus on those worries and what sucks for you about your kid intermarrying. It's equally possible to focus on the good things that can come out of this union. Do you like your future kid-in-law? What great qualities do they have and bring to your family? What do you actually want for your family? Great holiday celebrations, beautiful quality time together, and a continuation of Jewish traditions? Make those wonderful and inclusive so they happen and are meaningful to everyone. Approach newness with openness and you're more likely to get what you want out of this situation. Focusing on what's hard is almost always a way to bring more hardship. Focusing on what's good is almost always a way to bring more goodness.

Opportunity

If there's one takeaway from this entire book it's this: *Intermarriage presents an opportunity for learning, growth, depth, and beauty.* This opportunity is there for the couple, their families, and their communities, including the broad Jewish community. I grew up hearing about the "crisis" of intermarriage. That didn't get the community very far. It encouraged a whole bunch of people to leave what they felt was a closed, closed-minded, and somewhat tribalistic culture. What if I had grown up hearing about the "opportunity" of intermarriage? I wonder what doors might have stayed open for me? And I am one of the ones who said "Who cares? I'll do it anyway!" I got a Jewish education, found Jewish community, became a rabbi, did a lot of Jewish stuff. But many people are not like that. Their attitude, rightly so, is "if you don't accept me, my values, my partner or spouse then what do I need you for?" Those people are the ones who deserve to hear this particular nugget of truth: Intermarriage is an opportunity to explore and expand your Jewishness if you want it to. It'll push you to examine what is important about being Jewish and learn about practices that you value so you can teach them to your partner. Judaism itself grows and is enriched when we learn from others. We have picked up laws, customs, languages, traditions, and learning from the many cultures amongst which we've lived. Now is no different.

I was recently meeting with a couple planning a wedding; he is from a family that is Greek Orthodox and she is from a family that is Conservative Jewish. They are both relatively secular, interested in their cultural backgrounds but not the religious rites and obligations with which they grew up. We talked about the Jewish custom of breaking a glass at the end of a wedding and the Greek custom of breaking a plate at moments of celebration. I asked if they might want to break one of each, as a way to highlight the similarities between their cultures and showcasing how lovely and complementary bringing cultures together can be. The symbolism of the breaking works particularly well: When you get married, you are changing your identity. You are still who you are, of course, but you have adopted a new identity as a person who has committed to another, binding your lives in some way. Just as the plate or glass breaks irreparably, your life is never exactly the same as it was. Rather than seeing it as something that has been broken, you can see it as something that has fallen away, making way for something new. Intermarriage is exactly that: making way for something new. For you, for all of us.

Oppression

Oppression is tied to systemic and structural practices that are harmful to minority groups. Jews have historically been one such group. I think it's important to state that some of the anxiety of intermarriage for some Jewish folks is a fear of antisemitism. Many people grew up believing that people who aren't Jewish would never fully understand or accept Jews, that there would always be some stereotyping or hatred. For that reason, it scares them to think of these people joining their family, the one place where they had always felt secure and accepted. That's a real dynamic and should be taken seriously. I do think it's important for folks who aren't Jewish to understand antisemitism and work to ensure they are confronting any biases they picked up along the way. That goes for Jews too if they are entering families with their own history of oppression. A Jewish person (of any background) marrying into a family that is Black, Indigenous, racialized, queer, or any other group that carries a history of oppression similarly needs to learn about that community and its history, and work to unlearn internalized biases. The risk is there, of course, that someone will say something wrong or make a mistake. With clients and families I work with, I have sometimes had to explain how something that got said was antisemitic in nature, even though it was unintentionally so. I've also explained the politics of marginalization and minority culture to folks who might not realize what the "big deal" is about certain cultural practices.

A great example of this is circumcision (see "C" for "Children"). I once worked with a couple who had a really difficult experience with a family member around this practice. One of them had a brother who wrote a long letter to the couple while they were expecting their first child. In the letter he explained that he was opposed to circumcision and was really worried about this child being subjected to this "barbaric" practice. I explained to the brother that calling the practices of minority cultures "barbaric" is something that has been done for a long time. It tends to "other" people and it tends to stoke hatred. I also explained that for many folks, circumcision has been the mark of belonging to a people, and that belonging is sometimes a matter of survival if you are surrounded by hate. I'm not saying this here to talk about the politics of circumcision, but to talk about how oppression sometimes shows up in sneaky ways, even in families who are loving and accepting. So, it's good to be vigilant and watch for the biases, to be open to being corrected on something, and to remember that love only trumps hate if we are purposeful about fighting hate of all kinds.

Having said all that, love really can win out over hate! Intermarriage itself can be a tool to fight oppression, for it shows that people can learn to love across difference. It can also be a tool to understand oppression: when you learn about the history and beliefs of your partner, you remind yourself that there are so many other cultures and practices out there that we can all better seek to understand.

By the way, there is so much to say about the work that needs to be done *within* Jewish communities to unlearn biases about other groups (see "U" for "Unlearning" and "W" for "Whiteness" and "Wokeness"). Issues of gender, race, (dis)ability, and more are only beginning to be understood and taken seriously in our communities. Check out the awesome organization Be'chol Lashon; writers like Tema Smith, Rebecca Pierce, and Nylah Burton; and the many other rabbis, activists, and thinkers addressing these issues.

Optimism

Openness, and battling oppression as a team, can lead to optimism. You can actually change your fear-based worries into action that produces a positive result. Optimists typically have an outlook that reassures them that things will be okay. For example, if you're having a fight over the holidays you can either retreat into fear – "I'm going to lose out to your traditions; my culture always gets the short end of the stick; things won't feel joyous for me" – or you can push towards optimism – "My partner loves me and we will work together, to make sure things turn out right; whatever we do together, the most important thing is time with each other; sometimes good enough is much better than perfect if perfect will lead to stress and sadness." In my experience, holidays turn out beautifully. Folks worry so much in the lead up and then are happy on the day. We might as well let the worry go and trust that things will be fine.

I also see this a lot when people are getting married and someone's parent is upset about the upcoming marriage. It creates sadness and stress to know your parents or your future in-laws don't approve of you or your union. However, I strongly suggest taking an optimistic approach; remember that people usually turn it around and almost always behave themselves at the wedding. Don't waste too much time or energy on the stress and sadness of others. Decide that you're going to have an amazing wedding no matter how others feel and hope for them that they can do the same. If they can't, that's not on you. It'll all be fine. Optimism comes to me naturally, in spite of my tendency to worry. Both are true for me: I worry a lot but I also tend to think things will be okay. I have had to train my brain to be optimistic with some dedicated hard work, and I continue to do so. I focus a lot on mindset and goal setting. I work to let go of the things that are hard or imperfect. I still worry too much, but I'm much happier for my optimistic outlook. And when it comes to intermarriage, trust me – based on my personal and professional experiences – most of the time families work out their stuff and everything really does turn out just fine.

Ordained

I was so lucky to attend a Jewish seminary that took optimism and openness as its starting place when it came to intermarriage (and most everything else). There was never a question that I could be intermarried and become a rabbi. There was no question that I would perform weddings for intermarrying folks, serve all kinds of families in all kinds of ways, and that the religion/culture of any family member would never be an issue. I have never once had to ask a family which parent is Jewish in order to decide which rituals are appropriate. I have never, ever told someone they couldn't say or do something they wanted to do in a life-cycle celebration, holiday service, or anything else because of the rules around who gets to do what, Jewishly. In my community, we have folks who are not Jewish but are partnered with or parenting Jews who serve in all kinds of ways: as board members and presidents, as service readers, as co-creators of programs, as full participants in rituals for weddings, B Mitzvahs, and so on. No barriers, no rules.

Most rabbis and other religious leaders were ordained in places where this is not the culture. Ordination matters because the attitudes with which you're trained usually filter into how you practice. The culture of our institutions is reflected in the kind of Jewish practice we offer and foster. So, ask a lot of questions of the rabbis or religious leaders. Find out whether they have rules, barriers, or attitudes around intermarriage, and determine whether they work for you and your family. Every single person deserves to find a leader who will make them feel affirmed and included. Luckily, we are at a time when there are many more options in terms of clergy.

I was married by an amazing rabbi named Miriam Jerris. I trained with the wonderful rabbis Eva Goldfinger and Karen Levy. Even Conservative rabbis are beginning to officiate joyfully (see *Joy: A Proposal* by Rabbi Amichai Lau-Lavie). Terrific officiants are out there. Find yours.

Originality

See "C" for "Creativity" and "D" for "DIY."

Oscillation

In all the talk under the letter "O" about optimism and openness, it's useful to remember that very rarely does change happen in a linear way. Think about any mindset or habit you've ever had to build. My guess is if you've ever tried to exercise regularly, for example, you start out strong, then fall off a little, sometimes stop for reasons of injury or irritation, then you start up again. You get a little more consistent and things are flowing. Then you stop for a bit because of vacation or injury. Then you pick it up once again and it becomes even more a habit that you can't live without. It's not like you start and get consistently better all the time. There are hiccups and that's normal. Expect the hiccups. So too with adopting a new mindset around intermarriage. It's not always going to be easy. You're not always going to feel great about everything. Optimism is only realistic if it falters sometimes. It's not about being naive, it's about having a positive outlook. So, expect a little oscillation. Expect some good times and bad times with your family, with your partner, with your own thoughts. Trust that you're on a good path; it isn't linear, but it's moving towards getting better all the time if you're putting in the work.

Oxygen

This is a tip I give all my wedding clients, whether or not they are intermarrying: the week of your wedding, go on a date together, do something you both will enjoy and is a little special, and vow not to talk about the wedding or family dynamics or anything stressful. My husband and I went to see a great musical that week (*Billy Elliot*) and then spent time in the park. We talked about so many things we hadn't talked about for so long: our work, politics, art, fun memories. We had been so consumed with talking about wedding plans, family stuff, guest lists, and budgets that we hadn't had a chance to talk about regular stuff. It felt so nice to reconnect in that way, and it was a great reminder of what all the wedding planning was for: the marriage.

We needed a little oxygen, literally and figuratively. We opened up space to breathe, talk, and rest. At the end of the date, after this time to reconnect, we sat down separately but together in the park to write our vows. It came so naturally after this time together and was a beautiful and fun way to approach this thing that had been stressing us out.

So, wherever you're at in your journey, whether about to get married, already married, the parent of someone getting married, or anything else, ask yourself right now: How can I get a little oxygen to open up my perspective? What do I need to be able to breathe and relax?

I hope you are passionate about your partner. Use that passion! Be passionate about being part of an intermarriage! This section covers parents (as in, the parents of the adults in a relationship) and also parenting. Sometimes our parents put pressure on us to marry someone from our own culture or faith. Sometimes our parents give us a hard time. Shout out to the parents who love and accept their kids no matter what! Parenting is a big subject (see "C" for "Children"). I have learned so much about parenting from becoming one myself. You have to decide how to raise your kids religiously/culturally. Also, this section will encourage couples to consider their parenting style and how it will reflect or be informed by culture. There are a lot of stereotypes and jokes about "Jewish mothers." These will be considered. "P" is for "partnership." I like the term "partner" because it evokes both a state of being and an ideal. Your partner's happiness affects your own and vice versa. Also covered is the very sticky topic of patrilineal descent. In Jewish law, one is Jewish if one is born to a Jewish woman. I'll talk about my objections to this rule, especially in the contemporary context when there are many families with a committed Jewish father, with two men as the parents, with children being from blended families, adopted, or raised by relatives who aren't their birth parents.

Pandering

Pandering is the close cousin of paternalism (see below). Sometimes folks who are well-meaning but perhaps a little paternalistic will pander. They put a *dreidel* on the Christmas tree and feel like they deserve some sort of trophy. There are many fake efforts at inclusion. This happens by and to Jews. Everyone is at risk for this sort of pandering. Watch for it.

Parenting

In the natural cycle of intermarriage, you barely get over tensions with your own parents before becoming a parent yourself. And that's when the real fun begins! Parenting is the very best and very hardest thing to do in the world, in my view. Of course, not everyone becomes a parent. But many of the fears around intermarriage have to do with how to parent children, so it's important to take a look at it here. We've already addressed some of the intermarriage-related choices you'll make as a parent (see "C" for "Children"). Here, I want to spend a moment talking about some of the non-specifically intermarriage-related choices you'll have to make. Why? Because sometimes we spend so much time and energy on the intermarriage stuff that we forget about the billion other choices we have to make. Here are some examples of things that would have been dealbreakers for me when seeking a co-parent:

- An anti-vaxxer (don't get me started)
- Someone who wanted to put our kids in private school (I work in, support, and really believe in public education)
- A laissez-faire, loosey-goosey, free-range parenting type of parent
- A really strict and, *oy vey*, wanting to use corporal punishment type of parent
- Someone who expected kids to be seen and not heard
- Someone who cared about kids getting really good at sports

And so on. If you are described by one of the above points, then all the best to you. This list doesn't describe someone who is a bad parent, just someone whose parenting style would have been incompatible with mine. None of this has to do with culture/religion.

Sometimes people meet me to plan their wedding ceremony and have literally never talked about parenting. Um, not great. Nothing will test a marriage like becoming and being parents. You can't fully know what you'll want to do and what your style is going to be until you're in it. But you should have discussed certain basics! Are you going to be attachment parents? Helicopter parents? Hands-off parents? How strict are you and how will rules be enforced? How do you envisage spending time as a family? What are your plans and priorities around activities, childcare, discipline, and so on? Talk this stuff out!

The last thing I'll say on parenting is that there are a lot of stereo-types and jokes about "Jewish mothers." As someone who both has (hi, Mom!) and is a Jewish mother, I want to say this: if you rely on the mama to do too much, then you are encouraging her martyr complex and also possibly being a jerk. (See "E" for "Emotional Load.") Having said that, most of us mamas need to learn how to chill. I include myself in that. We come by our neurosis honestly: Jews and moms are noto-riously (stereotypically) the most neurotic people there are.[6] But, still, let's rededicate ourselves to our yoga and meditation practices (like the temple was rededicated after Chanukah) and learn to let go a little. And for everyone who's not a Jewish mother: stop telling those jokes and call your mom right now.

Parents

A lot of this book is inspired by a response to parents who don't under-stand or support the intercultural relationships of their kids. To quote DJ Jazzy Jeff & the Fresh Prince, sometimes "parents just don't under-stand." It isn't great when parents make us feel yucky about our choices, particularly our choice in a partner. The love we have for our parents and the love we have for our partners becomes a mishmash of weird feelings. Parents feel replaced. Partners feel excluded. The kids who are adults feel caught in the middle. There's lots of love and also lots of other feelings like fear, resentment, anger, sadness, shame, and guilt.

Being a parent is wild. You love your kids more than you love air and yet they drive you batsh*t. You spend years feeling overburdened and stretched and then your kids don't need you anymore and so you feel abandoned. I'm still in the overburdened and stretched years but I already see it coming: the distance between "I just want to shower without someone needing something from me" and "Why don't you want to spend time with me anymore?" is about two minutes.

I have some sympathy for parents for whom intermarriage rep-resents significant change for them in the cultural life of their family and in some deeply held values. Change is hard for folks, it really is. I get it. And, at the very same time, I don't get it.

Your kid is in love, is independent enough to make their own choices, and is choosing to include you in their lives. Celebrate! Your kid made a choice you wouldn't have made and that's hard for you? It's their job to decide who they are and what they believe. If they are able to do that, you did a good job parenting. I am not being glib when I say "I don't get it." I mean, truly, when people create family rifts and hurt their own children by excluding or judging or being mean to them, I really don't understand it. This is your kid! As I said, I love my kids more than I love air. I would gladly lay down my life for them if needed. There is absolutely nothing they could do to make me stop loving them. I wouldn't love their actions but I'd always love them. Some very Orthodox Jews will sit *shiva*, the Jewish mourning ritual, for children who intermarry. They act like their kids are dead. This is something I will never understand. I hope to always be in my kids' lives and, for that to happen, I have to respect that they are going to turn out different than any ideal I have in my head about them. I will do my best to instill good values, a sense of rootedness and identity, a love of some of the things I love. I'm a left-leaning, feminist Jew in Canada. They might turn out to be politically conservative, born-again Christians living in Texas. I will always want to be in their lives and will have to accept their choices. Most of the time, kids share similar values as their parents. Chances are, the life partner someone chooses shares many of the same values and characteristics, regardless of religion/culture, as the parents who are unsure about them.

My family learned this when my now-husband entered our lives. They were never the kind of parents who insisted I marry Jewish, but I knew they'd prefer it. But Charlie is a kind, loving, generous, and funny person. They were charmed by him fairly early and grew to love him. He is very lovable! They were surprised that despite any "differences" in background and culture, he shares a lot of their values: he's family oriented, interested in politics, a believer in education, loves books and travel, and so on. We as humans tend to fear difference but, actually, when you get to know someone, you're likely to find you share a lot in common despite any differences. My parents also enjoy the benefit of having me at all Jewish-related holidays and dinners. My brother is often at his Jewish in-laws for Shabbat and holidays. If you're Jewish parents, remember that a real benefit of intermarriage is always knowing your kid will be at your Passover table. One thing my parents didn't anticipate about their kid (me) intermarrying is that they'd always get me on Jewish holidays. It's nice that we never have to decide whose house we're going to for Christmas or Chanukah (or any other holiday).

Everyone gets to do their own childhood traditions with their own family of origin. It's a real plus. That is, of course, unless you sit *shiva* for them or otherwise treat them badly. Then they won't want to come. Obviously.

Partnership

When I describe a significant other, I like to use the term "partner" instead of "spouse" or "husband/wife" because it evokes both a state of being and an ideal. You are not just someone's "significant other," as "other" implies that they are outside you. You are someone's "partner," as in, their happiness affects your own and vice versa. This is important to remember in an intermarriage. There are no winners and losers in a debate over how to lead a homelife that is culturally rich and/or spiritually significant. If you have an unhappy partner, I guarantee that your own happiness will be affected. That is, unless you're a jerk and don't care. Don't be a jerk. Be a *mentsch* (see "M").

Passion

I hope you are passionate about your partner. Use that passion! Learn about them, help them create the homelife they want, defend them to suspicious outsiders. Be passionate about being part of an intermarriage!

Paternalism (aka Mansplaining, Jewsplaining, and Beyond)

Have you ever had someone explain something to you that you already knew very well? That's a particular brand of paternalism. It happens to me when people assume I don't know much about Judaism because I'm intermarried or I'm a woman or who even knows why. Paternalism can also be a weird protection thing where someone is trying to make you feel like you are a precious little baby in need of coddling. This is an intermarriage thing because sometimes the dynamics of intermarriage include a certain type of paternalism. I've seen the partners of Jews be talked down to. I've seen Jews be told that they will get harmed joining families that can never fully accept or understand them. There are all kinds of weird religious chauvinisms that go on, with people thinking their backgrounds are superior to the backgrounds of others. This can manifest as paternalism.

Patrilineal Descent

This part is going to be controversial, but I believe what I'm about to say deep in my bones, so here goes: the rules around matrilineal descent defining who is a Jew are ridiculous and outdated and if I could wave a magic wand and change one thing in Jewish life, it would be this.

For those who don't know, Jewish law says that there are two ways and only two ways one can be a Jew: to be born to a Jewish mother or to convert. That's it. The people most likely to bring this up about how Jewish dads don't make Jewish kids are people who routinely flout approximately 597 of the 613 Jewish commandments but, for some reason, think the rules around matrilineal descent are the most holy and important thing ever to come out of rabbinic thought. I call it BS. These people are being gatekeepers of something they neither particularly value nor understand. I've heard kids who don't practice or live Jewishly in any meaningful way say to other kids that they're not "really Jewish" because it's their dad who brings home the bagels. For some, they might think they practice Jewish values and tradition and hold them dear, and it's from that belief that the gatekeeping instinct comes. I still call it BS and here's why: some of the most sacred and important Jewish teachings are that we not shame others, that we treat others as we'd want to be treated, that we care for and love the stranger. If you value your Judaism so much, then you'll stop using it to make others feel bad. Also, if you do believe that matrilineal descent is the end all and be all of who is a Jew, then fine, but you'd better be fully inclusive and kind to my pals with Jewish moms who are fully secular, have no interest in Hebrew, march in slut walks, dance to reggae, and drink to excess. If it's only about having a Jewish mother, then stop bringing other non-rules into your definition.

Nothing drives me nuts like Jewish gatekeeping. We're so very worried about who's in and who's out that we forget to ask whether what we're doing is actually meaningful, joyous, and beautiful.

Consider some of the ramifications of rules around matrilineal descent. Children with an active and engaged Jewish father and a mother who isn't Jewish will often be told:

- You're not really Jewish (again, often these folks do way more Jewish stuff than their accusers).
- Your parent can't stand with you on the *bimah* (religious alter) at your B Mitzvah or stand under the *chuppah* (canopy) at your wedding.
- You should convert if you want to be taken seriously as a Jew (this is someone who has called themselves Jewish their whole lives).

How hurtful. How absurd. There are folks who have a Jewish mother but don't feel Jewish, don't do anything particularly Jewish, and might even resent any implication that they are Jewish. You really think they're "more Jewish" than someone with a Jewish dad and a mom who never converted but got involved in synagogue life, makes Passover every year, and plays mahjong with the Kibbitz Klub every Thursday? What about kids of two dads who are both Jewish? Should they have to convert when they've been identified and raised Jewish from birth?

Different movements and branches of Judaism have different rules around patrilineal descent and Jewish definition. Whether or not you have one or two Jewish parents, I encourage all Jews to push for these rules to be relaxed. They encourage a lot of blaming and shaming and cause a lot of harm. Why? For the sake of Jewish law? Okay, but then, again, you'd better be following those 612 other commandments to the letter or you're a hypocrite.

Poetry

I am a fan of good poetry. Nothing else in language can be so incisive and precise while also being emotionally evocative. I have read a lot of poets who have inspired me, but perhaps my favorite is Marge Piercy. You might know her work. She is a celebrated poet who has been active in Jewish life. Her poems are read throughout the year, such as those from *The Art of Blessing the Day*, which contains compositions on Jewish themes and holidays, pieces about the Holocaust, and daily prayers, blessings, and meditations. I use her poems in my services quite regularly, as do many other rabbis and Jewish communities. What they often don't mention is that Marge Piercy's mother was Jewish and her father was not. She is a celebrated Jewish writer who constructs deeply moving poems on Jewish themes. She is the product of an intercultural relationship. Deep Jewish wisdom and beauty can come from an intermarriage. We have other examples in poetry too.

Shaul Tchernichovsky was an important Zionist writer and poet. You might be familiar with the words from one of his poems, "Creed." Debbie Friedman used this in her song "Laugh at All My Dreams." Here is Tchernichovsky's original verse:

Laugh, laugh at all my dreams!
What I dream shall yet come true!
Laugh at my belief in man,
At my belief in you.

Freedom still my soul demands,
Unbartered for a calf of gold.
For still I do believe in man,
And his spirit, strong and bold.

And in the future I still believe,
Though it be distant, come it will.
When nations shall each other bless,
And peace at last the earth shall fill.

So important was this Zionist poet that his image was put on Israel's 50-shekel bill in 2014. But Tchernichovsky was married to a Christian woman and so, despite his moving Zionist poetry and contributions to the Jewish state, a Sephardic Haredi rabbi ordered that religious people not look at his image on the bill.

I ask you, who is a greater threat to Jewish continuity, the poet who intermarries or the rabbi who condemns him? I'd argue it's the latter. Tchernichovsky is a Jewish hero. He was intermarried and he remained committed to his people and to the ideals of a Jewish state. Being intermarried did not make him a traitor to his people. The religious leaders who create division and harm amongst Jews are far more destructive.

What do the cases of Marge Piercy and Shaul Tchernichovsky show? Parentage aside, our choice in partner aside, we are who we choose to be. When we live out our identities in a way that is consistent with our values and ideals, it's poetry.

Possibility

Although you'll sometimes find paternalism and pandering, many families are really successful at avoiding these pitfalls and truly expanding and growing as a result of an intermarriage in the family. Intermarriage presents many wonderful possibilities for folks. See "O" for "Opportunity."

Principles

However you are raising your kids, you are teaching and modeling certain principles. I think of them as beliefs. Just as some folks have very dear religious beliefs that deserve to be taken seriously, there are other beliefs and principles that deserve to be taken just as seriously. For me, these beliefs include the need for gender and racial equality, the belief in humanity's capacity for good, the principle of authenticity and being true to oneself, the principle that telling the truth is hard but necessary, the belief that all of us need and deserve human connection and community. Life gets busy, so it's a good time to check in with yourself: Are you living your life according to your beliefs? If you believe in justice, do you spend your time and money in a way that reflects that? If you believe in fairness, are you modeling that fairness in how you speak to your spouse and kids, barista and server? If you believe in gender equality, do you divide household responsibilities in a way that is truly equitable? How we spend our time and money are particularly indicative of our values; they indicate whether and how we are putting our principles into action.

Questioning is a very Jewish practice. There's a joke that the Jewish answer to "How are you?" is "How should I be?" Here, we talk about why questioning can be good and how you can use questions to power your quest for a culturally meaningful life. Queer: The many couples I've worked with who are in LGBTQ partnerships, or are from the LGBTQ community, have often had to negotiate coming out twice. First they tell their family they are gay/bi/trans, whatever the case may be, and then they tell their family they are marrying someone who isn't Jewish (or, if they are the partner who isn't Jewish, they tell their families a Jew is joining the family). Each coming out story, in either the identity or the intermarriage scenario, can be a moment of pain and conflict. Sometimes these stories are not that – families are welcoming and accepting. But I wanted this book to name specifically those people who often have to navigate familial discussions around multiple points of identity, and kudos to those who do this with courage and grace. This section will cover some quagmires and quandaries that intermarrying people might find themselves in and provide some helpful ways to get out. If we take advice on how to escape quicksand, it turns out we can find some important relationship tips. And quotables are included about love and life that intermarrying families can use in weddings, as affirmations, as discussion questions, or as topics to learn about.

Quagmires and Quandaries

Sometimes the quarrels and conflicts in our relationships will take time to resolve. As much as I'm a champion of intermarriage and a believer in the opportunities it presents (see "O"), I also think it's important to be real about how there might be some real points of tension and difficult conversations along the way. Sometimes we have to defend our inter-marriages so much that we don't make space to talk about the problems. There are problems and points of tension in every marriage.

If you're in a quagmire or quandary together, my advice is to take your time figuring it out. Working out the hard stuff is a process. You can make the lists. (See my suggestions for this under "N" for "Negotiation.") Ideally, you can also find a leader or support person to talk it through with. One of the nice things about there being more and more intermarried rabbis[7] is that there are leaders with experience, personal and professional, to bounce ideas off. I spend a lot of time with wedding or baby-naming clients doing this kind of talking. Of course, there are also therapists and other support practitioners to reach out to if you're really stuck (see "T" for "Talk Therapy"). In my experience, all the quagmires and quandaries can be resolved if both people come from a place of respect and love.

Quality

Sometimes it's less about quantity (see below) and more about quality. The reality is that there are a whole lot of Jewish holidays! If you're doing something for many or most of them, the quantity may seem unfair. Sometimes it's more about the quality of the holidays or practices, not how often you do them. Quality means whether you're doing them the way the partner who chose them wants to, whether they are imbued with meaning in your home, and whether each person's identity gets affirmed in a sincere and significant way.

Quantity

Sometimes when people figure out how to blend or share their cultural or religious holidays, traditions, and practices, they divide it up as "equally" as possible. Making sure there are an equal number of visits with both sides of the family, making sure there is lots of hoopla and fanfare around both sets of identities in the home. Folks often like to say "less is more," but sometimes more is more. More celebrations, more rituals, more religious/cultural communities to belong to, more of all of it satisfies everyone's needs.

Quarrelling

Sometimes in marriage, you're going to find that you're not your best self. There's going to be bickering, fighting, and occasional hurt and harm. This isn't what people picture when they decide to get married, but it's a real part of marriage. Of course, it's best to avoid hurt and harm, and abuse is not to be tolerated. The killer of a marriage isn't that someone gets hurt, it's when someone gets hurt and there isn't adequate repair.

It is sad that folks fight over religion and culture. It means that there's a conflict between two really important parts of their identity: their cultural identity and their partnership. That's really difficult.

Try your best to honor all aspects of your partner, including and especially their identity as rooted in tradition, practice, community, or ritual – whatever it is for them. You may not like everything, you may not wish to participate in it, but you do need to respect it.

Quarrels will happen and people will get hurt. How do you work to fix it? Listen, seek to understand, and take seriously that this person has trusted you with their lives; that is, they have made you their most important friend, confidante, and witness to their lives. Approach each other with love. In a marriage, truly, no one ever wins an argument. You can't get a win at your partner's expense; it just doesn't work like that. Do your best to make it so that everybody wins. The happier your partner is, the happier you will be and vice versa.

Queer

Shout out to all of the queer intermarried folks: You have had to "come out" twice in many cases, first in terms of who you are and then in terms of whom you're partnering with. The good news is that the experience of one coming out can often make space for the other. There's nothing in this book that is for heterosexual couples only; all the same tips and experiences apply. However, we live in a heterosexist and homophobic world, and you face that extra layer of quagmire to wade through. The kids of queer intermarried folks get all the same "you're not a real Jew" stuff as the kids of straight couples, and they also get the homophobia that runs rampant at school and camp. I just want to say I see you and we're working on making this much, much better. Again, shout out to you living your lives authentically and beautifully.

Questioning

It is a Jewish tradition to ask questions. To answer questions with questions. To question to the point of irritation. The Talmud is basically a compendium of ridiculous questions posed about other questions (see "T" for "Talmud"). Questioning is good! It causes us to find out both the "what" and the "why" of aspects of culture, religion, or anything to do with life. And an inquisitive nature can lead to interesting learning and knowledge (see "L" and "K"), and also some great questions to discuss with a partner. When I work with couples, I encourage them to always know the "why" of what they are doing. If you want to put lights on your house at Christmas, why? If you want to celebrate Chanukah with latkes, why? Discussing these "whys" will help solidify your belief and negotiate your "must-haves." It will also help your partner come along with you because they'll understand both the practice and its importance to you.

Quicksand

Sometimes being in a marriage feels like sinking. Things spiral downwards fast. You can feel a little like you're losing yourself. People don't like to talk about that stuff but it's true for all the married people I know. Here are some tips for getting out of quicksand (literally) that I think apply nicely to the quicksand of marriage and intermarriage:

- Make yourself as light as possible. With real quicksand that means ditching your coat, bag, and so on. In marriage, it means lighten up: share a joke, take a break, go on a date, share a kiss. These small gestures can make the moment feel less heavy.
- Try to take a few steps backwards. In real quicksand, it's better to go back than forward to get out of it. Sometimes in marriage we need to walk a conversation back when it's going too far into the realm of hurt. Sometimes reverting back to how things were for a while opens up space to chart a new path.
- Reach for a branch or someone's hand. Sometimes we need help to get out of something. This is when to talk to a rabbi or a religious leader or a therapist or a good friend and get perspective.
- Take deep breaths. Enough said.
- Move slowly and deliberately. With quicksand, fast movements exacerbate the sinking. In marriage, sometimes when we're upset we make quick and impromptu decisions or say things without thinking. This rarely helps us out of the quagmire.

Quid Pro Quo

What I don't recommend is a "quid pro quo" approach where you say something like "well, if I get x, you get y." There is no scorecard in marriage, and it's better to give because we want to give rather than because we want to get. Try to be generous with each other. A tit-for-tat marriage is rarely satisfying.

Quirks

There will be things you don't understand about your partner. I promise. Try to embrace their quirks and the quirks of their culture/religion that may be foreign or new to you. Human cultures all have beautiful elements as well as aspects that are bizarre, especially when people see them for the first time. Quirks are what make cultures and individuals interesting. See what you can love about them.

Quotables

There are many quotations about love and life that people choose to insert into their wedding ceremonies as part of their relationship's foundation. Some of them come from religious sources and, if couples are choosing to incorporate them, I always want to ensure the messaging is true to their relationship and values. I've included here a number of common examples.

From 1 Corinthians 4–5: "Love is patient, love is kind. It does not envy, it does not boast, it is not proud. It does not dishonor others, it is not self-seeking, it is not easily angered, it keeps no record of wrong." I fully understand why people choose this one for their weddings; it is a nice intention or goal. However, in my experience, it doesn't always feel genuine. For example, "it keeps no record of wrong." Again, ideally, yes. However, most couples I know in fact do keep some record of wrongs, for better or worse (if you'll pardon the expression!). My husband jokes when he does something wrong that it goes "into the grudge drawer" to be pulled out and wielded at some later time. Please understand, this is not good nor is it a guide for how to be in a relationship. It is, however, very human. I'm also not sure that love "is not self-seeking." I think we ultimately form relationships and need to work at them precisely out of a sense of self-interest. There are simply going to be times when marriage is hard or a relationship is strained. Sometimes what gets us through those times is an awareness that being in partnership is better than being without it. Of course, for some folks, being self-interested means ending a loving relationship. Perhaps the relationship is abusive or the two people can no longer get along or make it work. But staying in relationships is also self-interested, and that's not a bad thing. You can't be married to someone for their sake alone.

A quotable proverb that almost never finds its way into weddings is from the Yiddish: "Man plans, God laughs" (*Der mentsch trakht un Got lakht*). This one is more true to the experience of marriage. Not because a god laughs at us literally, but because for almost everyone, things don't go as planned. Whatever you think your life will be when you marry, it will surely turn out differently. For example, someone gets ill, your job situations fluctuate, having kids is harder than you expected. There are often reasons why things go off-plan. Marriages get tested in these moments. Is the bond strong enough to withstand those tests? Can you roll with the punches together? We can never anticipate exactly what the challenges will be, but we can certainly anticipate challenges.

A common selection from the Bible (common to both Jewish and Christian canons) is a verse from the Song of Songs. The Song of Songs (also known as *Shir Hashirim* in the Jewish community and as Song of Solomon in the Christian community) is a fascinating text. For Jews, it often gets explained as a love letter from God to Israel, and for Christians as a love letter from Christ to the people. What it really is, though, is a piece of erotic love poetry that made its way into the biblical canon. The writing of the poem is attributed to King Solomon. The history around it is fuzzy but most biblical scholars agree that this was essentially a secular of text that was so beautiful it got included in the biblical canons.

I love the Song of Songs but, again, it's good to consider whether the words resonate. Here are some examples of what people include: "Arise my darling, my perfect one, come away with me" (2:10), or "How sweet is your love, how much more delightful than wine!" (4:10). Or the classic, "I am my beloved's and my beloved is mine" (*Ani l'dodi v'dodi li*) (2:16). While I do hope you find your partner's kisses to be sweeter than wine (although I really like wine) and that the other is perfect, if we are being strictly literal these may not apply. Metaphor has its place for sure and I have no objection to folks using these beautiful bits of poetry if they are meaningful. What I don't love is a nod to tradition that is not rooted in the actual sensibilities of the couple. On my *ketubah* (Jewish wedding contract), it says "*Ani l'dodi v'dodi li*; I am my beloved's and my beloved is mine." I like it for the beauty and the inclusion of tradition. I did pause for a moment over using it; I don't actually agree with the idea that I *am* my beloved's or that he *is* mine. Marriage isn't possession, and it can be dangerous if it's assumed to be. However, it was close enough to a sentiment I share that I chose to include it. My goal is that people choose sayings that truly reflect their beliefs and values.

A great quotable for marriage, which I've never seen included in a wedding ceremony, is from the Sage Hillel. When asked how to summarize the whole Torah, he said: "If I am not for myself, who will be? But if I am only for myself, what am I? And if not now, when?" This becomes the Jewish "golden rule" and applies beautifully to marriage. In marriage one has to care about their own needs, the needs of their partner, and be continually doing the work to make sure both partners' needs are met. Sometimes the less romantic quotable is actually more apt for marriage.

There is a false dichotomy in philosophy between reason and emotion. I like to think that I'm a reasonable person, and I see myself as leading with the heart. Reason is there to help us when we need to work through a problem. Love is there to make sure we stay connected and on track. Respect is the basis for all relationships. It should be the minimum requirement. Part of respecting your partner is respecting their cultural and ancestral origins. This section talks about relatives (family) and relativity (as in, everything is relative). I get into the idea of rules. Rules aren't all bad, as they keep things consistent, instill discipline, foster accountability. Having said that, religion is too rife with rules that can sometimes obscure meaning. I consider Judaism and other cultural affiliations to offer tools, rather than rules, for living a meaningful life. Renewal is a really complex and compelling Jewish idea. Read on to find out more ...

Reaching Out

In my experience, when folks have difficult relationships in families, sometimes time is all you need. Eventually, people mellow. Eventually, they want to meet their grandkids (if applicable). Eventually, the fuel of the fire of their anger or fear dies down and a new space for love and respect appears.

My advice to families who have been harsh with their kids or in-laws for any reason – for our purposes, because of intermarriage – is to reach out. It's amazing how we as humans will go so far out of our way to avoid apologizing or taking responsibility for our damaging actions. Sometimes reaching out and genuinely seeking to understand the family members with whom you are in conflict can lead to a beautiful reconnection and even reconciliation.

Realism

We need to have a positive outlook and also remain realistic. It's possible the relatives (see below) will never come around. Our job is to create the marriage, family, and homelife we want, within circumstances as they are, not as we'd wish for them to be. Sometimes this is easier said than done. But you can only control what you can control. We can be hopeful that difficult dynamics will change, but we need to live with those dynamics and make our lives as joyful as possible. We also need to be realistic about who our partner is, what their values and needs are, and what committing to marriage with them really means. Hint: Whatever drives you bananas about your partner now will make you even more bananas ten years from now. Count on it. Lots of couples idealize marriage. Marriage is beautiful and wonderful and also plenty of hard work. Realism helps make it manageable and may help you avoid being disappointed when things aren't perfect. Try to be grateful for what is good.

Reason(ableness)

In the Humanistic Jewish movement in which I was ordained, we really pride ourselves on using reason. Got a problem? Reason it out. Reason can be the basis of your system of belief. For a long time, reason was considered the opposite of faith. But plenty of people are finding ways to incorporate understandings of science, rationality, and philosophy with their faith (the classic Jewish example is Maimonides, who brought Aristotelian ideas together with Jewish faith and practice).

Reason can also be a communication technique: Speak reasonably and rationally to your partner, as opposed to letting emotion cloud your judgment and words. I don't recommend telling your partner they are being irrational (even when they are). Rather, ask questions, seek to understand, explain your perspective as rationally as possible.

I do believe in reason but I also believe that sometimes it is reasonable to be unreasonable. Sometimes we lead with our emotion or our heart. Sometimes we are overwhelmed and, in the face of illness, crisis, grief, or conflict, we can get a little unreasonable. I want all of us to see and love that part of ourselves. Then, as gently as possible, get back to reason as soon as we can. There's a big myth out there that reason and emotion don't mix. Untrue! The most rational thing in the world is to feel our feelings, and when we do, we are more likely to make sense of them and return to rational next steps.

Reconnection

If you have reconnected with someone after a lengthy or intense conflict, I suggest putting an action plan in place. Of course, be kind and respectful. Also, however, try your best to engage in meaningful action for active repair. As you reconnect, really get to know your in-laws (whether that's your kid and their partner or whether that's your partner's parents). Do your best to meet them where they're at in terms of experience and comfort. You don't have to sacrifice your own well-being to make things comfortable for others, but it's nice to give people the benefit of the doubt. Share the gifts of culture – holidays, food, celebrations, traditions, values, teachings, stories, music, art. Be prepared to learn and to give. Reconnection is possible and sometimes people and relationships are much stronger for having been through the process of conflict and repair.

Relatives

They say everything is relative, but you know what sometimes doesn't seem relative? Your relatives. Some folks really struggle with not being accepted by their partner's family. I've seen this happen with many of my clients. They try to connect, but the difference in religion or culture is too much. Or it is some other issue or point of tension that creates problems. It is so hard for folks when they don't feel included or welcome or have a sense of belonging in their own family. This is some of the worst damage caused by people who oppose intermarriage: their own kids often feel they no longer have a place in the family, the one place they should always feel a sense of home and belonging. It is also very hard, of course, for the partner who is unwelcome with in-laws. I speak about these dynamics throughout this book (for example, see "G" for "Grandchildren" and "M" for "*Mentsch*").

Relativity

Science does teach us that everything is relative. You've heard of my buddy Einstein? Note, he was deeply committed to his Jewish identity and also pretty secular and into science (but I digress). He came up with the theory of relativity, which I thought I had some understanding of until I started writing this section and now, an afternoon later, I still don't really understand. The point is, there is some connection between humans and space and time. And, because of all this, we like to say "Everything is relative!" What do we mean when we say that? I think very often the point is something like "stop worrying, there are bigger problems in the world." Again, I think it's important, especially in the context of a committed relationship, to feel our feelings. We shouldn't downplay them or ask our partner to do so.

Still, I like the idea from the theory of relativity that our space and time conflate and connect (I can't wait for the letters I'm going to get telling me how I fundamentally misunderstand this theory!). Metaphor, people! I like the idea that, in marriage, as we choose to somehow cosmically align our lives with our beloved, we create a sense of our own space (our home), our own time (the rhythms of our lives).

Indeed, everything is relative. If you are struggling or stressed out, try to have a sense of perspective. The other thing the theory of relativity tells us is that we are very tiny and insignificant compared to the vastness of space and time. Yes, feel your feelings; they're real and important. And remember that our little dance on this earth is, always, sort of miraculous and unlikely. We are lucky to be alive and to be in a position to have the consciousness to wonder about stuff like intermarriage.

Renewal

Renewal is an interesting concept in contemporary Jewish life. The idea of renewal is a part of the Jewish New Year, Rosh Hashanah. At this time of year, we talk about "*cheshbon hanefesh*," which means something like an accounting of the soul; taking stock of who we are and who we want to be. There is always the chance for growth and betterment.

I often speak of every Shabbat as an opportunity for renewal; each week we get to consider how we did and how we can do better, what we want and how to get it, who we are and who we wish to be in the week ahead. We also are reminded that the work isn't linear; we don't continue to get better without snags and setbacks. We can't keep growing unless we take time to rest.

Christianity and other religions also offer beautiful teachings on the opportunity for renewal. Whether through confession, pilgrimage, prayer, discipline, good deeds and acts of kindness, one of the things religion and culture can do well is to give us ways to be intentional about how we renew ourselves.

Intermarriage offers renewal for both partners, as it challenges us to plan out our life by paying attention to what we value and why, how we want to practice and live our cultural identities, and how we do all this in a loving relationship. Rather than being a barrier to renewing one's sense of identity, it can be a real motivator to this kind of spiritual or cultural renewal.

Resilience

What I see as a by-product of a lot of hurt and pain that folks have experienced in an anti-intermarriage environment is an amazing amount of resilience. Countless couples I've married note that they grow much closer and their bond becomes much stronger because of the resistance of others. Truly, the best revenge is living well!

I notice this trend in other ways: Many women, racialized folks, and other minorities have accomplished amazing things by working hard to break down barriers and then go beyond. Jews, as a marginalized group, have achieved great success as a community. There are other examples. Of course, this doesn't make racism, sexism, antisemitism okay. But it means that people can be remarkably resilient. It's good to hold on to that when things are tough.

Respect

Respect – this is a pretty basic one but it needs to be in here. Respect your partner. Respect the whole family. Respect people's beliefs and choices. Demand they respect you in return. We all do better in an environment fueled by and imbued with respect.

Rules

I am sort of equal parts rule follower and rebel. Sometimes I try to uphold rules because I generally like a sense of order and, let's face it, I am a teacher and a parent so rules work for me. However, I also really balk at rules that make no sense or don't have value. So it's these two sides of the same coin of "rules" or, if you like, commandments that fuel my thinking and work on the issue of religion and culture. Sometimes following religious rules can add a nice sense of structure, discipline, and meaning to one's life. If you are in the habit of giving *tzedakah* (charity) on Shabbat, that's a nice rule to follow that adds depth to your life and goodness to the world. If you like following dietary restrictions (religious or otherwise) because they help you live out your values, great. I think that also makes life more meaningful. What I don't love is following rules for the sake of it, particularly if those rules are actually harmful. For example, Judaism and other traditions ban same-sex partnerships. Following that rule, and expecting others to follow that rule, makes life a good measure worse for many good people. It's a bad rule. For more on rules, see "K" for "*Keva/Kavannah.*"

My hope is that intermarriage provides the container and landscape in which people create their own rules. You are almost certainly doing things a little differently than how you grew up. So now you get to make up the rules. This is a great situation for someone who wants the rules but wants them to be meaningful too.

If you are Jewish or marrying a Jew, you may wish to join a synagogue. Will you be welcomed? Will the rabbi officiate your wedding? Will non-Jewish partners be able to participate fully? This section will provide practical things to consider and questions to ask when looking to join a community. *Shavuot* is a Jewish holiday when we read the Book of Ruth, which includes the famous line "Your people shall be my people and your God shall be my God." We'll look at the story and what it says about changing cultures, for better or worse. Shopping: Intermarriage may mean you need more stuff. What stuff? I'll tell you. And I'll also tell you about what happened when *Skymall*, the in-flight shopping magazine, published an ad for a Star of David Christmas tree topper. This section considers sex and sweetness and softness all together. There are many kinds of sexual relationships and it's not my place to judge them. However, in the context of committed partnerships, I hope there's a sweetness to the sexual experiences and connections you share. And silliness. One of my favorite things to hear when I interview wedding couples to create their ceremony is when they describe their partner or relationship as 'silly.' Recently, one client told me they love their partner because "she knows when to be serious and when to be silly." That balance really is the stuff a strong marriage is made of.

Sensitivity

I like the double meaning of sensitivity. Have you ever met anyone who is so sensitive that they become insensitive to others? The person who is so fragile that others have to go to great lengths to accommodate them? Here are my tips: Be sensitive to the needs of your partner in a meaningful way. Try to avoid being so sensitive about your own needs that you stifle theirs. That's it. Be sensitive, but not insensitive.

Serendipity/Synchronicity

Two of my favorite things as a wedding officiant are serendipity and synchronicity. I love when a couple finds that one member's cultural practice of handfasting (Celtic) can work with a Jewish tartan. I love when we discover that the Jewish *chuppah* is similar to the Hindu *mandap*. I love when Easter and Passover coincide and people use Easter eggs as the egg on the Seder plate. As I write this, it is the start of a new Jewish month, *Adar*. This is supposed to be the happiest month of the year! It's the month of the silly and playful holiday Purim. It is also a month that in a Jewish leap year, we get twice over. *Adar* ends and then starts right back up again. This is because the Jewish calendar follows the lunar cycle and things could get so far off course that eventually Passover would be in winter and Chanukah would be in the fall. Right now also happens to be Fat Tuesday/Mardi Gras. I like the idea that people everywhere are having pancake dinners, which are joyful and fun. Mardi Gras/*Adar* work together nicely in terms of both Christian and Jewish cultural practices. A few years ago, American Thanksgiving and Chanukah coincided. Christmas and Chanukah sometimes do as well, as do Easter and Passover. Look for the serendipitous moments of synchronicity for you.

Sex/Sweetness/Softness

Sex isn't an issue specific to intercultural couples; rather, it's usually a feature of any couple or committed romantic relationship. There are all different kinds of sex and I want people to have fulfilling sex lives, whatever that looks like for them. I hope that when you are in a committed relationship, sex, sweetness, and softness are all bound up together. This section is just a reminder that for many people, the intermarriage isn't the principal feature of the relationship. Sex, sweetness, and softness, being your partner's soft place to land, is much more important to most of us, at least most of the time. Partnership is a powerful force in our lives. Don't let any issues relating to intermarriage cloud over the good stuff that you share in the relationship.

As a particular example of sweetness, one of my community members in SecularSynagogue.com posted photos of her family's Chrismukkah prep with such gusto. They went big! They had all the stuff you can imagine ... menorahments, the Elf on the Shelf, the Mensch on a Bench, the lights, the Star of David tree topper, silver stars, tinsel, the whole shebang. It was so important that their house look like an explosion of holiday magic and glee. She was so happy and it was so tender. I found the whole thing very, very sweet. There is such sweetness in bringing traditions and customs together, and creating a home full of joy. Don't forget to create such sweetness in your home. It amounts to a lot.

Sharing

If you have kids, my guess is that you know the phrase "sharing is caring." It really is! Sharing in your partner's cultural stories, songs, practices, and rituals really is a way of caring for them. I can tell you that my partner knows a lot more about Jewish history, texts, holidays, culture, and practice than he ever would have if he hadn't married a Jew. I find it extraordinarily sweet when he sings Shabbat songs with my kids. He will tell you that, although he isn't Jewish, being in proximity to Judaism has added to his life. He loves how my community does Yom Kippur, telling stories of real-life heroes who have transformed the world. He finds Shabbat meaningful. He enjoys spinning *dreidels* and dancing around with our kids. Judaism, like all cultures, is there to bring meaning and joy to life and, I believe, that extends to the people who aren't Jewish and are part of our families and communities. The same goes for the Jewish folks learning about and experiencing the religion or culture of their partners. When we share, we grow. When it comes to sharing, there's no give or get. It's all win-win. It's fun to share your own experiences, and it's fun to learn about others' experiences.

Shavuot

Shavuot is the Jewish holiday when we read the Book of Ruth, which includes the famous line "Your people shall be my people and your God shall be my God." Ruth is speaking these words to her mother-in-law,

Naomi. Naomi is an Israelite; Ruth is not. Sadly, Ruth's husband (Naomi's son) dies and Naomi tells Ruth to go back to her people, for she can't take care of her. But Ruth loves Naomi and tells her, nah, I'm sticking with you ("Whither thou goest, I will go"). For anyone struggling with weird dynamics with in-laws, consider this: Ruth and Naomi stick together. This moment of text is Ruth's conversion, essentially. She is not required to undergo a year of study and sign a pledge that she'll raise exclusively Jewish children. She simply decides she wants to be part of Naomi's people and then, well, she is. This is my community's approach to conversion into the Jewish people. We require nothing except your identification with the history, culture, values, and fate of the Jewish people. And we don't require you to declare yourself a Jew in order for us to welcome you; it's truly a choice.

I love the beautiful identification between Naomi and Ruth in this story; and I love that Ruth declares herself loyal to the people as well as to Naomi herself. The rest of the Book of Ruth is worth reading; there is a ruse and sex and all kinds of things relating to bizarre Jewish law (google "Levirate marriage") and what folks do to survive.

Shavuot is a holiday for which the significance has shifted over time. It was once an agricultural holiday. Later on, rabbis imbued the holiday with a new significance: we learn that Moses gave the Torah at Mount Sinai on Shavuot and so Shavuot became a holiday devoted to Torah study. There's a tradition called Tikkun Leil Shavuot in which folks study all night long. In Toronto, where I live, the Jewish Community Centre puts on an amazing program of all-night learning that includes every subject under the sun, from Jewish farming, to meditation, to text study, to Hebrew practice. It's for anyone and everyone and gets hundreds of people out for all-night learning and cheesecake ... it's traditional to eat dairy on Shavuot. Bonus.

I love the story Lex Rofeberg, co-host of the popular podcast "Judaism Unbound," tells about one Shavuot. Taking up the challenge of Torah learning, he and his partner, Valerie, who isn't Jewish, began to explore the YouTube channel BimBam. BimBam has a short animation for each weekly Torah portion. Lex and Valerie began to binge watch this particular Shavuot and made it through each and every video – essentially taking in the whole Torah in one night. Lex was moved by Valerie's commitment to watching and the fact that they both found it meaningful and fun. For Lex, his love for Valerie was and is enhanced by Judaism, and his Judaism was and is enhanced by sharing it with Valerie. Of course, she was getting something out of sharing in Lex's culture too. The whole experience flew in the face of all Lex had heard growing up about intermarriage. Lex proposed that very night – Shavuot. The resonance is perfect, as the central text of that holiday is about conversion/coming into a culture for love. Just as Ruth commits to Naomi in the story we read on Shavuot, Lex and Valerie committed to each other.

Shopping – Stuff

Intermarriage may mean you need more stuff. For some folks, this is fun! If you're like me and would rather eat your own arm than go to the mall, getting stuff is stressful. Look, strictly speaking you don't need much. But here are some items you may wish to consider having in your home:

- Holiday stuff – Christmas and Chanukah/Chrismukkah: You might want lights. Some do green/red some do blue/white, some do a mix. These work for Diwali too! People include many items for decoration, including *dreidels* and Christmas ornaments, sometimes made a little more Jewish with a Star of David or *menorah* (people call them "menorahments"). Many people have a *menorah* in their window or on their table. There's also the Mensch on a Bench and the Elf on the Shelf; some parents place these on a shelf or the mantelpiece and tell their kids the Mensch and the Elf are watching them. (Note: There are no built-in cameras.) See my "December Delights: Creating and Crushing Chrismukkah" guide in the appendix for more.

  You can also get Star of David tree toppers, which I think are a particular stroke of genius. These toppers are fairly mainstream now. You can buy them from small artisans via Etsy, an online selling site for artists. I've seen them at Bed Bath & Beyond stores and at Home Depot. And, get this, it was number-one-selling tree topper on Amazon in 2011! The person who created it, Morri Chowaiki, cited that his incentive was the 47 per cent intermarriage rate in America. He had a marketing background and realized there was an underserved market. He was right! You are that market and have a lot of buying power as a result! You may know the story of when Skymall, the airline in-flight shopping magazine, featured the Star of David tree topper in its catalogue. Some more traditional Jews on those flights were enraged! Some tried to organize a boycott of Skymall itself. I found the whole thing so telling because there are few places where people are forced to get in close proximity with people who are different from themselves, but airplanes are certainly one such place. They symbolize contemporary cosmopolitanism, making it possible to cross boundaries, borders, and oceans. More traditional Jews in enclosed communities sometimes have little access to life outside their world. Enter Skymall, forcing folks to confront things out of their orbit and comfort zone. The symbolism is sort of delicious.

- Other holiday stuff: Shabbat candles, *kiddush* cup, and Seder plate are the usual ones. You can get a Havdallah set if you want to go big.
- Ritual stuff as needed: In my house we don't wear skull caps (*kippot* or *yarmulkes*), but get some if it's something you want people to wear at Shabbat or Passover.
- Books: It's useful to have a few books explaining holidays or practices. Sometimes people get Passover *Haggadot* (the service booklets) for Seders. You might want children's books. Check out PJ Library (pjlibrary.org). It sends free Jewish-themed children's books and adult resources to families in the US and Canada each month. Reading can be a great way to learn about your culture or that of your partner and share in the learning together. (See "L" for "Learning.")
- Whatever else you may need for the holidays in your house from any cultural or religious background.

Of course, the cultural life of your home should not be heavily dependent on stuff. I am a minimalist by nature and keep very little around. My Shabbat drawer, with a *challah* plate, *kiddush* cups, and candlesticks, does get a lot of use, but, honestly, that and a *menorah* would do for "stuff" in our house (oh, and a billion books). I'm not saying you have to go out and spend your life savings on gear. I'm saying that finding stuff that serves you can be a great way to solidify your cultural practices and commitments as a family.

Shopping – Synagogues

If you are Jewish or marrying a Jew, you may wish to join a synagogue or community space. There are many creative and wonderful communities that are cropping up in places big and small. Sometimes what you want is a legacy synagogue with a traditional feel. Sometimes it's a small group (often called a *havura*). Sometimes it's a place that meets in pop-up locations and does creative services and programming. Sometimes it's an online space. When I started SecularSynagogue.com, a digital community for those wanting a cultural Jewish experience and community, I was intentional about the use of the word "synagogue."

Being online, secular, and non-traditional in a whole host of ways isn't what people think of as a "synagogue." And that's exactly the point: what we consider synagogues to be is changing.

This is partly for reasons that are a little bit sad or challenging for some. Like religious institutions everywhere, many synagogues are having a problem of too few in the pew. There aren't enough people coming or supporting the synagogue financially to keep the lights on. For people for whom the synagogue was the center of their spiritual and cultural life, this is very hard to understand and to accept. I have a lot of sympathy for those people.

Having said that, a lot of what has driven people out of synagogue life is a damaging and exclusionary attitude to people who intermarry. It is absolutely no wonder that people wouldn't come to or support places where they, their spouse, or their child is made to feel unwelcome. It is counter to the whole ethos of what a synagogue should be, having gatekeepers who are fiercely unwelcoming of people, even while their institutions are dying.

The "unwelcome" feeling is different in different places. Personally, I wouldn't go anywhere that had any sort of barrier or rule around the participation of my partner. He may not choose to participate in all of the potential activities and roles, including service leading, board participation, and ritual roles, but the choice should be his. Some people are fine with having a non-Jewish family member be able to do most things, with a few off-limit items. For example, perhaps all members of the family can come up to the *bimah* (alter) for services or for life-cycle events (their own child's baby naming or B Mitzvah, for example), but not do a Torah reading. Plenty of people who aren't Jewish prefer not to do a Torah reading anyway, so if this works for you and for the synagogue and its community, great. It's up to each person and family to determine which barriers they can live with, and which are dealbreakers.

It's especially important to be aware of the rules and ask a lot of questions. Many communities, becoming aware that they *need* intermarried folks and their kids if they are to survive, will now claim to be "welcoming" of intermarried people. Some are, some are not. Sometimes the community is welcoming but the clergy is not, or sometimes it's the opposite.

Here are some things to consider when "*shul* shopping," as they say:

- Will you be welcomed with genuine warmth?
- Is intermarriage handled with a "don't ask, don't tell" kind of policy or are you allowed to be fully authentic and open about who you are?

- Will the rabbi officiate your wedding? I find it very obnoxious when a community is "welcoming" but a couple and the family can't be served by the rabbi. Sometimes this isn't the fault of the rabbi or clergy; their own associations and movements have rules. But it still doesn't mean you have to subject yourself to the exclusion.
- Will the rabbi officiate your child's baby naming or B Mitzvah? (Especially check this if it's a father who is the Jewish parent; see "P" for "Patrilineal Descent.")
- Does the community and clergy require that you are a "Jewish-only" house and, if so, does that work for you?
- Will non-Jewish partners be able to participate fully? How about as ritual leaders? How about as committee or board members?
- Will clergy, educators, leaders apologize to you if someone says something that isn't okay? Will it be communicated to the whole community that intermarried families are valued and that the traditional narrative against intermarriage is unwelcome in community spaces?
- Is being intermarried seen as a lesser choice in the community?
- Are you the minority as an intermarried family, or are most folks like you?
- What happens if your kid draws a Christmas tree as part of the Chanukah card-making? Because that happens. A lot.

Every person and family deserves a community that works for them! It's worth it to do some shopping and find one that meets your needs and wants you to be part of them not because they need your membership dollars but because they know you will enhance the life of the community, and the community can enhance your life in return.

Silliness

Sometimes what a relationship needs is a little bit of silliness. Sometimes when I'm sitting down with a big work project, or haven't left the house for a while because of winter storms, or for some reason or the other I'm experiencing that feeling of being stuck, I dance around. I recommend YouTube's "Fitness Marshall" for silly dance routines to popular music (this isn't a Jewish tip specifically). Being a little silly is a really good cure for being stuck. Apply this to your relationship. One of the best things about my partner (don't tell him I'm saying this, okay? We don't want it going to his head or anything) is his ability to be silly in the face of tension. He's the kind of person to bring out water guns to settle a dispute. Sometimes I'll bring up something he did that was, you know, less than ideal, and he'll respond by doing something like initiating a pillow fight. He reminds me to laugh; usually things aren't so serious after all. And we are always better able to solve a problem if we are smiling.

Stifled

Sometimes in an intermarriage one partner ends up feeling stifled. I want to mention that this can happen because it is a dynamic I have seen many times. It's when your partner feels unable to express something they want. And, fellow Jews, this is often on us. For example, I have felt so strongly about protecting my Jewish identity that my partner has sometimes felt unable to express his own cultural needs. He knew I'd be unhappy about putting Christmas lights on our house so he didn't bring it up for a while, even when it was something he really wanted. *Mea culpa*. I'm not saying we *have to* put lights on our house, but we do have to have the kind of relationship where we can both express what it is we feel or what it is we want.

Struggling

I don't want to pretend that the sharing and blending and negotiating go smoothly all the time. Sometimes there are struggles. Sometimes, someone feels outside their comfort zone. Sometimes the way the traditions and practices play out isn't exactly as someone would have liked. Sometimes, we feel genuine loss (see "L"). Sometimes life is a struggle. You're not abnormal and, importantly, your relationship is not a mistake or a failure if you're struggling from time to time. Everyone is struggling from time to time. This is a fact of life, a reality, regardless of how things look on social media. Note that although everyone struggles, for many people things get easier (see "H" for "Hope" and "Z" for "Zone").

The letter "T" gets into some of the weighty matter that makes up intermarriage. Tradition – what we keep and what we discard – is really at the
heart of how all Jews, including intermarried ones, determine their Jewish
future. The tension between tradition and change informs all cultural and
religious life, including ours. This letter considers *tzedakah*, which means
charity and justice. This value often unites couples in spite of cultural differences, because both partners appreciate that creating a more just
world is a worthwhile cultural and spiritual goal. Related to the idea of
tzedakah is the idea of *tikkun olam*, which means "repairing the world."
Find out what it has to do with the earth's creation in Jewish mysticism
and what it has to do with intermarriage today. And therapy, which can
be a terrific tool to help people in their marriage, including the dynamics
of intermarriage.

Talk Therapy

Therapy. I believe in it! If there are struggles in intermarriage negotiation, or in the marriage generally, therapy may help. There are different types of therapists a couple could see. Clergy may be a great option, particularly if your clergy person is supportive of intermarriage. There are also life coaches, psychotherapists, and social workers. They all take a different approach or use a different model. I encourage you to ask a lot of questions before you get going.

Once my partner and I went to see a therapist. It was a disaster! Her approach was really traditional in terms of gender roles, she was judgmental, and she wasn't empathetic. Right at the very end I noticed she had both a Christmas tree and a menorah. I had a glimmer of hope that, perhaps, she would understand us after all! But, sadly, she said that her ex had been Jewish, that she valued the "exotic" nature of Jewish culture, and that she could "help us with the difficulties of intermarriage." See "N" for "Nope." I'm never going to see a therapist who takes as a starting point that intermarriage is difficult. Being intermarried has never been something my partner and I experience conflict over. I also took as a red flag her exoticization of Jewish culture via her ex. The whole thing was pretty bad, but it actually did help because it made us realize exactly what we *don't* want in a therapist and gave us something to laugh and bond over.

Therapists can be damaging and so it's important to check them out fully. Having said that, one of their most important roles is just to create the space for people to talk. Sometimes simply saying something out loud and giving it some oxygen (see "O") is what's needed to create the space to feel love or joy or relief.

Talmud

You may have heard of the Talmud as a book of commentary and laws based on the Torah. That is both true and untrue. The Talmud is a wacky compendium of conversations of early rabbis. Yes, they are engaging with biblical text, but they are also telling stories and disagreeing over what the stories mean and how human behavior should be changed based on them. Yes, there are laws in there, but there are also many contradictions and some laws that were never practiced or, perhaps, never even meant to be. What is most fascinating about reading the Talmud is the way in which you get to follow a conversation through time and space. It's not like all the rabbis of the Talmud wrote the content while sitting

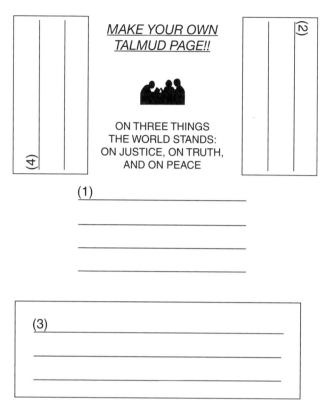

Figure 1. "Make Your Own Talmud Page" exercise

together at the same time in the same place. There are commentaries on commentaries spanning centuries.

Figure 1 is an example of a Sunday school activity created by my colleague Rabbi Adam Chalom. It takes a little snippet of the Talmud – the three things on which the world stands: truth, justice, and peace – and it asks students to replicate the process and form of the Talmud by creating their own commentaries. In this way, students are responsible for internalizing the content of their learning and becoming a part of the conversation itself.

Intermarried folks can learn from the way the Talmud is formed and works. Everyone gets to have their own take on any point in the discussion. The different opinions and experiences don't have to eclipse one another. They can all stand, side by side, united (as on the page of the Talmud) while retaining differences. You don't have to agree with your partner, believe in all they believe, share everything in terms of ritual and practice. You have to hear them and respect them and create a cultural mosaic in your home that works for everyone.

By the way, you may be wondering what the Talmud itself says about intermarriage. Like most things in Talmud, it varies a lot! But if anyone ever tells you that the rabbis of the Talmud were uniformly against intermarriage, send them these passages (taken from Sefaria.org, which uses the William Davidson Talmud in English translation):

Taanit 30b:8–12

The mishna taught that Rabban Shimon ben Gamliel said: There were no days as happy for the Jewish people as the fifteenth of Av and as Yom Kippur. The Gemara asks: Granted, Yom Kippur is a day of joy because it has the elements of pardon and forgiveness, and moreover, it is the day on which the last pair of tablets were given.

However, what is the special joy of the fifteenth of Av? Rav Yehuda said that Shmuel said: This was the day on which the members of different tribes were permitted to enter one another's tribe, by intermarriage. It was initially prohibited to intermarry between tribes, so as to keep each plot of land within the portion of the tribe that originally inherited it. This *halakha* was instituted by the Torah in the wake of a complaint by the relatives of the daughters of Zelophehad, who were worried that if these women married men from other tribes, the inheritance of Zelophehad would be lost from his tribe (see Numbers 36:1–12).

What did they expound, in support of their conclusion that this *halakha* was no longer in effect? The verse states: "This is the matter that the Lord has commanded concerning the daughters of Zelophehad, saying: Let them marry whom they think best; only into the family of the tribe of their father shall they marry" (Numbers 36:5). They derived from the verse that this matter shall be practiced only in this generation, when Eretz Yisrael was divided among the tribes, but afterward members of different tribes were permitted to marry. On the day this barrier separating the tribes was removed, the Sages established a permanent day of rejoicing.

Tu B'Av, a holiday celebrating love, is still practiced today. It is notable that on this day in particular, intermarriage is permitted! So, as Jews celebrate love, we should be celebrating love in all its forms and iterations. In that, I include same-sex and queer love, intermarriage, and love between people who celebrate each other in all kinds of ways. The mention of the daughters of Zelophehad makes this bit of text especially wonderful. These women stood up for their inheritance rights, speaking out in the pursuit of justice. The fact that the intermarriage ruling is based on this biblical story of women fighting for gender rights highlights another important idea: more justice leads to more justice.

Avodah Zarah 36b:5

It was stated that the prohibition against marrying the daughters of gentiles was decreed on account of idolatry. The Gemara raises an objection: But the prohibition against marrying their daughters is prescribed by Torah law, as it is written: "Neither shall you make marriages with them" (Deuteronomy 7:3). The Gemara explains: By Torah law intermarriage is prohibited only with the seven Canaanite nations, but intermarriage with the other nations of the world is not prohibited, and the students of Shammai and Hillel came and decreed that intermarriage is prohibited even with the other nations.

This text reminds us that the "rules" around intermarriage were formed when Jewish leaders had some fairly different concerns. Rarely do we hear people worry about whether an intermarriage is between a Jew and someone from one of the seven Canaanite nations. The point the rabbis are discussing here is how to appropriately differentiate the Israelite/Jewish people from their surrounding peoples. This becomes even more important post-exile. The concern is the same for rabbis today: how to make sure the Jews stay a distinct group so that Jews and Judaism continue to exist. My suggestion is that the answer has never been to ban intermarriage but, rather, to strengthen Judaism.

Teaching

I find that teaching a concept, a text, or a skill is the best way to reinforce my own learning or practice of it. When I taught history, boning up on my knowledge of, say, the pre–World War II period really helped reinforce what I had learned about it. If you are Jewishly educated, it'll help deepen your own knowledge and connection if you share what you know. It'll also help make others feel welcome, a nice goal in itself.

Terminology

There's a lot of Jewish terminology that can make someone who isn't Jewish or educated Jewishly feel like an outsider. When I lead Jewish study classes or community events, I always ask people to avoid Hebrew words or other "insider" terms or acronyms without explaining them.

We casually throw around sentences like "I'm looking forward to hearing the *shofar* at Rosh Hashanah." If some in your family or community don't know all those words, you could say instead, "At the Jewish New Year, Rosh Hashanah, we blow a ram's horn, the *shofar*, which reminds us to wake up and calls us to action. It's a beautiful part of the service and I look forward to it each year." Notice that this is not only accessible for a newbie, it also helps remind you of what's meaningful.

Things in the Attic

My teacher-turned-friend and occasional drinking buddy Rabbi Adam Chalom, who created the Talmud sheet above, and Israeli writer Amos Oz both give this analogy: Judaism is like an inheritance. (Note: This applies to Jews by choice, Jews by birth, people joining the Jewish family by marriage.) Let's say you inherit the home of a family member and have to go through the stuff they've collected over time that is now stored in the attic. As you begin to explore the attic, you're going to find treasured family heirlooms. You're going to find junk. You're going to find some stuff that seems important or meaningful but you might not yet be sure exactly how or what you're going to do with it. Judaism is like this. There are elements we value and treasure, elements we keep and are still figuring out, elements we have no more use for.

Tikkun Olam

Tikkun olam is an idea from Jewish mysticism, known as *Kabbalah,* the central text of which is the Zohar (Madonna is a fan). The theology behind it is that when the world was created, God had to contract himself into vessels of light to make room for the world. But the vessels shattered and bits of God were scattered throughout the world. Now, each time we do a good deed, we are reassembling a shard of glass in the mystical realm. Whether or not you believe this, it's a compelling narrative for doing good in the world. As we do good, we are repairing the world, and we can all agree that the world needs some healing and repairing.

As you make others feel welcome and included, you are doing good deeds. Jewish teachings tell us that we are to love our neighbors and love the stranger. This can be understood as loving others like us (other Jews), near us. Many understand it as being kind and loving people who are unlike us, other nations. It is my goal that people who aren't

Jewish feel seen, welcome, and included in my Jewish community and that they also get something out of what we're doing.

Tradition

Tradition. You likely know the song from *Fiddler on the Roof*. Tradition matters. But does it get a vote or a veto in your home? In my branch of Judaism, Humanistic Judaism, we often say that tradition gets a vote but not a veto. I never do anything for the simple reason that it is traditional. Something being traditional might help imbue it with meaning. I like that Shabbat is celebrated by Jews all over the world and has been throughout the ages, for example, but it is never the only reason to do it. Shabbat brings me a sense of peace, a rhythm to my week, a way to connect with my family, sensory delights including candlelight, delicious wine, and satisfying challah. I love sharing what our favorite parts of the week were and reliving special moments. I like that it is special and precious time. If I weren't getting anything out of Shabbat, I wouldn't do it, in spite of the fact that it's traditional. There are plenty of things that are traditional that I don't do. I choose not to follow all the rules of Shabbat, including avoiding electricity, for example. I certainly don't follow traditions I find outdated or even harmful. An example of this is the "three blessings" that Jewish men traditionally say every day. They thank the deity for not making them a woman, a gentile, or a slave. I should say that there are plenty of traditional Jews who don't say these blessings at all, or modify them if they do. Still, they're in the prayer book and they're offensive.

I recall being at my brother's *aufruf*, a time before a man gets married and is given a special recognition and celebration at a synagogue. He chose an Orthodox synagogue. This is a reminder that even when families are made up of all Jews, they can still be intercultural/interfaith families. I am an intermarried secularist and my brother and his wife are in-married traditionalists. This is as intercultural/interfaith as any family created by marriage. It was the first time my husband was with me at a Jewish service or space where we weren't together. I choose places without segregated seating but, of course, we'd both attend this Orthodox synagogue for a family event. I was sitting in the women's section above and he was with the men's section below. As I followed in the *siddur* (prayer book), and saw the three blessings, I realized I hadn't prepped him. We were both about to be equally insulted in this passage: I, a woman, he, a gentile. I wondered what he would feel as a gentile trying to be part of his family's religious/cultural life at a moment of celebration and having the prayer book highlight his inferiority. I was embarrassed.

Tradition has its place, for sure. To me and many others, however, tradition is only meaningful if it is congruent with our contemporary values. When it isn't, we should opt for change.

Tradition and change is a tension that all Jewish movements and communities grapple with. Some groups call themselves something with the word "traditional" in the title/identification: "traditional egalitarian," "traditional but not religious" (I don't know what the latter means but people say it a lot). The truth is that if there is one thing that is traditional in Judaism, it is change. We started out as a people with priests conducting animal sacrifices at a central temple. If we had clung to that as the one true "tradition," we'd have ceased to exist. Almost every single thing that is recognizable as "Jewish" today is rather new, from a historical perspective. A lot of people don't know that Orthodox Judaism is a reaction to Reform Judaism, not vice versa. They had been fine with change up to a point but then felt things went "too far" and then they decided to freeze Judaism in time. Ever wonder why some groups of Jews dress like they're in the middle of a Russian winter around 300 years ago? That's why. They chose to freeze things like traditions, practices, and rituals. But even making that choice is a change from the way it had been! It's not like the Israelites wandering the desert were depicted as wearing black hats and long coats in the Bible. Everyone has to change and adapt, and some groups and individuals change more than others. It's really a quest to stay relevant and meaningful. For me, more change means my Judaism is more meaningful to me and corresponds more fully with my values. But whenever folks publicly criticize others because they're too "untraditional," honestly, they're being a little hypocritical. We all change. We all respect tradition. It's a question of degrees.

Truth

You need to be authentic in choosing the traditions you want to keep and what you want to discard. Sometimes learning more about what you find up in the metaphorical attic (see "T" for "Things in the Attic") will help you make that choice. You can't value something if you don't know what it is or what it means. Sometimes we keep something less because it is significant to us but because we know it was significant to the person who left it to us. Some people recite traditional prayers, even when they don't usually pray or recite traditional blessings, because it was done with their mother. Another example is attending a synagogue service with family, when it wouldn't be your choice or style of service. It's perfectly legitimate to do things because of family connection, history, or "tradition," however it is understood. What I value is truth. For me, it's really important that I say what I believe and I believe what I say. I can't recite prayers when I don't believe the words.

My hope is that anyone reading this spends some time finding their own truth: What do you need to feel spiritually nourished? Are you getting it? What are your dealbreakers or red lines? Where are you flexible? We can't be honest with our families and partners unless we are honest with ourselves.

Turtle Island

To many Indigenous Peoples, if you are in North America, you are on Turtle Island. The phrase comes from their creation story. It's a pretty different story than Adam and Eve. All peoples have a creation story, and very often one story is very unlike another. That makes some people doubt the validity of other peoples and their stories, and it makes some people question the veracity of their own. I tend towards the latter. Wherever you fall on that spectrum, I would encourage you, if you are currently situated on Turtle Island, to be respectful of the people who were here before we were. The treatment of Indigenous Canadians and Americans has been shameful. As Jews, we understand the plight of minorities who are lacking adequate resources, rights, and respect. As a settler Canadian, I see it as my responsibility as a human being, a Canadian, and, yes, a Jew to make the country more equitable. Love the stranger. In a sense, that's us as newcomers. In a sense, that's the people here with fewer advantages.

Tzedakah

The Jewish concept of *tzedakah* is often translated as "charity" but actually means something closer to "justice." This is important in today's context. Many people are starting to understand charity as a necessary evil that releases the pressure valve of human guilt over inequality by making us feel like we're helping. Anti-poverty activists will tell you that food banks aren't the solution to hunger, addressing income inequality is.

Many religious institutions do a good amount of charity work. Many are also engaged in advocacy and activism around a variety of social justice or action projects. This is wonderful. I do hope that, more and more, our approach changes to working for justice over charity, and to better realizing the Jewish laws and teachings on these issues. There are many labor laws (allow a part of the land or crops for the hungry, mandatory time off, fair pay expectations) in Jewish law. So too are there laws and teachings around respecting the environment (for example, if the messiah is coming and you are planting a tree, first finish the planting and then greet the messiah). Using Jewish ethics can make us more effective at working for a better world. This is an area that many intermarried folks find unites them. Lots of religious groups work to feed the hungry. Many have clothing drives. Many do blood donation campaigns. Getting involved in the justice work of your and your partner's community is a great way to live out an intermarriage.

It's important to always keep learning, and some of that process involves unlearning. We all grew up with harmful stereotypes, and these can show up in intermarriages (and elsewhere). It's good to confront our own biases. This can make us better partners, better parents, and better forces for goodness and justice in the world. The goal in relationships should be understanding. I really believe that one of the primary needs we have as humans is to simply be and feel understood. A partner can be the person who best understands you, and that is a truly wonderful aspect of intimate relationships. Universality is something people mention a lot. Ideas like "universal values" sound good, but they need to be interrogated, as do all the other ideas we are trying to unlearn. This section considers the idea that being who you are and loving who you love might make you unpopular with your particular community. I'm inviting you to be strong and brave in the face of that. It's more important to please yourself and your partner than it is to please others. And "unorthodox" is a fun word to play with. I am proud to be unorthodox in many ways! This isn't about defining ourselves in opposition to observant Judaism, but rather exploring how being unorthodox invites new perspectives and opportunities.

Ugliness

Being understanding (see below) helps when our partner does something, shall we say, less than desirable. We're all going to mess up sometimes. It's so easy to get sucked into the drama of a moment, or of a person, or of our own feelings. There can be real ugliness in relationships. It is easy to say, as an officiant or as a rabbi, "avoid saying things you'll regret." But it's not realistic. We all sometimes say things we regret; sometimes the regret comes in the exact instant the words leave our mouths. For that reason, it's useful to seek to understand your partner not just at their best but also at their worst. When someone is behaving badly, can you seek to understand their frustration or motivation? It's okay to say at the same time: "It's not okay to behave like this" and also "I see that you are really hurting or angry or sad right now." Note: I am speaking of dynamics that arise in all relationships and assuming that the bad behavior comes from both parties. I'm not talking about abuse, which involves other dynamics of power and control. While I think it is kind to seek to understand the motivations of abusers, it neither justifies nor excuses their behavior.

Undercutting

When we're in the weeds of difficult times, we may be tempted to undercut our partner by making a jab about their religion or culture. I really, really, really advise against this. Slights meant to cut to the core of who someone is usually do just that. It's really hard to repair that kind of damage.

Understanding

My suspicion is that most people walk around the bulk of their days feeling wildly misunderstood. It's so difficult to accurately communicate our feelings and intentions, and so much gets lost in all the noise of life. One of the benefits of being with a loving partner is having the potential to be understood by someone close to you. This is just potential because even, and sometimes especially, in committed partnerships, we can feel really misunderstood. It's important to really seek to understand your partner, including the aspects of their identity that you don't know much about. Sometimes when I've been in the thick of a difficult conversation (read: fight) with my husband, I say something like "I'm not looking for you to agree with me; I just want to be understood." I bet that resonates with you a little. All we want is to be understood, so we all need to do our best to be understanding.

Unity

The goal here should be unity without uniformity. That is, not all people in a family or in a society should be the same. We can stand united with folks who are different from us. In families, the idea of unity is really central. There's an idea in Judaism – *Achdut Yisrael* – which means "Unity of Israel." The concept is that Jews may be different from one another, may disagree with one another, may sometimes even despise one another, but we are all part of the same family and thus are united. I agree with this! It's too bad that the issue of intermarriage has caused so much division and dissension amongst Jewish people and groups. It has really been ugly. The idea of unity without uniformity is really what we as Jews need. We need it for our survival and also for our well-being as individuals and as a people. I also believe that folks who marry Jews are included in that big, wacky, and disharmonious united family of the Jewish people. We understand when we marry that we marry not just a person but their family.

Universality

Universality is a tricky concept. It seems to me that very little is truly universal; we are all the products of our time, environment, and culture. And yet some things are universal, such as a need for safety, for fulfillment, for laughter. Sometimes people make claims towards a need for a universal religion, culture, or language. That sounds nice for a minute. It's a great concept to imagine everyone sharing so much in common. If you really think about it, though, it would require the erasure of many precious cultures and traditions.

Once, a long time ago, a boyfriend I had who wasn't Jewish was talking about how during December it'd be great if there was one, universal, common holiday, with common songs and symbols. I was like, "Err, what would an example of a symbol be?" And he was like, "I don't know ... a star? A tree?" Look, he wasn't particularly sophisticated in the argument, and his heart was in the right place for sure, but it does show how when we think of things being "universal," we tend to be thinking through the very limiting and limited view of our own experiences.

In my previous working life of teaching African literature, I had a fun game with my students. We would see who could first find the word "universal" used to describe a book we were reading. Would it be on the back cover of said book? A review? Something an interviewer would say? It seemed that Western audiences could only be persuaded to read a book by someone from Africa if it was described as being "universal." What's that about? We want to know that it will not be so "foreign" to us that we won't understand it? We want to believe that people from Africa are here to teach "us" something? It's especially funny because most of the time the themes of the book were really not universal. Not everyone has experienced slavery, colonization, family division, exile, political oppression. I suppose those forces have shaped all of our lives in some way, but I'd argue that the specificity of the stories is what gives them their power, not their universality.

All of us have a particular narrative and set of experiences, individual and communal, and they are all equally special and worthy of celebrating. We have a lot in common as humans, but we aren't all the same. It's better to find out about your partner rather than try to erase differences.

Unlearning

Sometimes we cause harm unintentionally, for we have all learned and internalized harmful stereotypes. Unlearning can be as important as learning (see "L"). Do you have negative stereotypes about the culture of the person you're marrying or married to? Do you think Jews are irrational or too loud or cheap? Do you think Christians are soft or obsessed with power? Do you think Muslims are inherently sexist? It's so uncomfortable for me to write those stereotypes, but I know they are out there. Honesty moment: Do you ever have a flash of some horrid thought cross your mind? Examples: A racist thought about someone's driving, judging someone's character based on religious garb. I bet they happen to you. Look, they happen to all of us. It's a sign that we have some unlearning to do. If you love someone, you owe it to them to unlearn some of the stereotypes about them, for they can show up in relationships even when there is a lot of love there. All of us have a responsibility to unlearn the attitudes and ideas that harm others and to teach future generations better so there is less to unlearn.

Unorthodox

If you've read a good chunk of this book, you likely have a sense that I'm a touch unorthodox. I'm actually unorthodox in many ways, Jewishly and otherwise. In Judaism, there is a movement called "Orthodox," meaning that they follow Jewish law closely. Of course, amongst the Orthodox, you will find many groups and degrees of orthodoxy. They aren't immune to the divisions amongst Jews and Jewish groups. Orthodoxy works for some folks: it provides structure and discipline, it tends to create close-knit communities, it keeps tradition going as a powerful force in people's lives. It also can create too much rigidity and choicelessness for some.

I like to think of myself as radically unorthodox. I don't believe in rules, but rather tools, for living life. The metaphor of being unorthodox can help couples feel okay about letting go of some traditions and traditional expectations. If you accept that you are unorthodox in some ways or many ways or all ways, you will be less harmed by the judgments of others. You will ask yourself important questions about what you believe and how to practice those beliefs. You will find ways to be true to yourself without changing too much to meet the expectations of others. Being unorthodox (even for those who would call themselves religiously Orthodox) can be a really powerful and freeing thing.

Unpopular

Sometimes being unorthodox (see above) will also make you unpopular. I'm sorry, but it's true. I'm pretty unpopular amongst some groups of rabbis, for example, who are trying to prevent ideas like the ones in this book from reaching a wide audience. (Note to those rabbis: Too late!) You might find yourself holding the minority or unpopular opinion within your family, at your holiday dinner, out in your own religious/cultural community, or anywhere out in the world. You should know that being the minority voice and holding true to your values is actually very Jewish. Holding true to your values and beliefs on intermarriage, in the face of judgment, criticism, and shaming by others, is actually, it seems to me, a really Jewish thing to do. We are known as the "stiff-necked" people; we don't bow to gods in whom we don't believe. Neither do we adopt positions that are not right for us just because it's the will of the majority. So, you're Jewish in your approach and openness when it comes to intermarriage. The irony and paradox are delightful.

Sometimes it feels good to be the unorthodox one, the outlier, the one with the *chutzpah*. Sometimes it doesn't feel so good, because we are hardwired to seek belonging. On this subject, I recommend wholeheartedly the work of Brené Brown, particularly her wonderful *Braving the Wilderness: The Quest for True Belonging and the Courage to Stand Alone*.

Urgency

There's an urgency to some of this work of unlearning and understanding each other (see "Understanding" and "Unlearning" above). We are seeing a tremendous uptick in the expression of racism, white supremacy, and antisemitism. I am hopeful that intermarriage is a force for good in the world for many reasons, not least of which is that if you have someone join your family and they are different from you, you might just look at your own stereotypes about the one joining the family and, in so doing, unlearn some of the stereotypes you hold about this new family member and their cultural/religious background.

The urgency is also felt within relationships. There is an urgent need for us to be accepted and valued as our whole selves. Sometimes intermarriage is not a significant factor in problems within a relationship, and sometimes it is. It's useful to pay attention to your particular dynamic and ask, What is it my partner needs me to understand about them?

We need to seek unity without uniformity in our own homes and lives; I know that my house feels unified and harmonious even though not everyone in it calls themselves Jewish. We also need to seek unity without uniformity in the broader Jewish community; we disagree over many important issues, but we are all connected. Lastly, we need to work towards unity without uniformity amongst all the peoples of the world. We really do. We can stretch ourselves to imagine a time when we don't let difference divide us the way we do now. If we operated from a belief that we are all interdependent and that if we work together we can make sure there is enough to sustain all of us, we really could be unified and diverse at the same time.

Utopia

You may think that unity (see above) is impossible and simply a utopic dream. Maybe so. People have shown themselves to be vicious throughout history. But you're not, right? You, reading this right now, you don't see yourself as a bad person. Few people do. Most of us want to be good and do what's right. To do that, we have to do a lot of un-learning so that the good in us overtakes the bad and so we can find ways to live our lives peacefully. It would take work, it would take leadership, and it would take a lot of education. It might even take a revolution, but I don't think it's impossible.

Do you have a vision for what your relationship, family, and life could or should be? Some people actually write a mission or vision statement for their relationship/their family to crystallize what's most important to them. Part of constructing this vision is to center on your values. Each couple and family needs to determine their values. I encourage conversations just about what values are shared and how they can be enacted. This will always center a couple and their family if negotiations or problems arise. Veils are like masks we wear, sometimes concealing who we are for we fear we will not be accepted or understood. Viewpoints are like values in that they are culturally informed. Sometimes we are unaware how much our cultural upbringing affects our point of view. It's worth checking in and asking whether our viewpoint can shift or change as we learn and grow with our partners. This section also talks about victories! So much of what we hear about intermarriage is negative so it's important to focus on the triumphs and wins we experience in our relationships and lives!

Vacations

A great way to understand your partner's values, points of view, and vantage points is to plan a vacation and travel to the place where they or their family come from. There are some people who have been living away from their ancestral place of origin for so long it doesn't hold much meaning, but for lots of us, it's a meaningful and exciting journey to trace our routes. People do trips to Spain and Latin America to trace the origins of their Sephardic family. People visit synagogues in places like Poland, Rome, and Argentina to see what feels familiar to their own way of practicing, and what might feel different. Lots of people do learning trips to sites of relevance to the Holocaust. Many people go to Israel and/or Palestine to learn about its history and political situation. Lots of Jews go to Scotland, China, Japan, Mexico, or Estonia, anywhere that their partner's family is from and learn about the particular histories and cultural attributes of that place.

I always enjoy learning about new places and cultures, and have spent quite a lot of time (and, when I was younger, pretty much all of my student loan money) traveling. There is no doubt that it's been meaningful for me to visit places where I have a family connection: South Africa, Israel, Palestine, Poland. It's so enriching to go on these kinds of journeys together with a partner: to taste the foods, hear the languages, share in the experience of museums or art galleries, and really get a feel for a place. It's a benefit of intermarriage that isn't often discussed: the world opens up to you in a new way, offering new places with which you share a connection and a desire to explore.

Values

There is a whole lot of noise about what you'll "do" as an intermarried family, including celebrating holidays, educating children, and crafting ritual and practice. I don't actually recommend starting by visioning or planning what you'll do. I think it's easy to think that if we just do stuff, our lives will click into place. I suggest starting with exploring and discussing what your values are.

Many couples who intermarry find that, although they grew up doing different things in terms of religion and culture, those things were inspired by the same values. Here are some examples: Some Muslim families grew up with the tradition of fasting at Ramadan. Some Christian families adopt the practice of giving something (or many things) up for Lent. Fasting is part of other cultures/religions too, such as Buddhism. In Judaism we have several fast days. The one most commonly observed is on Yom Kippur. There may be different reasons in scripture to fast on the various holidays but my guess is that there is common ground.

Most religions and cultures have other things in common too. Many have a set of principles based on some version of "the golden rule" – that is, treating others well. Most have a set of standards meant to encourage respect for elders. Most instill an understanding of the need for, and a disciplined approach to, acts of charity or giving.

If you're intermarried, it is tempting to go straight to the practices. But by explaining the values to your partner, you are much likelier to get buy-in, find common practices with which they are familiar, and design a vision for your home that is really driven by values.

Think about it like this: Someone really wants a Christmas tree but their partner isn't sure. Why not approach it from a values-perspective? What does the tree mean or symbolize? Maybe some common ground can be found. Is the tree about celebrating nature? Perhaps you'll have one and also make sure you make a big deal about the Jewish environmental holiday of Tu B'shevat. Is the tree about maintaining traditions the person grew up with? Talk about the value of tradition for both of you and how you can weave it into your home. Do you like the tree because it is beautiful and smells good? Consider appreciating beauty to be an important value to you and see how everyone's cultural practice can fulfill that need and express that value.

This may sound a little bit existential, but at the end of the day, your life amounts to what you do. You want what you do – your practices big and small – to be a reflection of your values. If you are what you do, be thoughtful and intentional about all that doing.

Vantage Point/Viewpoint

Viewpoints are like values in that they are culturally informed. Sometimes we are unaware how much our cultural upbringing affects our point of view or vantage point. It can lead to tension if one person is oblivious to something that is obvious for their partner. It's worth checking in and asking whether our viewpoint can shift or change as we learn and grow with our partners. What did we always take for granted and what new perspectives can we incorporate into our own ways of being and doing?

Intermarried folks often find that their approach to family and communication is different from that of their partner. These are sometimes simply individual differences, and sometimes there might be some ways in which family dynamics are culturally informed. Does your family of origin tend to talk things out? Yell to resolve problems? Use passive-aggressive behavior or give the silent treatment? Is the vibe in the home loud and boisterous or quiet and reserved? Sometimes it's easy for us to assume that all families are just like our own, and we are a little surprised when the mood or tone is different. Part of marriage and partnership is considering how we confront the ways of being and doing that seem natural and obvious to us, and consider how our partner's ways of being and doing mesh with ours – or don't. Sometimes someone has to change. Often, both people do.

Variability

They say that people never really change and I find that to be very true and very untrue all at once. I do think that often there is a core to our personalities that is rather unmovable. If you are someone who loves organization and systems, you're just never going to be happy becoming the kind of person who teaches skydiving professionally and lives in a messy house. If you are someone who teaches skydiving and lives in a messy house, chances are you are never going to decide that you really want to be a desk jockey. If you are adventurous by nature, or a homebody, or very extroverted, or very introverted, most of that stuff is going to stick with you through your life. So, yes, people don't really change. Except people do change all the time! I'll use myself as an example. My natural way of being is unathletic, bookish, and pretty nerdy. When I was a child, you'd be more likely to find me curled up with a book than playing soccer. I was never one of the super popular kids and, indeed, I survived some years having few friends at all. This is me as I naturally am. However, I am also in charge of my own life.

I remain unathletic in terms of natural ability, but I have learned that through disciplined practice one can actually develop muscles. I'll never win any 10k races or triathlons, but I have run them. I even found that, although I started out dreading every single second of a workout, now my body *craves* movement and I hate periods of time I go without exercising. You can change.

I was naturally someone who was content to stay inside and read. Did I mention I like to read? But a series of life experiences and choices taught me that I'm happier if I get outside a lot.

I was naturally a little socially awkward, but I have learned to be quite social indeed. People who meet me often assume I've always been an extrovert, but that's not true. I actually have more characteristically in common with introverts (like staying home alone and reading all the time) and have had to work on being social and developing public-speaking skills.

Why am I saying all this? Well, because one of the many garbage "reasons" people give about why intermarriages won't work is that your viewpoints are culturally informed and thereby fixed and, as a result, marriages work better if you marry someone more like you.

That wouldn't even be true if people really did stay the same forever. Hello? Being married to someone just like you in terms of values and viewpoints? Sounds a little boring. It also sounds impossible; no matter how much your families of origin had in common, my guess is you'll find some pretty big differences with any partner. But the reality is that people do change and grow.

I have seen countless couples I've worked with adopt radically different perspectives on culture, religion, family, communication, practice, lifestyle, and beyond because they opened up to the ways of being that their partner showed them. People are shockingly variable and can accommodate all kinds of new learning and growth. Not only is this good for our partners, as we adapt to include aspects of their lives, but it's good for ourselves because we avoid stagnating in our own perspectives and lives.

Veils

Veils are like masks we wear, sometimes concealing who we are because we fear we will not be accepted or understood. There are literal veils too. In a traditional Jewish wedding, there is what is called the *bedeken*, when a bride's veil is lifted. The tradition is a nod to the biblical story of Jacob and Rachel. Jacob thought he was marrying Rachel but her older sister was behind the veil instead, placed there by her father who wanted his older daughter married first. So now grooms have to check that it's the right bride. Of course today many brides do not wear veils, many weddings don't have a groom at all, and there is little anxiety that the bride's dad has switched out the sisters. Many of my couples do not do a *bedeken* at all. But, if they wish, I do a version of it where I have them stand back to back, and then turn around to face each other. This is the face, unveiled, and unbridled (excuse the pun) that you will be waking up to. Look at that face. Always feel free to be transparent, unveiled, with your partner. Indeed, we are so used to wearing a mask or a veil in our daily lives that we forget to remove it when we are with our partner. This is the most deeply intimate relationship of your life; your partner must really see you, including all of your beauty and all of your faults and all of your gifts. It's challenging to let ourselves be seen so nakedly, but it is also the greatest gift of marriage and committed partnership to know that you are loved in the fullness of who you are. This includes culture, religion, values, and viewpoints. All of it has to be visible to your partner for your marriage to be fully affirming and as beautiful as possible.

Venting/Ventilation

You deserve to vent. You deserve to complain about the ways your partner drives you up the wall, even as you love them and the variability and values they've brought to your life. It's a very important part of marriage that you feel secure enough with your partner that you can express how they drive you bonkers. It's a very important part of being in a community, that you feel included enough that you feel entitled to *kvetch* (complain). Obviously, try not to complain all the time! Find joy! (For more on lessening the *kvetching* and complaining and finding more joy, see "J" for "Joy.") But, sure, sometimes you need to vent a little and you're entitled. *Kvetching* when done artfully can be a great way to make positive change (I'm not referring to the people who do it all the time, like the boy who cried wolf, but to the ones who are committed and joyful and awesome and then form a real complaint). When my partner, who is generally quite agreeable and kind, tells me I've screwed up, I listen. When a congregant, who is generally active and amiable, tells me they didn't like something, I listen then too. When you are fully and equally part of a family or community, your voice matters. Then, once you're done with your vent or *kvetch*, let it go. Get a little ventilation going. (See "O" for "Oxygen.")

Vicious Circles

There's a tragic feature of a lot of Jewish life, which I think of as a vicious circle: Synagogues are anti-intermarriage; clergy rail against intermarriage in sermons; synagogue policies make life uncomfortable for intermarried folks, imposing barriers and rules that are designed to exclude and exude a community vibe that is unwelcoming, and so on. But then, uh oh, the communities realize that these unwelcoming places are no longer able to attract the membership they need to survive (imagine that!), and so they start a campaign trying to undo all that damage they previously did and recruit intermarried folks. This is like going back to a bad boyfriend. Their narrative is similar to "I was wrong to have treated you that way! I've changed!" So you give them another chance but then, of course, nothing has meaningfully changed. Things are pleasant at first and then you find out that the clergy still has some attitude towards you, the rules are still inflexible, and some members of the community continue to say hurtful things. So the intermarried families who rightly don't want to subject themselves and their kids to this nonsense leave. This causes the board and staff, clergy and committee leaders, to feel confirmed in their original bias that intermarried folks aren't "serious" about Judaism. They go on spouting their misinformed diatribes. More of an ethos of being exclusionary is created. This loop goes on forever and ever – until it doesn't. Many synagogues are closing and it's clear that people are voting with their feet.

If you are intermarried, I really encourage you to ask questions about how welcoming a community really is. If you hear something like "We have determined that we must welcome intermarried families here as a matter of our own survival," then you should run away as fast and as far as possible. I really want you to find a place that welcomes you because they value you, not because their survival depends on it. You are not a means to an end in a community. You deserve to be part of the life of the community, fully and completely.

Victories

Even though it's true that folks come from different vantage points (see "Vantage Point/Viewpoint" above), sometimes it's good to celebrate the wins that come with fluidity and congruity. For example, there are a large number of "Jewpanese" families who find that their viewpoints on things like family, tradition, and education are remarkably similar. Despite having grown up in fairly different cultures, they discover that there are certain values that are deeply shared between them. Of course, this dynamic extends to many folks beyond those in Jewpanese communities. Celebrate the victories when everybody wins.

Visibility

I was at a dinner recently and we were discussing the schools people send their kids to. One person suggested that her child, highly gifted and also someone with some learning disabilities, wasn't doing well in the public system but had found great success at the Jewish day school housed at the local Jewish Community Centre. Sadly, the program ends before middle school. Someone else suggested a private middle school program for high achievers but the parent said, "That wouldn't work for our family. What I love about the JCC program is that there are so many families who are mixed-race and intermarried like mine."

This was one of those moments when I knew that the world had changed forever and ever – and for the better. Here's a mom, parenting children who are mixed-race and visible minorities. She wants to ensure her kids are visible and appreciated and have peers who are visibly like them, so she sends them to the Jewish school at the JCC instead of secular, unaffiliated, private education programs, which tend to be too homogenous. Amazing. Why aren't all Jewish spaces equally fantastic?

Everyone deserves to be in a space where they feel seen. I mean really seen. Where their family, be it intermarried, intercultural, mixed-race, or some combination of these, will be accepted, understood, and reflected in the population of where they are. Given the diversity within Judaism, it should be a given that all spaces are like this but, sadly, that's not the case.

Intermarried folks often feel they have to hide their identity. Many synagogues have a kind of "don't ask, don't tell" policy about being intermarried. You have to keep quiet about who you are and what goes on in your home. This is supposed to be your spiritual community where you connect with others and your highest self, but you must be inauthentic. Of course, folks who are racialized don't have the choice to hide, and often couldn't be invisible even if they wanted to. But the point is that no one wants to. The feeling of being invisible in a communal space is awful. All of us deserve to be seen.

Vision

It is a useful exercise for people, when they are considering marriage or perhaps early in a marriage, to spend some time envisioning what they want their lives to be like. This goes better if you draw on certain strengths you already possess. Some people are big-picture thinkers; they focus on grand plans, big goals, and an overall sense of how they want their lives to look. Some people are better with details; they are great at making the day-to-day of their lives soulful and beautiful. They are usually better at anticipating challenges and proactively dealing with them. Sometimes this corresponds with speed: big-picture types tend to be a little bit impatient and want to get a lot done quickly, in service of their grand plan. Detail types are usually a little slower in

181

the process, trying to ensure that things are done well. I am definitely a big-picture, do-it-fast-and-see-what-sticks master-plan kind of person. I need people around me who force me to pause and make sure that gaps in the plan are addressed, things are going to be smooth, and, most importantly, that people involved in this plan feel comfortable.

What does this have to do with intermarriage? Well, I think it's useful to come up with a vision for how your homelife will look. Judaism is a home-based religion/culture with lots of things happening without ever stepping foot into a synagogue or communal space. What do you want your homelife to be? What practices are inspiring? How will the education of children (if you have them) look? If, like me, you're a big-picture person, it's easy and even fun to imagine and discuss future scenarios and decide on one that you want your life to look like. If you're more of a details person, then it might be easy and fun to focus on creating daily or weekly rituals and practices and seeing which ones work. You may not foster a five-year plan right away, but you will slowly and methodically cement really important and grounding practices for you and your family.

Either way, you'll need to come up with a sense of what your homelife, and your life in general, is going to be like. Some folks use vision boards, collaging words and images that help keep them focused on their goals. Some folks spend time visualizing the life they'd like to have. Sometimes this all just happens over dinner in conversation with your beloved. I do think that doing a little visioning in marriage goes a long way to set you up for a life you want to live.

The "wandering Jew" is a great metaphor for exploring your identity and community. Wandering with a partner deepens the experience. "Wokeness" – what is it? Why do we need it? We'll talk about it generally and in the context of questions about Judaism and whiteness or white privilege. This section considers wandering and wondering. Because of the stories and histories that comprise and inform Jewish culture, we often speak of the "wandering" Jew (wandering in the desert in the Exodus narrative, and wandering across lands during periods of exile). I think that many Jews today are not so much wandering as wondering. We wonder whether there is a way to connect with our Judaism if we are untraditional. We wonder if being intermarried or in an intercultural/interfaith partnership prohibits Jewish engagement. We wonder if our partner's culture can have a central place in our home and lives without betraying or cheapening our Judaism. I think this type of wondering is necessary for healthy relationships. And we'll talk about weddings and what they involve. See below for a full guide on planning a wedding for an intermarrying couple.

Wake-Up Calls

Sometimes in a relationship there's a certain "wake-up call" you get about something that isn't working or isn't okay. With an intermarriage, sometimes it is that subtle form of antisemitism or racism that comes out unintentionally. When a holiday gets belittled, or a stereotype gets replicated, or an act of hate or contempt is brushed off, it can be a sign that a conversation is in order. Within our intimate relationships, it's important we try to be open to these corrections, because these are the people who should make us feel safest and most seen.

It's also important to be open to being corrected out there in the wider world. I'm part of many Jewish groups online, and it happens quite often that white Jews respond really negatively when challenged on a racist assumption or statement. The work of Robin DiAngelo in *White Fragility* explains this phenomenon better than I can, but I've seen it often. We want our community, the big and broad Jewish family, to feel like a caring and supportive place, and it's hard to be wrong in public. However, avoiding correcting someone if they make a racist mistake, or reacting defensively if we make such a mistake, only works to create further divisions and hurt in the big tent of Jewish community. We all need to work on this stuff, and someone correcting you is simply a wake-up call that you have more unlearning and learning to do (see "U" for "Unlearning" and "L" for "Learning").

Wandering

There is a metaphor in Judaism of the "wandering Jew," coming from the story of Jews wandering in the desert, and extended because of the centuries of exile and displacement. Many Jews feel like we are wandering. Intermarriage may mean agreeing to wander with someone, exploring and meandering through choices around how to practice, what to believe, where to belong, and who you are. I suggest wandering into many different types of communities and seeing where you fit. Wandering, exploring, and trying are all part of the beauty of cultural life and can enhance the bond of marriage beautifully.

Weddings

In our society, we make both too much and too little of weddings. We make too much of them because we (literally) buy into the wedding industrial complex, making weddings outrageously lavish affairs with all manner of bells and whistles (same with B Mitzvahs; see "B"). Please know that I don't mean to take away the pleasure in all that. It's real. If it's your thing to plan the wedding of the century, and you want to spend your life's savings doing it, that's nobody's business but yours. I've been to those weddings; they're super fun. Equally, if it's not your thing at all to do that and you want to get married in a park with two witnesses that you met on the bus that morning, that's also great with me. We make too much of the party, the reception, and all the other stuff around the actual marriage ceremony in general. It can be as big a deal or as not big a deal as you make it. We *don't* make enough of weddings in their significance, to ourselves, our families, and our social circles. Last year, I officiated a wedding of a friend of mine from elementary school (it was an intermarriage, but for the purposes of this story, that's a bit beside the point). This wedding was a multiday affair, with a spa day, wine tour, gorgeous dinners, day trips, and the wedding itself, which was lavish and extraordinary. It was really fun to be part of all that. But unlike some weddings that involve many parties and occasions, this was all in the service of creating a beautiful sense of community around the couple and their special day. The goal wasn't showing off or acquiring things or making themselves the center of attention for as long as possible. The goal was that on their wedding day, everyone would feel comfortable and close with others; everyone would be part of something magical. And it really was magical! As we did the ceremony, and this couple gazed at each other lovingly, and stated their vows with such a heartfelt and earnest intensity, their love was palpable and so was the love from everyone in the room.

Weddings are one of the only times in your life, very often the only time until the very end of your life, when everyone (or almost everyone) you care about gathers in one space. It's strange in our guarded culture to be bold and celebratory of emotion, but that's what weddings are all about. People laugh, cry, kiss, hug, dance, and sit with others, reflecting on love, friendship, intimacy, and partnership. It's really an extraordinary thing.

When I meet with couples, I advise them to do whatever they want with the reception elements of their wedding. I've seen it all, from cheap and cheerful country-western to opulent royalty-themed celebrations. I've seen venues ranging from barns to beaches to backyards to banquet halls. It's all wonderful and lovely, especially if it fits and reflects the couple. But, ultimately, none of it really matters. What really matters, I believe, is what gets said during the ceremony. The whole party revolves around this declaration of love and commitment – you might as well get that part right!

First, it's deeply important to get the officiant right (see "O" for "Officiating"), someone who will meet your needs and speak words that are true to you. Second, I think it's great if you have input into the ceremony. I meet with my couples, talk over options for the ceremony, and get a feel for them. I write the ceremony based on all of that, and then I give my couples the ceremony by email so they can edit as they wish, telling them that I want every word to feel true to them. Third, and this is important, I encourage you to actually give some thought to what it is you are committing to.

I recently met with a couple planning their wedding. One of the partners was a therapist whose primary research is on healthy relationship dynamics. She was so clear about not wanting to commit to things that, to her, are impossible to commit to. For example, she did not want it said that they'd "love each other every day for all their lives" because, in her research and experience, couples don't actively feel love every single day and some people fall out of love permanently. I know to some people, this seems like a strange and perhaps foreboding thing to have brought up at their wedding meeting. Not me. I think that couple has a better shot than most at long-lasting love because they were realistic about what love and commitment are (and are not). Sometimes folks enter a marriage doe-eyed and invested in fantasies about how marriage will solve all their problems. Marriage is actually really hard work.

You might want to talk about undying love and forever commitment. You might want to talk about how you'll never go to bed angry (although the people I know who have been married a long time have all done this, and many do it regularly). You might want to talk about the particular things you love about your partner. You might want to keep it a little more about love and commitment more broadly. You may write your own vows, or say something from your tradition, or do something else to express your vows. There are lots of choices to make. What I suggest, simply, is that you be intentional about it. All that time you're spending looking at flowers and tablecloths and doing tastings and venue-shopping is great, but few people will remember those details and, later on in your life, those choices won't matter. The love and commitment with your partner does matter. So spend some of your time and resources making sure the ceremony part of the wedding really does reflect you.

For intermarried folks, there are a few things I suggest, which begin with Jewish options.

There are several traditional elements of a Jewish wedding. I always pose these each as choices that couples can include if they wish. I explain their significance to the couple and then during the ceremony so that people in attendance all are included and know what's going on. Here are some of those Jewish elements you could include:

- *Bedeken* (see "V" for "Veils"). This is traditionally done before the wedding ceremony.
- *Ketubah* (the Jewish wedding contract). These were once the legal marriage contract but now most people also sign a civil marriage license. *Ketubot* (plural of *ketubah*) can be more traditional or radically untraditional in what they say. They're a neat thing to sign because you get a beautiful piece of art for your home with your commitment on it.
- Circling. Traditionally the bride circles the groom, but in my ceremonies, the partners walk a circle around each other as a sign of honor and love regardless of gender.
- *Chuppah* (canopy to get married under). These can be made out of different types of material, including prayer shawls, tartans, and beyond – a nice way to incorporate different cultures into the literal and figurative fabric of the ceremony.
- Vows. The Jewish tradition is to say, "I am consecrated unto you according to the laws of Moses and Israel." Most of my couples don't say that but, rather, find vows of meaning to them, like a version of "I do" or something totally different. One of my couples were very into musical theater and they sang their vows to each other in an incredible duet!
- Rings. Traditionally, the man places the ring on the woman's pointer finger and she signals her assent by moving it to her ring finger. Most of my couples, regardless of gender, exchange rings with one another, and both say something. I give options from biblical texts or something simple about what the ring symbolizes.
- Wine. Jews drink wine as part of the ceremony, and you can include a traditional *kiddush* cup if desired.
- Seven blessings (*Sheva Brachot*). There are traditional ones or some officiants have alternatives. Mine are fully secular, egalitarian versions. Sometimes people invite family and friends to come up and say these blessings.
- Breaking the glass. Traditionally, the man does it and often the rabbi says something about how it symbolizes the destruction of the temple in Jerusalem. I let both partners, or one or the other if they prefer, do it and talk about how it symbolizes the shattering of the old and beginning of the new.
- *Yichud*. Originally, the story goes, couples would consummate the marriage straight away. I usually joke with couples that they've

spent too much time and money getting all dolled up for that! But the tradition of being alone right after the ceremony is actually great. Traditionally couples would fast on the day of their wedding (but don't do this! Seriously! It's never good when people keel over under the *chuppah*) and *Yichud*, their time of seclusion, would involve some food to break the fast. Many of my couples choose to go to a private room, bridal suite, or other area and share a little food and champagne, celebrating in a private moment before rejoining their guests. It's often the only time they are alone together the whole of their wedding day and it is often really meaningful.

In my intermarriage ceremonies, we take these traditions and do the ones that resonate. We also add in many other options from other cultures. I've done unity candles, a *mandap*, handfasting, poetry and other readings, and betel nut throwing – traditions gathered from the cultures and religions represented at the weddings. It's amazing when you can create beautiful synchronous ceremonies by using a Jewish tartan in a *chuppah* or handfasting, or talking about how the *mandap* and *chuppah* have a similar resonance.

At my wedding, we did the Jewish traditions (in a secular/cultural way), and we had readings from the Song of Songs and from Pablo Neruda's poetry. To honor my husband's Scottish heritage, we had a Scottish blessing (secular) and he wore the traditional thistle. Everything that got said in Hebrew also got said in English. Everyone in the family was represented and everyone in attendance knew what each symbol meant. The ceremony really did feel like us, and I'll always be grateful.

Whatever you choose to do with your wedding, make it yours. Make it joyful. Make it feel like you.

White Dresses

Now that I've talked about weddings, I need to include a reference to the proverbial white dress. In North America, there's a cultural idea of the white dress as whiteness that symbolizes purity (see "Whiteness" below). This of course, begs the question: Why can't the color black mean purity or peace? We have to wear our virginity on our sleeve on the day we gather with everyone we know. It's weird. A lot of women go with an ivory or other off-white color. Sure, but, to me, it's just as weird to announce that you're not a virgin as it is to announce you are one. It's not even the virginity thing and the sexism and patriarchy contained in that whole construction that bothers me. It's the idea of purity beyond that.

None of us is pure. I don't even know what it means to think that people can be. We are all incredibly weighted down by our own luggage/baggage (see "L"), we are all screw-ups in our own ways, and we are all full of faults and foibles. No one arrives at their wedding day unsullied by harsh lessons of life. Also, there is no purity of race or religion. Everyone is a mutt. All of us inherit vast cultures through time, some of which we know about and many of which we do not. Purity is a myth.

Okay, so I did wear an off-white color to my wedding. When I went dress shopping with my mom, I tried on some other colors. I liked one green gown, for example. My mom was having none of it. And, anyway, sometimes doing the traditional thing feels fun – it gets a vote, not a veto! (See "T" for "Tradition.") So, I wore the dress. But I have no illusions about purity in any way. Our intermarriage is a mixed marriage in the same way all marriages are: two mixed-up folks, with their mixed-up lineages, mixing up their lives. Ain't nothing "pure" about it.

Whiteness

What does whiteness have to do with intermarriage? A lot! Most of what I'm talking about in this book has to do with the coming together of different cultures, and sometimes cultures are racially defined or inflected. Many members of our community are Jews of color. Many white Jews are married to people of color, sometimes becoming parents to kids of color. Our families and communities are diverse in all kinds of ways, and that is beautiful and wonderful. What is not beautiful and wonderful is that we as individuals and communities have a lot of work to do to unlearn (see "U") our racism.

Over the past several years, there have been a lot of debates about Jews and white privilege, white fragility, white passing, and whiteness. These are too complex to gloss here, but are important enough to me that I spend a lot of time with the communities I serve discussing issues of racism in the Jewish community. They were also important enough to comprise a large chunk of my learning as a fellow with Rabbis Without Borders. I think it's important that we look at our internalized racism. All of us have it, regardless of our race. And as a good starting point, I recommend the organization Be'chol Lashon, which does great trainings and offers wonderful resources on this important issue.

For white Jews marrying people of color (Jewish, not Jewish, doesn't matter) and becoming parents, we need to take seriously that we've internalized some racism, because when it shows up in our homes, it's devastating.

Wisdom

Wisdom, to me, is a deep sense of understanding and knowing. There are many people I know who are wise, and perhaps I have known my own wisdom – but here is the key, one should never really think too much of one's own wisdom. We are always learning. In Judaism we have a set of our biblical texts designated as wisdom literature. The Book of Job, Ecclesiastes, the Song of Songs, the Book of Proverbs, these are biblical books that involve stories or teachings that are less about law and more about wisdom. That's not to say that everything in them is true or useful. Job, for example, is a bit of a wild ride. Ecclesiastes includes some real gems but, by Job, it can be dark. The Song of Songs is erotic poetry (see "Q" for "Quotables"); Proverbs has some great ideas but there are some I'd avoid. The point is that I think wisdom is found both within and outside of our wisdom literature tradition. I take wisdom from leaders and writers I admire, Jewish and not Jewish, secular and religious, contemporary and historical. I think we are all on our own path to finding wisdom, to becoming wiser.

Wishlists

People create gift registries and Amazon wishlists for their wedding – things needed for the wedding reception or presents needed for their married life. That's all fine. Why not also make a wishlist for the marriage? This could be a list of what you hope to do together, things you want in your home to make your cultural life meaningful, and characteristics that you plan to bring to the marriage and that you hope your partner will bring. Wishlists are very powerful. I am not someone who believes that when you write a wish "the universe" provides it. I am someone who believes that when you write down a wish, you solidify your commitment to going after it and getting it. It reorients our intention, ambition, and direction towards that which we care about. Oh, and while creating an Amazon wishlist, consider your holidays and what you'll need. Might as well get that Seder plate or Star of David tree topper now (see "S" for "Shopping – Stuff").

Wokeness

When someone is "woke," it usually refers to being aware of language and practices that ensure inclusion, that combat racism, sexism, and homophobia, and that confirm a commitment to combating oppression.

Some people are "woke" on the outside, through virtue signaling via social media, for example, but not "woke" with their partner. Learn what is hurtful to them and avoid it. Be fully awake to the needs of your partner. If your intermarriage is between a person of color and a white person, it is important to learn about racism and its many forms, from the structural to the subtle, and to work together to combat them.

Wondering

Part of wandering (see above) is wondering. Part of the journey is really asking questions and considering what your values are, what you want out of life. I spent a lot of my youth wondering about Judaism and my place in it, wondering about and wrestling with belief in God, sexism and patriarchy, communal affiliation, learning and education, and more. I think the wondering really set me up to live a meaningful Jewish life because I asked a lot of questions. I also wondered about whether I could have that meaningful Jewish life if I intermarried, for I had few models and a lot of negativity coming from the community about the whole issue. If you're wondering right now, wondering what life might be like, what's possible, what you even want, you're on the path to something great. I always prefer people who are in a state of wonder. They're reaching for something. People who never wonder seem to be a little stuck or, at least, disinterested. The wondering is part of it.

Worldliness

One thing I'll say for intermarried folks: intermarriage makes us worldly in a cool way. We learn new languages, cultural idioms and lexicons, holidays, practices, places, and traditions via our partners. We become acquainted with vantage points far from our own. Intermarriage is the product of a world that is getting more cosmopolitan. In a diverse and free society, you simply can't stop people falling in love with people who are different from them (not that you should want to stop them. I'm just saying that those who have wanted to stop them haven't been successful). The way cultural contact works now, online and in person, means that we interact with a lot of different types of people all the time. I live in one of the most diverse cities in the world. I know for sure that the folks around me represent ideas and ways of being that are unlike my own. I know my life is enriched by the diversity around me. I also know that I'm worldlier for my interactions with people who are unlike me. We all win when we get to know people who are different from ourselves.

These dynamics go on in people's own relationships and homes. We become worldlier, more cosmopolitan, and more able to understand and work with others across difference because we do it daily. Some intermarried folks have almost everything in common and some have very little in common from a cultural perspective. But most intermarried families find they do become a little worldlier with the coming together of cultures in their own homes.

X / Y

In this section, we will talk about finding your "X factor" in a relationship, a sweet spot where you no longer have to do so much negotiating and figuring out, and you can just live out the values and practices you've determined are right for you. We'll talk about Xmas and the feelings it can provoke in Jews and Christians, including a fear of being excluded, often linked to xenophobia. Xenophobia is a fear of others. Jews have historically been the target of xenophobia. Rising rates of intermarriage are a sign that this is no longer so much the case. This is a great point to make with grandparents! Yom Kippur is the traditional Jewish Day of Atonement, when we seek forgiveness from those we have hurt. My partner and I find it meaningful to use this holiday to talk over ways we have hurt each other during the past year and how we can work on repairing that hurt. Yelling – does it ever have a place? The answer might be partly culturally determined. Sometimes things come up in an intermarriage that one wouldn't expect.

Xenophobia

Many minorities, including Jews, have felt the sting of xenophobia. It's so hard to know that you are being perceived as "different." There has been a recent uptick in antisemitic threats, violence, and graffiti and so people are right to feel cautious. First, we need to make sure in our own families and relationships that we are standing up to xenophobia. No matter which group of people is the target, xenophobic language and attitudes (rightly) make Jews feel unsafe. Second, we have a responsibility if we are Jews to be kind to the stranger for, as the Bible repeatedly says, we were strangers in the land of Egypt. One of the wonderful things Judaism can do is to make us more open and accepting of others. Some Jews and Jewish communities choose to ignore these lessons in our texts and history, just as some other religious groups ignore similar lessons in their own teachings. At their best, religion and culture can be forces for coming together in common humanity, each offer their own particular inflection and way of practicing, but with respect for all. When religion starts to instill a sense of xenophobia, it can become a dangerous force. Intermarriage is the very act of coming together across difference, and it can be a hopeful and positive force for changing xenophobic attitudes.

X Factor

What makes us fall in love in the first place? It's such a strange alchemy and set of circumstances that causes us to pick one person to whom we commit ourselves and with whom we commit to live our lives. Whatever that "X factor" is, use it in your conversations about intermarriage.

One of the things I really value about my partner is his humor. He is able to cut tension by being silly or making a joke right at the perfect moment. I also really love him for his kindness. These are the things I fell in love with him for and so, naturally, they come in handy when any cultural differences or conversations about compromise occur.

The "X factor" for us is that even though I tend to take things far too seriously, he tends to make me chill out. It works. What's your X factor? What do you love about your partner? What are the strengths they bring to your relationship that can be useful when navigating any difficult terrain?

X Marks the Spot

I often tell clients who are getting married that couples tend to find a "sweet spot." After discussions about how to handle holidays, how to raise and educate children, how to deal with any difficult family dynamics, life just sort of keeps unfolding. There will be a time when the things that are stressful now are no longer stressful. There will be a time when your life will feel full and meaningful without there being a struggle. Marriage often settles into a rhythm. You've done some of the tough work to chart the course for your life together, and now you just get to live it (see "Z" for "Zone").

Xmas

Christmas is the thing that makes a lot of Jews feel really freaked out about intermarriage. It seems to be the dealbreaker for some people: intermarriage is okay as long as there is no Christmas. Of course, lots of intermarried folks, including me, do some version of Christmas. And there are some who don't. All of that is up to each individual family.

What I want to note here is why Christmas is so threatening for some Jews, not as a justification for any anti-intermarriage nonsense, but as an explanation for where hurtful attitudes sometimes come from and what can be done about it.

A lot of Jews grew up seeing Christmas everywhere – on the street, in school, in the stores, on television, just everywhere. It felt like they didn't belong and it reinforced a sense of being an outsider that was already part of their familial life. A lot of their parents were immigrants or had been raised with a sense that being Jewish meant you were different and, importantly, would never be accepted by the broader society.

Growing up like this and feeling like the only kid not participating in the spectacle and large-scale celebration of Christmas made some people feel they needed to double down on their Judaism, for their Jewish communities were where they were safe and accepted.

For many of these people, the idea of doing Christmas is therefore really antithetical to how they view Judaism and their own familial lives. It feels like their families are being taken over by this Christmasizing, if not Christianizing, force. And they feel as threatened and excluded as they did when they were kids.

Of course, if your sense of being Jewish is simply that you don't do Christmas, then you are not living a very meaningful Jewish life.

Judaism has much more to offer and is defined by much more than what it is not or what it opposes.

I grew up with a sense that Christmas didn't have to be such a big deal and that being Jewish could be cool. I don't share that same anxiety over Christmasizing. For me, I can see how having a little tree in my house does not need to detract from all of the deep and meaningful Jewish rituals and practices in my home, which we do with much greater regularity and much more emphasis. The way we grew up has a big impact on how we feel about these dynamics.

So, if you are someone wanting to do Christmas (either as the Jewish person or the partner of a Jewish person) and someone in the family objects, I suggest approaching with a sense of understanding. Reassure them that the way you do Christmas does not have to eclipse the way you do Jewish. Ask them to trust that the days when they were excluded are gone, that they are a valued part of the family. If it's your partner who is freaked out about doing Christmas, you'll have to do some negotiation (see "N"). Similarly, approaching with a sense of what makes them feel nervous or threatened is a good way to go. You want to show your family member that you are empathetic towards them and their experience as part of a minority culture.

For notes on Chrismukkah, see "B" for "Blending." There is lots more information on holidays under "C" for "Children" and "Communication" as well as my "December Delights: Creating and Crushing Chrismukkah" guide in the appendix.

X-Ray Vision

It's kind of wild that we invented machines that can see through our skin to check out our bones. If only we had a similar machine that could probe the depths of our relationships to find out what is going on beyond the surface where it's hard for the light to get in.

I want you to imagine you have x-ray vision for your relationships: your partner, kids, anyone with whom you may discuss intermarriage. What's going on behind or beyond the surface? What might be hard for you to typically see?

I think a lot of the work of intermarriage comes from pulling back layers. Yes, it's about conversation and compromise, but it's much more about challenging our own assumptions. It's so hard to really hear and understand someone, and that's without different cultural frames of reference. Sometimes it's useful to stop and wonder what it is that we can't see, and how things would be different if we could see them.

Yearning

A lot of my work in Jewish communities has led me to the idea that people are yearning for something that contemporary life doesn't seem to provide. We want real meaning, not clickbait or sound bites. We want real community, not superficial groups without meaningful connection (in person or online – each space can be meaningful, or not). We want real cultural identities rooted in a sense of history, the global community, and our own personal beliefs and practices. We want real ritual and ceremony that imbue our life with depth and elevate the everyday moments into something special. We yearn for spiritual nourishment and fulfillment that is often not served and nurtured by traditional institutions, religions, groupings, or practices. Sometimes we just yearn for people to be kind and show empathy. The yearning is real.

My advice to those who are yearning, who are longing for belonging or connection, is to seek out what you need. It's possible it will differ from the needs of your partner and that is okay! Identity and culture can be individualized, even if some of what you do happens with a partner. In my own life, my Jewish communities and practices are deeply meaningful. I engage with many of these communities and practices without my partner, because they serve my yearnings and not his. And there are some that we engage in together because they serve us both. We are part of communities, both online and in person, that do provide a sense of meaning and a circle of care. And we are also on our own path to find what we need to live a fulfilled and purposeful life. We don't have to do it together, but we do have to support one another in the journey.

Wherever you are in your journey, I wish for you an identity, a set of practices, a community of caring support that can help nourish you. I wish for you a resolution to yearning and striving that culminates in a deep sense of belonging and satisfaction. I don't believe we ever fully stop yearning, for that would mean we'd stop growing, but I do think we can find a comfort zone, our sweet spot, where we feel settled in a happy and fulfilled way.

Yelling

Some stereotypes are based in truth. One such stereotype is that Jewish families are often loud. Sometimes my husband thinks I'm yelling at him when I am just excited or arguing a point passionately. I need to work to understand how he receives my words. He needs to work to understand how my culture might affect my delivery of those words.

Sometimes things come up in intermarriage that one wouldn't expect. This is why the "x-ray vision" metaphor (see above) is important. We all need to ask ourselves what it is we might not be seeing in our partner, and how shedding some light on that could make a difference. I'm not saying it's good to yell at your partner in anger, although that sometimes happens. I'm saying that what feels like a normal range of voice to one person is intolerably loud to another. It's a reminder that, although we share a lot in common, we are different from each other.

Yiddish

Cultural differences are often encoded in language. I come from an Ashkenazi background with a father who speaks Yiddish and so some of the inflection is encoded in how I see the world. Yiddish is notoriously good for cursing and cussing. It's a language of wit and insight. Other languages might be better for romance, accurate descriptors, or poetry.

Once in an English-language classroom I saw a sign that read, "The limits of my language are the limits of my mind." It's worth thinking through how our cultural differences might be encoded in our languages and what might be revealed if we probed some of their limits and constructs. For more on specific Yiddish words and their meanings, see "K" for "*Kaput*," "M" for "*Mentsch*," and "Q" for "*Quotables*."

Yom Kippur

Yom Kippur is the traditional Jewish Day of Atonement. On this sacred day, we seek forgiveness from those we have hurt. My partner and I find it meaningful to use this holiday to talk over ways we have hurt each other during the past year and on ways we can repair that hurt. Find ways to use culture and religion that will support and enhance your partnership. It is also a good time to work on repairing relationships with extended family. If there have been tensions or issues arising from someone's intermarriage, this is a great time to reach out and apologize for any harmful or hurtful words or actions. It is a great time to reaffirm that love is more important than division.

The Jewish resonances of this holiday can also be meaningful to spouses who aren't Jewish. In my congregation, we tell "stories of transformation" on Yom Kippur; stories of real people who have made a difference in the world. We use the holiday to remind ourselves that we all have the power to make an impact. My husband loves these stories and this special time to focus on things he can let go of from the previous year and what he can focus on in the year to come.

You

Every time I officiate a wedding I talk about how a couple is a coming together of two complete individuals. You know that famous moment in the movie *Jerry Maguire* when Jerry (Tom Cruise) tells Dorothy (Renée Zellweger) "you complete me" and it's supposed to be the most romantic thing ever? Well, it's not. Honestly, we all need to be complete on our own. Our partners may complement us, but they shouldn't complete us. A real partnership is a partnership of two whole people who seek their happiness together because together they are greater than the sum of their parts, but not because the parts are themselves deficient. It's an important distinction to make because, at the end of the day, the only person who can really make you happy is you.

You are responsible for your own life, in your choices and your actions. Just you. Whatever your yearnings (see above), find a way to satisfy them. Whatever your cultural or religious needs, ditto. Your partner might be part of these journeys or they might not. You may find yourselves on very similar paths or very different ones. You will have to agree to do certain things together if you share a home or children, but a lot of your own life remains within your control. You decide how to spend your time, money, energy, and passion.

I love my husband very much. I love our kids endlessly. I love our home and our family traditions and our way of being. But none of that – absolutely none of that – can substitute for me being happy with who I am and what I do. You are the boss of you forever, no matter who you're married to or partnered with. How will you live your best life and be the best version of yourself?

A zygote is the nascent form of life. I often see people when they are planning to be married, which is, really, just the beginning of a long intermarried life together. My hope is that people focus on the potential more
than on any problems. Have you ever asked someone what their astrolog-
ical sign is? Or read your horoscope in hope or expectation that you might
glean something about your life? I'm not a believer in the zodiac. Are you?
I am a believer that a relationship can act as a kind of zipper, a place where
different parts come together and are made whole; the zipper (seam) of
intermarriage and love. Sometimes we need to zigzag around, operating
like the rhizomatic roots of plants that grow and extend out, seeking
nourishment. That can be a great metaphor for marriage. Finally, we will
talk about "the zone." My hope for you is that with your partner and family
you eventually stop "figuring out" the elements of intermarriage and just
get on with living a big, beautiful, wonderful life!

Zamboni

I got almost all the way through this book without a hockey reference. Pretty good for a Canadian, eh? If you've ever seen a Zamboni smooth out the ice of a skating rink, you know the wonder of it. The ice is all scratched up, bumpy, uneven, and perhaps a little dangerous. The Zamboni comes and a few swipes later the ice is smooth and clear and a thing of beauty. What's the Zamboni of your relationship? How do you smooth out the bumps and cracks? They are inevitable as you skate through life. How do they get repaired? For some people, their Zamboni is frequent date nights, or therapy, or the way they watch movies together. For some people, it's spending time apart because absence makes the heart grow fonder, as they say. For others, it's religion or culture, helping to add an element of the sacred and significant. All relationships will develop cracks and crags; there will be bumps along the way. Think about how you will smooth them over so you can keep on skating.

Zany

When life gets a little hairy, my partner gets a little zany. He makes me laugh in all kinds of ways, deciding to laugh in the face of stress and tension rather than to surrender to it. Life really is pretty zany, if you think about it. We are these complex beings made of atoms and stardust, wandering around this world as though our lives matter. I mean, they matter to us, of course. But in the grand scheme of things? People fretting over some types of humans marrying other types of humans? It all seems a little bit absurd. I think embracing the absurdity of life is a healthy thing to do. It's good to have perspective ... what are we all doing here, anyway? Might as well get a little zany in this zany ride called life. See "F" for "Fun"!

Zealous

My advice is to be zealous in your pursuit of a wonderful partner; one that is right for you. So many people pass up on the opportunity for love because of the expectations of others. Be picky. Be thoughtful about who you share your one, unique life with. At the end of the day, approach finding a partner, making your life with your partner, and creating the environment in which you live with the kind of zeal it deserves.

Zero Tolerance

It's good to have a zero tolerance policy on name-calling or bad-mouthing of your partner. If your parents or relatives like to talk to you about their issues with your partner, you need to put a stop to it. Your partner needs to know you have their back and you need your parents to know that you have individuated now and that their saying negative things about your partner drives you further from them, not closer. It also reflects badly on them, not on the person they're slagging. This is a time to be brave and bold; it can be easier to just let your parents or other relatives say what they want without challenging them but, at the end of the day, protecting the feelings of your partner is much more important than protecting the feelings of the people being rude.

Zigzag (Rhizome)

A type of zigzagging is common amongst intermarried couples. They explore, they circle back. I like the idea of a rhizome, the root systems of plants that go in all directions, connected but reaching outwards along multiple paths. Your marriage can zigzag rhizomatically: you are rooted together, grounded, but exploring and reaching new directions, searching for sustenance from many places.

Zipper (Seam)

Before I was a rabbi, I was an academic with a PhD in postcolonial literature. What's that, you ask? Google it if you want to know more than this one-sentence description: I was studying the literature of places that had been and are colonized. A lot of the theory, particularly from theorist Homi Bhabha, and *mestiza* writers like Gloria Anzaldua, focused on borderlands. The theory goes something like this: borders are sites of division but also places where cultures come together. Think of the Cuban influence on Miami, or the multiple languages spoken in European border towns. It needs to be acknowledged that for some people, borders are dangerous places. So, I'm not idealizing the border as a utopian space. Still, it's undeniable that what divides also brings together; one can view a border as a division or as a seam. Imagine a metaphorical zipper that sews the fabric of communities together.

In Jerusalem, there is a place called the Museum on the Seam, the dividing line between East and West Jerusalem, which is populated primarily by Palestinians/Arabs and Jews, respectively. The museum seeks to put on exhibitions relating to coexistence. The boundary between East and West Jerusalem can be seen as a division or as a seam. The people working for coexistence act as the zipper.

Your intermarriage too can be defined by divisions (what separates you) or by a seam (what unites you). Think of your wedding as the zipper, connecting the two pieces of fabric of your individual lives and joining them into one. Marriage is a coming together, your life on the seam, where differences become points of contact and connection, and a lot of blending (see "B") may occur.

Zodiac

I'll admit, I'm not very into astrology. I'll also admit that sometimes it's fun to read my horoscope and that of my partner and imagine that it's going to shed light on our current situation. I approach my horoscope the way I approach celebrity gossip: I assume it's fake but I am still somehow interested.

When I was growing up, I believed that one's sign and the sign of their partner could tell a lot about whether the relationship was going to be a success. I now believe that very little is written in the stars and relationships work based on mutual affection, shared goals, and plenty of hard work.

You may have a different belief about astrology, and that's more than okay. I could never be intermarried or work with intermarried families if I needed everyone to agree on matters of spirituality and the supernatural! What I'm saying is this: You get to blaze your own trail in this world. People who are intermarried are often trailblazers in their families and communities. Own that! Make your life what you want it to be. Obviously there will be circumstances beyond your control. This isn't about getting everything you want, and it certainly isn't about getting it without a struggle. This is about deciding what's right for you and not waiting for life to happen to you or around you. Don't ever let anyone convince you that you aren't in charge of your own life.

Zone

One of the final goals I want to stress in this book is that you find your own zone. Ideally, you get to a place where you've had the negotiations, talked through your values, created your practices and rituals, and now you can get on with your life. The zone is similar to the "X" in "X Marks the Spot" (see "X"). Obviously you are never done being intermarried as long as you are married, but you do get to experience the "zone" of doing what you do without it being a whole ton of work. Ideally, it's fun (see "F"), and you get to enjoy the work you've done in creating a strong, vital, full, happy, meaningful marriage. Marriage will always have its ups and downs but, in my experience as someone who is intermarried and serves people who are intermarried, we can find a way to experience much less *oy* and much more joy in our families and communities. I want joy and wellness and happiness for you (see "J" for "Joy"). In this shaky world, we should be celebratory of love in all its forms. There is nothing more sacred or precious.

Zoom

A typical day in my house involves a whole lot of zooming around. Today I woke up, did a workout, made breakfasts and lunches for four people, got two kids to two different caregivers, had three meetings, answered about a bajillion emails, wrote this entry about "Zoom," picked up kid 1, picked up a pizza, picked up kid 2, took kid 1 to ballet, entertained kid 2, put both kids to bed. My husband was there for the pizza-on-the-go-then-off-to-ballet part and we had a few moments to talk as the kids ran in different directions, constantly interrupting us, splitting our focus in a million ways. This is life, especially if you choose to have children. It is a lot of zooming around.

What is it all for? It all amounts to something. My advice is not to get overwhelmed and, above all, don't worry about the little details. Your hand-braided challah will be askew. You will be late for Sunday school. Your family will have a fight at some holiday dinner sometime. You will forget to pick up the important thing for that important occasion. Life is complex and messy, and we are supremely busy people (far too busy, in many cases). In all the mistakes and mess, you really are building something special. Creating a relationship, a home and a family, building traditions and cultural connections and community, all of that really does matter. It involves a lot of zooming around and it will sometimes feel like a lot. Hang in. And rest up when you can.

Zygote

To end, we begin. The zygote is the genesis of life. Just as Genesis, the biblical book, tells the story of our beginning, a zygote foretells a new beginning too. Each new life carries with it potential and power. Each coming together of two individuals is a remarkable gift. How special that two people want to commit to one another. Celebrate beginnings.

Every marriage is like a zygote in some way, pulsing with potential. You get to shape your future with your partner. Make it rich!

APPENDIX
December Delights: Creating and Crushing Chrismukkah
A Guide for Intermarried/Intercultural Couples and Families

The problem: This is supposed to be the most wonderful time of the year, but it can also be a stressful time. Not only are calendars over-booked and cheese wheels overconsumed, but for people who come from different backgrounds there can be conflict around the holidays.

The solution: Well, there isn't only one solution, but there are many creative and wonderful ways that people are approaching the "December Dilemma" and turning it into "December Delights"!

Here's what this guide is: It is for people looking for strategies and ideas. It is meant to guide you in having conversations with your partner and family and figuring out what will work for you this December. We'll cover ways you can do the holidays, from mixing traditions (think Star of David tree topper), to ways you can do both (think each set of in-laws gets you on their special day), to ways you can articulate why you're doing what you're doing (think, well, thinking about traditions and what they mean). We'll cover the important stuff – I call them the four Ls: Light (decorating), Latkes and Lasagna (food), Laughter (joy), and Learning (meaning). What if the decisions in December lead to a more fulfilling, more beautiful, more meaningful holiday for everyone? Sounds good, right? If so, this guide is for you.

Here's what this guide is not: The typical anti-intermarriage diatribe that you'll hear from most rabbis. I know you've heard that a Jew with a combined Christmas tree/Chanukah bush has sinned on the level of, say, a mass murderer. You know, scale and perspective. Or you've heard that your kids will be "confused" if you incorporate more than one culture in your home. Or you've heard some other boring and fear-based argument about how your life and family choices are somehow wrong. This is not that. The truth is that this isn't really a "guide" at all; you'll ultimately decide what's right for you.

As an intermarried rabbi who officiates many, many intermarriage ceremonies, one thing is perfectly clear to me: The narrative I grew up with in the Jewish community – that intermarriage will destroy Judaism – is very wrong. In my own life, and in those of the people I work with, it's clear that our Judaism is enhanced and activated by living with people from other cultures. In some cases, we blend. In others, articulating what's important to us about our Judaism helps us deepen our own attachment to it and helps to bring meaningful practice into our homes and families.

So, what does all this have to do with creating Chrismukkah? Well, here's your chance to have those conversations, to decorate your home according to your values, to involve your families, including children if you've got them, in practices that are fun and meaningful and that create light at the darkest time of year. This is a guide that will help you have the best December ever. Out with the "December Dilemma" and in with the "December Delights"!

Note: While this guide is mainly for families that have Christmas and Chanukah celebrations, it can also be applied to those who celebrate Diwali, Kwanzaa, or Solstice, or who are bridging other cultures and practices.

What is Chrismukkah, anyway?

For families that are blending religious understandings of the holidays, I think this is trickier. If you are celebrating the birth of Christ because you believe him to be the messiah, well, that is contrary to Jewish thinking. It's still doable! People talk about Christ as a prophet. They talk about how there are different cosmological beliefs in the world and that, as a family, not everyone holds the same ones. In that way, families model coexistence and cooperation.

For most people I work with, Christmas isn't so much a religious but a cultural experience. Same with Judaism. And cultures blend all the time! How did we even get the practice of latkes? We stole it from the Eastern Europeans we lived near. Where did *dreidel* come from? We swiped that from the Germans. Judaism evolved based on the cultures around us and the people with whom we lived. And now, for those of us living in North America, it makes sense that the cultural Christmas traditions find their way into our celebrations.

The truth is, Chanukah is not a major Jewish holiday. It shouldn't be a big deal. Guess why it is? If you do Chanukah in a big way in your home, that's the influence of Christmas. So, let's embrace it. Find the light and lightness in the holiday(s) for you.

In my own life, I was also not super in favor of having a Christmas tree. I don't really want to call it a Chanukah bush. We had a separate (but equal?) plan in which we'd do Chanukah at home and Christmas at my in-laws' beautiful home. There our kids would decorate a tree and have Christmas dinner, and open presents Christmas morning. It was an awesome plan. Until my in-laws moved away.

My colleague, Rabbi Eva Goldfinger, who has officiated hundreds of intermarriages, likes to say that love is a necessary but insufficient condition for marriage. To be in a marriage means that sometimes we have to do things we wouldn't on our own. We redraw our boundary lines because it is almost always better to be happy than right.

There is an important Jewish value of *shalom bayit* – peace in the home. I take that value seriously. The holidays are meant to increase feelings of joy and togetherness in the family. There is no point letting strife get in the way.

What I'm saying is that, for the Jewish value of *shalom bayit*, I had to start being okay with having a Christmas tree.

We get a small one. Our kids help decorate it. We aren't big presents people but we put a few things under there. It's nice.

Here's the thing: My kids are still Jewish, our home is still filled with latkes, light, Chanukah delights. Sometimes "both/and" is more powerful than "either/or."

I used to think that it would be confusing for my kids to "do both." Or that Christmas would always "win" over Judaism (as if there's a cultural affiliation Olympics) because presents and Santa and trees are pretty fun. Here's what I know so strongly now: In a family, nobody wins unless everybody wins.

My Judaism compels me to act with *chesed*, lovingkindness, and to create a peaceful home. Those values are so much more important than the choice of a Christmas tree/Chanukah bush.

Also, these practices all need to have a meaning behind them. The truth is that Christmas does "win" if the Judaism we practice sucks. If you do a half-assed Chanukah with a smidge of candle lighting and soggy latkes then, yes, Christmas will "win" as the holiday of preference for your kids. But if your Chanukah is joyous, if your Judaism is active, engaged, alive, beautiful, enriching, and, importantly, a little more often than just Chanukah, then Judaism will absolutely be a meaningful identity and force for good in the lives of your family members.

Honestly, I imagine it's a little sad for people who want Christmas to be about the values of joy, togetherness, beauty, and goodness to see that it all becomes about "the stuff." It's the most commercialized holiday there is. If the way we do Jewish can't compete with the Christmas sold to us through the big-box stores, then we aren't doing a good job doing Jewish.

Here's the bottom line: You get to decide what you want to celebrate and what that celebration means to you. And here are some ideas for you to work with.

Light (Decorations, Family Traditions, Gifts)

In this section we'll consider light literally and metaphorically. It's no accident that we have so many cultural celebrations of light at this time of year: Diwali, Solstice, Chanukah, Christmas, and Kwanzaa. We need light on these cold, dark days. (If you are reading this somewhere that is not cold and dark, congratulations. And, know that I say this with love, be quiet about it. I live in Canada. But I bet you could use some light too, so read on.)

Fun fact: December 25th was most decidedly, historically speaking, not the birthday of Jesus. Fun fact: Early rabbis hated the practice of celebrating Chanukah and tried to stop it. Guess what? The people decided. We need good times, good food, good light. We need them now.

I've heard it all when it comes to how we bring light into our homes. There is, of course, the metaphorical light that comes with celebration. There's lots of that in this guide. But first let's address literal light. Here are some options:

- Putting lights up on or around the home.
- Lighting *menorah* candles and placing the *menorah* in the window.
- Having a Christmas tree (or Chanukah bush) and putting lights on that.
- Having disco lights and a disco ball and hosting a dance party. Look, that one's not traditional, but let's think outside the box a little.

Notice that most of the traditional options are two-directional: They bring light into the home to enliven and enlighten the people who live inside. They also are markers of identity – Christmas lights on the house signify to lots of people that this is a Christmas-celebrating home. *Menorahs* in the window are a declaration that Jews live inside.

In my experience, it's not so much the inside stuff that causes problems, but the outside stuff used to announce your identity and who you are. I'm thinking this is related to the way most of us grew up being told that intermarriage was wrong. Might we have internalized some sense of guilt or embarrassment? Might we be nervous to publicly declare something?

For me, I have a real thing about putting Christmas lights up. My partner insists that they don't have to be "Christmas lights" but just lights. But I don't buy it. (If you buy it, that's totally great. My way won't and shouldn't be your way!) To me, lights on the outside of the house is marking the house as Christian, and I feel weird about it.

Some people do blue and white lights. This is saying: "Hey, okay, we're doing the Christmas thing but also we're doing the Jewish thing." If that works, wonderful.

Similarly with Christmas tree/Chanukah bush lights, some people do blue and white, or all white, or any configuration basically that isn't red and green. How did Christmas co-opt all things red and green forever? I don't know ... but it's a fact. Red and green signifies Christmas, and blue and white signifies something Jewish. We can create a rainbow of lights for our homes if we choose. That works for lots of us.

Some people are not comfortable putting a *menorah* in the window for fear of antisemitism. And some people put the *menorah* in the window precisely to normalize that Jews are around in the neighborhood. We all need to figure out what works for us in terms of this internal/external lights dynamic.

In my own marriage, I've come a long way on the lights front. I used to be pretty hardline about it. I wasn't comfortable with lights. But then I had to ask myself why I wasn't comfortable and, to me, it was about wanting to mark myself and my home as a Jewish space. However, my marriage (sadly) isn't all about me and sometimes I have to accommodate the needs and wishes of my partner. For him, lights are joyful.

I'm open to lights on the house (preferably blue and white). We also have colorful lights up all year in our basement to de-Christmasify the meaning of them in our house. Chanukah is a festival of lights so you'd think this would be less weird for me. But, still, I don't love having lights up. Still further, it's an area in which I'm willing to compromise. For more on compromise and consideration, read on.

In our house we also do the *menorah* lighting for all eight nights of Chanukah. This means that for eight nights we have light, which increases with each night we light candles. We also make special dedications on each candle (we do a blessing but we also do a wish/intention for each candle). Along with the lighting we do singing, dancing, competitive *dreidel* playing, and more. The candles not only give light in themselves but they foster a lightness of spirit.

For many families, saying a secular blessing helps make the lighting inclusive. In my branch of Judaism we use ones like *Baruch ha'or Ba'Olam, Baruch ha'or Ba'adam, Baruch ha'or Ba'Chanukah* (Blessed is the light of the world, blessed is the light of humanity, blessed is the light of Chanukah). It helps bring meaning to the lighting – for everyone in the family – if you believe and understand the words you are saying.

The Christmas tree/Chanukah bush is another area of contention for lots of couples and families. Consider that this is the time of year for inviting light into your home. Is fighting over the tree worth it? For some it is. Some people are uncomfortable with the tree because it is a true symbol of incorporating another tradition into the home, and for lots of us it was the symbol that made us feel "other." I still feel like it's weird that there are Christmas trees in public schools. On the other hand, I know many (many!) Jews who are ecstatic to finally have the presence of a beautiful, fresh-smelling, present-laden tree in their homes. I mean, it's pretty great. The first time I had one was when I lived with a good friend of mine. One night we made popcorn strings for the tree while making a gingerbread house and watching the fine film *Elf*. Hard to beat. Trees add brightness and a sense of lightness to the home. You absolutely don't have to have one. If you do have one, make it yours.

Cultural traditions are complicated. There is nothing contrary to Judaism about any tree-related traditions. There's no prohibition on bringing living plants into the home or creating lovely popcorn strings for them. There's nothing contrary to Jewish law in watching *Elf* (unless it's Shabbat, but most of us watch movies on Shabbat anyway). It's just that we grew up with the sense that it was somehow anti-Jewish to do Christmas; that we'd be a "bad Jew" if we participated. I have a real bee in my bonnet about the whole "bad Jew" narrative, anyway. It isn't about following rules and practices for their own sake. The rules and practices are designed to make you a good person. I'm not sure abstaining from Christmas makes you a better person.

So, focus on the values. Come back to the value of light. Why do the Christmas tree? Why do the *menorah* lighting? Figure out what it means to and for you and your partner. Start there.

Or start here with this exercise (there are four exercises in this guide to help you work through the holidays).

Exercise 1

Write down what traditions you really value about your holiday this time of year. After writing them all out, give each of them a rating of importance from 1 to 10. Maybe having a tree is a 10 but giving presents is a 5. Maybe having *menorah* lighting is a 9 but eating *sufganiyot* (jelly-filled donuts that Sephardic Jews traditionally eat) is a 5. Maybe watching *Elf* is an 8. Maybe playing *dreidel* is a 3. Whatever your things are, write them down and assign each one a numeric value.

Switch lists with your partner. Look at it and see what they care about. Be honest with yourself about whether there is anything they've ranked as very important (say a 7 or higher) that you object to. Write down any that you feel you actually can't live with.

Discuss. Sometimes someone has to compromise. Sometimes you can trade: We'll do lights on the house if we can give Chanukah presents only. Sometimes you'll find that you're okay with everything that matters to your partner. Sometimes you're okay to do things at the in-laws' home or in a community context. Sometimes, if you're honest, you're excited to incorporate this tradition you didn't have growing up. See how it goes.

When there are sticking points, truly listen to your partner and what they want. Remember, marriage sometimes means doing something you wouldn't have expected. Try to map out the lights, decorations, and presents stuff in a way that works for everyone.

Come back to the values. For each tradition, articulate why it matters. This will make it so much more meaningful for you and help your partner get why it's a big deal. Working from the values, you can come out with a plan. Some examples:

- If we value increasing light, we'll do *menorah* and home lights.
- If we value the nostalgia and warm feelings of family traditions, we'll do some of mine, some of yours, and create new ones for our own family.
- If we value peace and justice, we'll spend time talking about those things at our celebrations and try to find community programs to help out at (maybe a holiday dinner for the homeless; maybe a toy drive for kids in foster care).
- If we value giving, we'll do presents for both holidays. What kind? How many?

Working from the values really will help make this the best December ever. Not only will you do all the things but you'll know why you are doing them (and so will your kids, if applicable). You also might let go of some things you used to do if you find they're no longer meaningful.

I used to give and get a lot of Chanukah gifts. I've decided I don't want the focus to be the presents. Now I'd rather we give to *tzedakah* (charity) than give elaborate gifts to each other. And while we're on the subject of gifts, examine some of the narratives around this time of year and if they are in line with your values. It makes me bananas when people use gifts to try to control the behavior of their children ... saying stuff like "good kids get presents from Santa." Not only does this leave non-Christmas-celebrating folks with some explaining to do, but it also sends weird messages about the point of presents.

Enter the Elf on the Shelf, the make-believe spy we put on mantles for surveillance and control (the kids think they have built-in cameras, but they don't). Jews responded with our own Jewish super spy to try to manage our sugar-high children: the Mensch on a Bench. Honestly, it's cute. But it's still contrary to my values. How about yours?

The holidays are a reflection and expression of values. Start there.

Latkes and Lasagna

One of the best things about being in an intercultural family is the exposure to new yummy foods. My partner claims the best thing about being married to me is that he got introduced to bagel and lox brunches (I'm sure it's not the *best* thing about being married to me, but it's pretty good). Food tells a pretty interesting story about a culture and how it has evolved. Everything we think of as "Chanukah food" really came from somewhere else. Different people have different types of foods at their holidays, so what does lasagna have to do with it? Read on ...

The history of Chanukah is pretty interesting. The "heroes," the Maccabees, were religious zealots. Yes, they defended their religion. But they were opposed to the Hellenization that was about to introduce new literatures, history, and sport into their community – things that most of us would actually want were we living at the time. It's such an irony that the Jewish Olympics is known as the Maccabee games! The Maccabees would have been so opposed to the whole idea. Anyway, Chanukah is a historical holiday about an unlikely military victory. Early rabbis didn't love that people celebrated it, as it didn't support the worldview they were promoting; they wanted people to celebrate biblical holidays, not historical or contemporary ones. Slowly, as the holiday evolved, new meanings were added. The story of the "miracle of the oil" gets added because it is more in line with Jewish theology ... now the story is about a God-given miracle instead of a human-driven one. Sorry if I just ruined Chanukah for you a little. ("You mean the Maccabees are weird heroes? You mean there was no actual miracle of oil?") Sorry. To keep things equal I'll also suggest that there's no real Santa Claus coming through your chimney. But! Upshot! All of this history is why we get to eat fried stuff at Chanukah! To remember the miracle of the oil, we eat delicious fried things.

This is like the lights. The real reason why it's good to eat fried things at this time of year is that it's cold outside and we are craving comfort food. There's nothing better than a snowy day outside, picture twilight, and the smell of latkes filling the home, a *menorah* about to be lit. So cozy.

There are other fried things you could eat. *Sufganiyot*, those Sephardic donuts I mentioned, are very delicious. And you can get creative! Some people fry up different sorts of foods to incorporate other cultures into their homes. People are doing creative latkes with sweet potatoes, chipotle peppers, zucchini, you name it! I'm a purist about my latkes though ... lots of potato, egg, onion, salt, and oil. Served with plenty of apple sauce and sour cream. It's once a year, people. Eat the oil.

Traditional Christmas dinners are beautiful affairs, often including ham, mashed potatoes, vegetables, and turkey. Sure, the ham isn't kosher, but many of us aren't kosher the rest of the year, anyway. And if you are, it'd be a fun challenge to see if you could make a completely kosher Christmas dinner. Shouldn't be too hard if you do turkey instead of ham and you make the mashed potatoes *pareve* (neither milk nor meat).

Part of being in a family where traditions are being blended or shared is that the traditions of your partner become important to you. One year, when my daughter was just a few months old, all of us got quite sick on Christmas. We didn't want to bring our germs to Christmas dinner so we skipped it. But I was so sad for my partner missing out on his feast that I found a fancy diner doing take-out turkey with the fixings and I got it for him. Another year when my in-laws moved far away, we didn't have anywhere to go for Christmas. So I organized for us to go to a friend's place (also an intermarried family doing some blending). My friend said: "This is perfect because we are honoring Christmas traditions and also the Jewish value of 'let all who are hungry come and eat.'" Love it. What I'm saying is, this rabbi will make sure Christmas dinner happens. You love your partner, get to love some of what matters to them.

I mentioned lasagna above. We do Christmas dinner most often at my partner's aunt and uncle's place. They know I'm a vegetarian and so they want a non-turkey option for me. A few years ago, Auntie Sam started buying me a lasagna. I explained that with the other food on the table, I didn't need anything extra. But she insisted. So now I associate Christmas with lasagna. Love you, Auntie Sam! What's the point of this? Well, a tradition is something that you start, find meaningful, and do regularly. It doesn't matter that it's a lasagna, which is traditional for neither Christmas nor Chanukah. The Christmas lasagna is a sign of me being cared for and included in the celebration. It's a beautiful and meaningful tradition for us! Make up a tradition of your own for your holidays.

If you are reading this, you likely know of the great Jewish tradition of Chinese food and a movie on Christmas. I'd say this is as serious for some Jews as celebrating Chanukah. See if you can work it in, if not on Christmas specifically then on Boxing Day or another day during the holidays. It's a nice blend of traditions that everyone can enjoy. (If you don't enjoy Chinese food then find something that works. But, I mean, everyone likes Chinese food, no?)

In my home, we do Chanukah with latkes, *sufganiyot*, and *gelt* (the chocolate coins you use when playing *dreidel*). At Christmas, we do Christmas dinner featuring lasagna. And on Christmas Eve, we do "Jewish Christmas" Chinese food and a movie. There is lots of family involved in all celebrations, which is, of course, the most important thing about them. There are all kinds of ways to blend traditions and make them your own.

One thing my parents didn't anticipate about their kid (me) inter-marrying is that they'd always get me on Jewish holidays. It's nice that we never have to decide whose house we're going to for Christmas or Chanukah (or any other holiday). Everyone gets to do their own child-hood traditions with their own family of origin. It's a real plus.

So, food. The sharing of it helps bind families together. The sharing of the cultural traditions around food do the same.

Here is Exercise 2 to help you build your tradition.

Exercise 2

Do a Chrismukkah dinner. This might be on one of the holidays and how you celebrate it, or you can choose a night that's around the hol-idays but neither Christmas nor Chanukah specifically. Make all the traditional foods from all the holidays your family celebrates. Throw in some family favorites and extra treats. This can be your special family dinner that celebrates both sides and the abundance that can come with blending families and traditions.

Laughter (Joy, Celebration)

What's the point of the holidays, anyway? Sometimes we get so caught up in the million parties and get-togethers and the shopping and prep that we forget what it's all for. It doesn't really matter to me how you do December, what traditions you incorporate and how. My one wish for you is that, at some point this holiday season, you laugh the kind of laugh that comes from your belly and shakes your whole body. I hope that you laugh until tears stream down your face and eggnog comes through your nose. The goal of all the prep and planning is that there will be moments when you are together.

Here's an example of something that happened one holiday to make me laugh like that. My mother-in-law saved certain Christmas crafts made by her kids through the years. Now there is no way for me to accurately describe this one particular craft made by my husband, but I'll try. It's a person made from a corrugated paper cone and a Sty-rofoam ball head. There's a mouth drawn on in a perfect circle. He's holding a little book made from paper. I asked about it one year, gently mocking my husband's crafting abilities (I too lack craft skills). I said something like "Um, your weird Christmas person has a very o-shaped mouth." He replied, "That's my choir boy, he's singing. Didn't you see the book?" I looked at the book and it said, so innocently and proudly, "sang's." It's a choir boy with a song book. Sang's. I can't. That mouth. I need a photo of this thing. Anyway, the look of that sad little choir boy craft and my husband's defense of it caused my sister-in-law to double over in hysterics. She joined in the mockery hard, the way only a sibling can. And then that big belly laugh hit me. Tears. Look, I get that this story isn't funny to you. It isn't even that funny to me, in retrospect. The point is, hanging out with family and creating our traditions is really all in the service of creating joy. That's it. If you achieve laughter and joy this season, you've done it right.

You know what facilitates joy for lots of people? Booze. One of the things I appreciate about Christmas is All. The. Booze. When I was twenty I spent Christmas in Thailand with some friends. I was the only Jewish person. I woke up in the morning, the hot Thai sun already beaming into the room. We had made the saddest little Christmas tree out of some tree branches – no evergreens there! And the first thing I heard was "Baileys with coffee or mimosa or both?" What? That's what goes on at Christmas? No wonder Santa is so jolly! (By the way, the right answer to that offer is "both.")

The stereotype is that Jewish holidays revolve around food and Christian ones around booze. Doing both means getting both. I know they say less is more but I say at the holidays more is more. Have both. Have it all. Make some mulled wine out of Manischewitz. (Okay, too far. Don't do that at all.)

If booze isn't your thing, of course that's just fine. What I'm saying is, create a situation for your family that facilitates joy, laughter, togetherness, fun. That's what it's all about.

In my family when we do Chanukah lightings, we always dance the *horah*. This isn't a tradition I grew up with. It started because we were singing "O Chanukah, O Chanukah" and there's the line "we'll all dance the *horah*." My daughter asked about an hour later, "When is the *horah* starting?" And so, just like that, a new tradition was born.

We jump and dance around the kitchen eight nights in a row. It's silly and fun. It also marks this holiday as a very special time of joy. Again, that's what it's all about.

Here is Exercise 3, which encourages you to write down your traditions.

Exercise 3

This is good to do especially if there's any tension around choices for the holidays or the usual family drama that tends to erupt when there's pressure for things to be extra nice and you're spending tons of time together.

Make a list of some of your favorite moments during the holidays since you've been together as a couple or family. Get detailed about it. Write down things you loved, great conversations, that awesome moment that your uncle revealed something about his salacious past, whatever it is. Just spend a little time remembering beautiful, hilarious, great times. Add to the list each year so you remind yourself that this whole business is about making memories.

Learning (Making Meaning)

Not to end this guide on a downer, but it's cool to learn about the holidays you're celebrating. If you have kids, it'll really help deepen their experience and the identities you're trying to instill. I mentioned earlier that the history of Chanukah is not what most of us learned as kids. If you haven't spent much time thinking about what the Greeks were after, who the Maccabees were, and what is with the miracle of oil thing, it might be worth looking into! And if you celebrate Christmas, it's equally fascinating to consider the story of Jesus' conception and birth and what to make of all that.

I'm pretty interested in religion (I guess most rabbis can say that). One Christmas Eve we were at a big party with many of my partner's childhood friends. There was food, drink, joy, all of it. One person announced she had to leave because she had promised her mother she'd go to Midnight Mass. I cheerfully declared that we were going too. My partner wasn't so into it (he's not really the church-going type), but I was so curious. So the Jew led the gentile to church that Christmas Eve.

I think it's worthwhile visiting all kinds of houses of worship even if, like me, worship isn't really the way you connect to your culture and identity. It's fascinating to read the prayer books, to hear the songs and hymns, and to hear the religious leaders speak.

That particular priest that night gave quite a guilt-inducing speech about how the holidays were filled with excess even when there are so many who are needy. I'm all for the value of giving back and *tzedakah* (charity and justice – I think it's our job to increase justice in the world). I mentioned I think participating in church dinners or gift wrapping for charity is a great tradition. But I also think sometimes celebration should be free from guilt.

I secretly loved this sermon because it's such a stereotype that Jewish holidays are downers and Christian ones are full of joy. Think about it. In April the Jews celebrate our freedom from slavery (joyful) with a four-hour dinner and the retelling of our suffering, complete with bitter herbs. Christians celebrate the death of their savior (sad) with bunnies and chocolate egg hunts. They know how to party and we know how to make things serious. But it turns out that priests also know how to take the most joyous night of the Christian year and turn it sad. Religion, you gotta love it.

Church services can also be gorgeous and wonderful. I went to my best friend's church when I was a teenager. She invited me and told me, and this is what I thought she said, "I'm so excited to be merry," but what she was actually saying was, "I'm so excited to be Mary." She played Mary in this silly, joyful, pageant with her Sunday school kids. Then the choir sang and beautiful bells were rung. It felt special and wonderful.

So, choose learning and also laughter. Are there ways to bring in storytelling, Bible study (if that's your thing), reading up on the history of the holidays, dinner-table discussions of the themes and meanings, all of that, into your joyful and fun celebration? I think there's room to be both serious and silly. It's an expansive time of year.

Here is the last exercise to help you keep your learning happening.

Exercise 4

Each year, plan one new piece of learning. It might be a trip to a service, or a family party at a community center. It might be a new book or YouTube video on the holiday (but vet sources because there's a lot of garbage out there). It might be a new children's book or folktale. Each year, experience something new about the holidays by learning more about them. And share your learning with others!

Resources

The purpose of this guide is to get you geared up for a great holiday. And what better way to gear up than to get some gear? Below you'll find ideas for holiday items that make it easy to blend holidays or DIY it to make some cool traditions. I'm also listing some fun videos/resources that I particularly like for this time of year. A note on the stuff. One year *Skymall*, the airline shopping magazine, put a Star of David Christmas tree topper in its catalogue. Some Jews lost their minds. There's still a real fear of "dilution," particularly for Jews who feel threatened because we aren't the dominant culture in North America. Don't operate from a narrative of dilution. Operate from a narrative of delight. This guide is meant to show how the holidays can actually increase in meaning and value when done right. So get the gear, but, more importantly, create a holiday and a home filled with joy, beauty, and wonder, to make it the happiest of holidays!

Gear for Blending

Search Etsy and Amazon for great decorations and other stuff for blending up your Chrismukkah, including ornaments (or, menorahments, if you like), clothing, books, and cards.

Fun Cultural Resources

Of all the Christmas movies to watch (and I love several), *The Night Before* starring Seth Roger is likely the best for Chrismukkah. Check out the scene when he wears a Star of David shirt to a Midnight Mass service.

Maccabeats, mash-ups, and other music can really set the tone. Seek out songs that add to the joy (Adam Sandler's Chanukah song always makes me laugh).

Jews love Christmas songs and movies! We have acted in, written, and produced lots of them! Check out Harry Belafonte and others. Ask yourself what Rudolph and his nose might have to do with the Jewish experience. And watch your roster of awesome Christmas movies. I like *The Holiday, Love Actually, Bridget Jones's Diary,* and the original *How the Grinch Stole Christmas!*

Tzedakah/Giving Opportunities

A great thing to do to blend is to give back. Here are some ideas:

- Mall gift-wrapping for charity (many malls do this)
- Church holiday dinners
- *Mazon/Hazon* food drives (or local food bank/shelter initiatives)
- Gift card drives
- Hospital visits/parties
- Random acts of giving – during this season of giving, I sometimes keep gift cards or other little gifts and give them out to anyone. The barista, the person looking down (literally and figuratively) on the subway, the person I pass on the street. When you give, you get.

Happy Holidays!

At a time when even the term "happy holidays" is politicized ("war on Christmas" and all), I want you to really focus on having a happy holiday season. Take the drama out of it. Tell any in-laws being difficult to have another eggnog and chill. Figure out what you need to have the best holiday ever and just do that.

Wishing you a holiday filled with the four Ls – Lights, Latkes and Lasagna, Laughter, and Learning. If you can bring them all in, you'll have a happy holiday indeed!

Rabbi Denise Handlarski, SecularSynagogue.com

NOTES

1. No population survey or census has adequately tracked numbers. The last major survey was *The National Jewish Population Survey 2000–2001*, which found that 47 per cent of Jews married non-Jews between 1996 and 2001. The Pew Research Center's *A Portrait of Jewish Americans* was not a census but did find similarly that the rate of intermarriage was just below or above 50 per cent, depending on one's age and generation.

2. Although the question/issue over authorship of the Bible remains debated, this author assumes it was written by people, according to our best archaeological evidence.

3. All biblical references are from *The Jewish Study Bible*, 2nd ed., edited by Adele Berlin, Marc Zvi Brettler, and Michael Fishbane (New York: Oxford University Press, 2004).

4. I'm using the term "B Mitzvah" as a gender-neutral way of including what we often call Bar or Bat Mitzvah. Hebrew is a gendered language, so many people are working to find inclusive expressions of traditional ideas and practices.

5. It is difficult to find a source for when and how intermarriage became forbidden. In the time of Ezra-Nehemiah, it is clear intermarriage is being forbidden between Jews returning from exile and people from other nations. The concern then, as today, is clearly for Jewish continuity. There is an anxiety that, post-exile, the Jewish people won't survive if there is widespread intermarriage. We are talking fifth century BCE. I'm going to argue that after 2,500 years of an anxiety that hasn't yet come to fruition, it's a good time to let it go. The rabbis of the Talmud use a prohibition against intermarriage from Deuteronomy (7:1–4) to enshrine the prohibition into Jewish law. Some parts of the Hebrew Bible are decidedly opposed to intermarriage. In other parts, there is no such prohibition (again, if it was good enough for Moses ...).

6. This is a stereotype. Stereotypes are usually unfair and sometimes recognizable. This one is recognizable to me but I get to say it because I am it. If you are not Jewish, not a mother, and not a Jewish mother, you don't get to use this one against anyone.

7. To be clear, it's still extraordinarily rare in the Jewish world to have inter-married rabbis. There are several in my movement of Humanistic Judaism, which was the first and has for quite a long time accepted and celebrated intermarried rabbis. Rules are shifting in other movements too, most notably in Jewish Renewal and Reconstructionist Judaism.

BIBLIOGRAPHY AND SUGGESTED READINGS

Brown, Brené. *Braving the Wilderness: The Quest for True Belonging and the Courage to Stand Alone.* New York: Random House, 2017.

———. *Daring Greatly: How the Courage to Be Vulnerable Transforms the Way We Live, Love, Parent, and Lead.* New York: Avery Publishing, 2012.

Brym, Robert, Keith Neuman, and Rhonda Lenton. *2018 Survey of Jews in Canada: Final Report.* Toronto: Environics Institute for Survey Research. https://www.environicsinstitute.org/docs/default-source/project-documents/2018-survey-of-jews-in-canada/2018-survey-of-jews-in-canada---final-report.pdf?sfvrsn=2994ef6_2.

Case, Edmund, and Ronnie Friedland, eds. *The Guide to Jewish Interfaith Family Life.* Woodstock, VT: Jewish Lights, 2001.

Cohen, Philip N. (2018, September 14). The Coming Divorce Decline. *SocArXiv Papers.* https://doi.org/10.31235/osf.io/h2sk6.

Cowan, Paul, and Rachel Cowan. *Mixed Blessings: Overcoming the Stumbling Blocks in an Interfaith Marriage.* New York: Penguin Books, 1987.

Crohn, Joel. *Mixed Matches.* New York: Fawcett Columbine, 1995.

DiAngelo, Robin. *White Fragility: Why It's So Hard for White People to Talk about Racism.* New York: Penguin, 2018.

Epstein, Greg. *Good without God: What a Billion Nonreligious People Do Believe.* New York: HarperCollins, 2009.

Goodman-Malamuth, Leslie, and Robin Margolis. *Between Two Worlds: Choices for Grown Children of Jewish-Christian Parents.* New York: Pocket Books, 1992.

Gruzen, Lee. *Raising Your Jewish-Christian Child: Wise Choices for Interfaith Parents.* New York: Dodd, Mead & Co, 1987.

Hawxhurst, Joan. *The Interfaith Family Guidebook: Practical Advice for Jewish and Christian Partners.* Kalamazoo, MI: Dovetail, 1998.

———. *Interfaith Wedding Ceremonies: Samples and Sources.* Kalamazoo, MI: Dovetail, 1997.

Kaplan, Jane. *Interfaith Families: Personal Stories of Jewish-Christian Intermarriage.* Oxford, UK: Praeger, 2005.

Katz Miller, Susan. *Being Both: Embracing Two Religions in One Interfaith Family.* Boston: Beacon Press, 2013.

Keen, Jim. *Inside Intermarriage: A Christian Partner's Perspective on Raising a Jewish Family.* New York: URJ, 2006.

Kim, Helen, and Noah Leavitt. *JewAsian: Race, Religion, and Identity for America's Newest Jews (Studies of Jews in Society)*. Lincoln: University of Nebraska Press, 2016.

Lau-Lavie, Amichai. *Joy: A Proposal*. New York: Lab/Shul, 2017. https://labshul.org/new-revised-joy-a-proposal/.

Lerner, Devon. *Celebrating Interfaith Marriages*. New York: Henry Holt, 1999.

Macomb, Susanna. *Joining Hands and Hearts: Interfaith, Intercultural Wedding Celebrations*. New York: Simon & Schuster, 2003.

Mayer, Egon. *Love & Tradition: Marriage between Jews and Christians*. New York: Plenum Press, 1985.

McGinity, Keren. *Marrying Out: Jewish Men, Intermarriage and Fatherhood (The Modern Jewish Experience)*. Bloomington: Indiana University Press, 2014.

———. *Still Jewish: A History of Women and Intermarriage in America*. New York: New York University Press, 2009.

Mehta, Samira. *Beyond Chrismukkah: The Christian-Jewish Interfaith Family in the United States*. Chapel Hill: University of North Carolina Press, 2018.

National Jewish Population Survey 2000–2001: Strength, Challenge and Diversity in the American Jewish Population, The. New York: United Jewish Communities, 2003. https://cdn.fedweb.org/fed-34/136/National-Jewish-Population -Study.pdf.

Olitzky, Kerry. *Making a Successful Jewish Interfaith Marriage*. Woodstock, VT: Jewish Lights, 2003.

Olitzky, Kerry, and Paul Golin. *How to Raise Jewish Children ... Even When You're Not Jewish Yourself – The Jewish Outreach Institute Handbook for Parents of Other Religious Backgrounds in a Jewish Intermarriage*. New York: Torah Aura, 2010.

Petsonk, Judy, and Jim Remsen. *The Intermarriage Handbook: A Guide for Jews and Christians*. New York: Arbor House, William Morrow, 1988.

Pew Research Center. *A Portrait of Jewish Americans: Findings from a Pew Research Center Survey of US Jews*. Washington, DC: Pew Research Center, 2013. https://www.pewresearch.org/wp-content/uploads/sites/7/2013 /10/jewish-american-full-report-for-web.pdf.

Reuben, Steven. *But How Will You Raise the Children? A Guide to Interfaith Marriage*. New York: Pocket Books, 1987.

———. *Making Interfaith Marriage Work*. California: Prima Publishing. 1994.

Roberts, Cokie, and Steve Roberts. *From This Day Forward*. New York: William Morrow, 2000.

Rosenbaum, Mary, and Stanley Rosenbaum. *Celebrating our Differences: Living Two Faiths in One Marriage*. Boston, KY: Ragged Edge Press, 1999.

Rosenberg, Roy, Peter Meehan, and John Payne. *Happily Intermarried: Authoritative Advice for a Joyous Jewish-Christian Marriage*. New York: Macmillan, 1988.

Rubin, Gretchen. *Better than Before: Mastering the Habits of Our Everyday Lives*. New York: Crown Publishing, 2015.

Sandberg, Sheryl. *Lean In: Women, Work, and the Will to Lead*. New York: Alfred A. Knopf, 2013.

Schneider, Susan Weidman. *Intermarriage: The Challenge of Living with Differences between Christians and Jews*. New York: Free Press, 1989.

Steinsaltz, Adin Even-Israel. *William Davidson Digital Edition of the Koren Noe Talmud*. Koren Publishers. Accessed via Sefaria.org, 2019/04/23.

Sweeney, Jon M., and Michal Wall. *Mixed-Up Love: Relationships, Family, and Religious Identity in the 21st Century*. Nashville: Jericho Books, 2013.

Thompson, Jennifer. *Jewish on Their Own Terms: How Intermarried Couples Are Changing American Judaism*. New Brunswick, NJ: Rutgers University Press, 2014.

Tobin, Gary, and Katherine Simon. *Rabbis Talk about Intermarriage*. San Francisco: Institute for Jewish and Community Research, 1999.